The Trolley Dollies
Dog Show Diary

Wishing you Well
Merry Christmas
2011

love
Shirley

The Trolley Dollies Dog Show Diary

Shirley Myall

ISBN: Softcover   978-1-4653-9179-7
               Ebook   978-1-4653-9180-3

To order additional copies of this book, contact:
Xlibris Corporation
1-888-795-4274
www.Xlibris.com
Orders@Xlibris.com
107854

Dedication

I dedicate this book firstly to my best dear friend Pat with whom I have had many fun adventures showing our dogs. Then I want to thank my husband Eric and my daughter Zena who without them I would never be able to go on all the trips that I have. They take care of the house and the dogs that I leave behind. Obviously can't take them all on every trip. I thank all the friends that I have made during our trips and all the people that have helped Pat and me on our journey.

February

Well the reason I thought I would write this book about us going to Dog Shows is because Pat, my best friend, and I were in a restaurant in Williamsburg talking about our latest trip and laughing!!!

We were laughing about Pat having her arm stuck down the toilet in her Motor Home!!!! We had taken both Motor Homes because Pat had her grandchildren with her. Her granddaughter rang me to say that Pat was having problems and could I come over.

When I got to her Motor Home she had her arm stuck in the toilet which was again blocked up!!!
The reason she needed help, because she had on one of those long arm rubber gloves and the top of it had got stuck under the flap of the toilet!!!!
Well yes we finally got her arm unstuck and then of course had to clean up the bathroom!! Wow a lot of bleach was used that day!! LOL

This and many other fun things that have happened led me to write it all down on paper!!!

My story starts with a trip to California in February to pick up Trixie who is a New Zealand Champion that my friend Mike Philip now owns. Her registered name is Salinacruz Drama Queen and you will see how that suits her!!!! Rather than Mike pay to ship Trixie to me it was $20 cheaper for him to fly me out there and then bring the dog back on the plane with me.

It was a fun trip but the weather was not conducive for the time of year. Lots of rain and cold, cold. Mike wanted me to show Trixie and Boysie, an English Import Papillon that he had just acquired. Wow lucky me and the show was a Specialty so should be good entries.

Mike picked me up from the airport and we went home to his house. Mike lives in a RV trailer which is about 38 feet long and very nice. I bathed the two dogs while Mike slept as he is a cardiology nurse at the local hospital and works nights. Trixie was easy to bath but she did not like the dryer so I took her out on a lead to see how she would react to me as showing her the next day. She was good for me and stood on the table real well. I was pleased.

Boysie is an English import Papillon, red and white and a very, very nice dog. He was fun to bath and even though he didn't know me just stood real well for me to brush and dry him. Will trim them up when Mike gets up.

While Mike was in bed I went outside with my cell phone to call Pat back in Williamsburg.
I didn't want Mike to hear me as didn't want to hurt his feelings but told Pat "You aren't going to like Trixie as she really isn't the type that we like. They must show a completely different dog in New Zealand is all I can say". I just hope she does well tomorrow.

Trixie must have her whiskers removed as they are black and curly!!! Not acceptable here, don't know about New Zealand but a lot of trimming needs to be done.
She did not like this one bit and it took Mike and me nearly an hour to do whiskers and claws and a bit of trimming of ears and tail. Now she looks like a show dog. I guess they don't trim them the same in New Zealand.

The first day I showed Trixie we got Reserve, which wasn't bad, as I have never shown her before. We were walking round the ring and she jumped up and spun round to attack the dog behind me! I nearly died as am used to them going down on the floor submissively when a dog comes up behind but not for Trixie. Hence the name!!!! Drama Queen.

Boysie got Reserve also which was nice. He really is a nice dog to show. Mike should have no problem finishing him.

The next day Trixie won and got two points, Winners Bitch which was very nice. This time, I had her on a short lead and went at the end of the line up so she couldn't do her attack thing LOL
Boysie got reserve again which was also very pleasing and yes we had a picture taken.

The next day Trixie won Winners Bitch and Best of Winners over a special and then got Best of Breed, being she won over a male special that gave her a three point major. That is one major out of the way!!!!! The worst part of this show was the judge wanted the male and the female on the table to decide on Best of Breed. My heart went in my mouth as I stood her on the table knowing what she was like yesterday. She stood very well but I did put my hand on her side between the two dogs. Phew that was hard work for a win!!!!

Yes Mike was thrilled and so was I. Thinking this is going to be a fun dog to show!!!
When I was given the Best of Breed ribbon all the people clapped and cheered which really surprised me. One man came running up to me asking me who owned the dog and where did she come from. I pointed him in Mike's direction. Turned out he was a judge and then offered Mike an open check to buy her!!!!! Yes he was very serious!!!! Of course, Mike said no-hum dumbass!!!!

Again I went on the end of the line up and the judge said to me when we had the picture taken "I wondered why you wanted to be on the end of the line but when I saw her move I could see why" I agreed but told her Trixie has more terrier in her than most Chihuahua's!!!! Yes it was a very nice picture.

We had the usual couple of hours wait to go to Group and then Trixie decided to try and eat the Pekingese behind me. Going to have to show this girl on a short lead so she can't do that!!!!
I had a fun time showing both his dogs and hopefully I can take Trixie home and make her into a Champion.

The next day we decided to go and tour Alcatraz in San Francisco. That was really fun but the rain was never ending. My jeans were soaking wet and so were my shoes. Alcatraz is a fun place. You walk around with headphones and a cassette player telling you all about the place. Just amazing that they still have a lot of the things still there from when it was a prison. When I get home I am going to order the video with Clint Eastwood in it about the Escape from Alcatraz.

It was fun and we went to a nice restaurant on the beach for dinner then off home after browsing the shops. Bought some neat gifts in the gift shop of course!!! Can't go home with just a dog eh!!

The next day we went to visit the Winchester House which was incredible, again in San Francisco. A beautiful house, the lady was married to the man who invented the Winchester rifle and she restored the house over many many years. She thought the spirits of the people killed by the Winchester Rifle were in the house!!! We must have walked up and down for seven miles. All the stairs are mostly called treaders which are only 3" high and about 12" deep. The house goes on forever. It again was a fun trip and something that I would never have had the chance to do if it were not for Mike inviting me to visit. At least today it wasn't raining all the time. The sun did shine a bit!

The next day was time to pack and leave for the airport.

Trixie travelled well and was real quiet. She is a good dog. Home at last but it was 1:30a.m. in the morning so I walked her round the garden and then put her to bed with some food.

The next day she had to be walked on a flexi lead as Trixie is a fence climber and as she wasn't used to me there was no way I was letting her off the lead. We got home Wednesday night and Thursday night oh Trixie decided to come into season so she will have to go in the laundry room. Guess I will be walking her round the back yard on a lead but it will give her time to get real dependant on me which is good.

March

I think it is now time to introduce you to our Motor Homes. Pat has a 38ft Coachman Sentara which is a 1996 model. It is nice because it has a slide out and we have put many many miles on it, and lots of laughs and fun trips. When we first started showing together I had a Ford Rally which was a 1995 model but it was only 28ft long. It was a lovely motor home but with us working together it really wasn't large enough and hard to take as many dogs as we are now showing. When we went to the Roanoke show last year a friend asked if I would be interested in looking at her motor home as it was for sale. Well I just thought I had died and gone to heaven. Firstly it is always best to buy a motor home from some one that you know or know the history of the vehicle. I went to see a 2000 Coachman Leprechaun 38 ft long. It doesn't have a slide out but so nice and has lots of storage on the inside, better than Pat's. It only had 16,000 and clean as a whistle inside. The stove had never been used. I got it for a very good price and we decided that Pat and I would use mine for long trips and hers just for the short trips or when we had to take Dee Dee, her grand daughter with us. I would never have been able to upgrade my motor home if this opportunity hadn't come along so it really worked very well for Pat and me.

Our first show of the year was to Kansas, Wichita. A trip of 1375 miles but we got to visit with our beloved friend Niki which is always fun!!!!
We had to drop of SuSu who I co-own with Niki and Pearl, a Chihuahua who also belongs to our friend Mike and Niki is going to breed her for the last time. Sure hope she gets as nice puppies as we got out of breeding her to Henry, Pat's male Chihuahua.

I took my Motor Home over to Pat's to load up the trolley and of course, fill up with water and get Pat's stuff. Oh my, the wheels on the trolley are all disintegrated. Will have to see if Eric can fix this and hopefully he can, as he is good at fixing my breakages!!!! Now we are going to be away for at least a week and we have no idea what the weather will be like so we need winter clothes, show clothes and then lounge around clothes. Don't forget the coats, waterproof shoes as well as show shoes. Plenty of towels so we can bath the dogs if they get wet in the rain.

Well gee Eric goes down to Ace Hardware and buys two new wheels but would you believe one of the wheels is put on completely different to the other three. Consequently a ten minute job ends up taking two hours back and fourth to Ace Hardware but yeah it is fixed. It will be interesting to see how they stand up compared to the original wheels.

Sunday

Today is our day to leave and as usual I get Eric to help me load my dogs in the Motor Home and also see me out of the driveway. I can only turn right out of the drive because there is a camber on the road and if I try to drive to the left we will get stuck in the middle. Not a funny site to see.

I get over to Pat's and we put stuff in the fridge and load up her dogs. Pat had already bought over most of her clothes so just had her meds and personal things to put in.
We get all loaded and the dogs are all nice and strapped in safe and sound and off we go.

We turn Lolla on our navigational system named after the movie "RV" with Robin Williams and off we go. We need to do as many miles as possible before we stop for the night.

Our first stop is in West Virginia to get petrol as always needed. We came out of the gas station and of course turned the way we came to get back on Rte 64.
Well Lolla (our navigational system) kept telling us to turn left and we kept saying "shut up we have to go back the way we came."
Well she was right and we were wrong as we couldn't get back on Rte 64 and she wouldn't speak to us any more so we had to turn her off and on again. We will know next time to do as she says as she is always right and we are wrong. Ended up having to turn round and go back the way she kept telling us to go, and trying to turn around in a Motor Home isn't exactly easy. Don't you hate it when a machine is correct?

The first State Park we stayed at was up on the top of a hill and had no cell phone service. Heavens forbid! Pat said she would go over to the building and then saw a pay phone. Guess they knew there was no cell service eh!! Luckily I had bought $5.00 in quarters for the toll roads etc so at least she could call Max and tell him to then ring my home and of course Niki as they would all be worried with us not being able to call. Always something? Next site we stay at we will check the phones before we park LOL. Also, the nice thing is we don't have to worry about the dogs barking as usually we are the only ones parked and if not we drive round till we find a spot without too many people close to us!!

State Parks are cheap because I am over 60 we get old people rates so only $17.25 Don't know why they have to charge the odd cents and as no one is at the office you have to put the money in an envelope. Good job we had the change.

Monday

We start out early in the morning heading westward. Before we leave Pat asks one of the Rangers if there is a better road down the mountain to get out of here, his response was "Lady that is the good road down the mountain". Well, at least we asked.

We turn Lolla on to get us back on the correct road and yes we listen to her this time. Hate electronics and when she throws a wobbly I have to ring Zena and ask her what to do!!! She can find any Wall Mart and gas station as near as possible to where you are on the road. Also can find ATM if necessary. Plus any State Park or motel if needed. And give phone numbers which is great.

Well we are full of petrol and we head in the direction that we left the interstate and Lolla keeps telling us to turn round. Of course we ignored her and told her to shut up but of course she was right as there was no ramp to get back on Rte 64 so we had to turn round again. Not easy to do in a 38ft Motor Home, this is the second time we haven't listened to her and it has cost us time!!!!

Of course Lolla was really cross with us and froze so we had to ring Zena and ask her what to do as neither Pat nor I are very good with electronics!!! Zena is my daughter and she looks after everything while we are away and she gets us out of trouble with our phones, Lolla, and usually if there is a hold up on the road we ring her and ask about the back up and she can pull it up on the computer. She is a great gal to have around. She tells us to push the reset button and wow Lolla is talking again. Thank you Zena.

Tuesday

After two days we have traveled 1000 miles and only have 375 to go. It has been a very smooth trip apart from the first State Park and Lolla not speaking to us. We start out and the wind has picked up, blowing right at us meaning we are driving into the wind which is not good. We are travelling through a place called the Flint Hills. There is nothing on either side of the road for many miles. The fields, if that is what they can be called are scorched black and there are no living things as the 40-60 mile per hour winds bombard us, at times you feel like you could be part of a horror movie!! I am driving with both hands clutching the wheel and my knuckles are white. We use more gas doing the last 375 miles than we used for the first 1000.

Finally we reach the camp site where Pat made a reservation that is only 5 miles from the Show site. The weather was just lovely when we arrived. No Wind Yeah!!!!!

The main reason for staying at this site was because they had a Laundromat. Well that wasn't good as the owner said they didn't open it till May 1st. Because of the cold weather!!! This was not good as of course we have dirty dog beds. Oh well there you go. Just shove them in the back hole!! The man knew we were coming from Virginia and he also knew that we needed the Laundromat because Pat kept asking him about the facilities. He never mentioned once that it would not be working!!!!! He told Pat he was worried about the pipes freezing!! Well gee what about our dirty dog beds??

We got all set up and I started bathing dogs and drying them. Seemed funny with men watching me even though they didn't think I saw them. The resident cat just keeps walking round and of course the dogs bark but I only have out the ones that I am bathing. Pat washed out all the dirty dog beds and we hung them on the fence to dry in the sun. Nice wind blowing so they should dry the same as the towels.

I finished Konaor, Sarah, and Grissom. Dinner was ready. Pat suggested a drink so we opened a bottle of Port. It was very nice to sit and watch the sun set. After dinner I was outside with the dogs and of course Trixie on a lead as she is a fence climber. Sarah was doing her usual barking but there was a resident long haired cat that really wanted to be inside our x-pen and of course the dogs didn't agree!!! I was handing the dogs into Pat when the owner came up and said he needed to talk to me. He informed me that next year we had to make other arrangements as he did not like the dogs barking. Hey, it was only 8:00p.m. and not even Pat was in bed yet LOL. Again Pat told him why we were staying here, go figure.

Pat was very upset over the situation and if we had not by now drunk the whole bottle of port we would have taken everything down and moved to the show site but we needed to empty tanks and fill up with water as there was no hookup at the show site. Still we had our showers watched a movie, and went to bed. Not like he didn't know we were coming all the way from Virginia to stay here as Pat had telephoned him several times to confirm our reservation!!! Idiot man!!!

Wednesday

In the morning we did not let the dogs out, just packed up and moved over to the show site. We didn't want the dogs barking again, and any more trouble. We had to stop and fill up with petrol as we will have to use the generator all the rest of our stay. Wow we were the third Motor Home to park. Guess they all knew the same as us to be early. Talking to the lady in the next RV she knew the camp ground we stayed at as she stayed there last year for the last time LOL Where was she when we made those reservations!

We finally parked and a great spot, only about 50ft from the building. As we set up the wind was just awful. Blew the mat up so we decided to take it up, couldn't have the chairs out as the wind just blew them over. Oh and then it started to snow. Isn't this just lovely? Guess this explains why he didn't want to turn the water on at the camping park.

Of course the dogs were dying to get out and they all ran to a corner and did their business. We always leave Henry till last because he eats all the food and pees in the water bowl. We got everyone in and put Henry out. The snow is now coming down real heavy. We start tidying up as we know that Niki and Barbara are coming to visit so of course we have to clean and hoover the floor so it is nice for them to visit. Hate having it cluttered. Oh my, Pat jumps up, we forgot to get Henry in and man is he pissed. Pat had to wade out in the snow to get him and he will not even look at her. Oh well we promise not to do it again!!! Yeah right!!!!

Niki finally arrived about 2.00p.m. and we visited for a couple of hours. Didn't stay for dinner but said they would take Pat shopping the next afternoon so that Niki could stay and visit with me. The snow had finally stopped and the sun was shining. Yeah but the wind is still blowing just awful.

Thursday

When we got up the next morning it was snowing again and blowing a gale. Well this is just lovely.

Still the good news was we didn't need to be over to the building till 11a.m. because it was a Specialty and they don't usually start early. We sat watching the snow come down and the rain mix and trying to figure out how we were going to get the dogs in the building dry and us dry of course. We decided that I would take the trolley over and then wait by the door and Pat would bring over a dog in a crate one at a time. So we both got dressed and looked out the window and wow the sun had decided to come out. Well sun but still wind but that is o.k. can deal with wind, it isn't wet!

Rhett showed first and was good except on the table but there you go it was their first show so to be expected. Still he won his class of two so we were thrilled.

Then it was Polly's turn and again she won her class but man is she bad on the table so we will have to work with this!!!

Then it was Trixie's turn and she ended up fifth out of seven dogs. Man this isn't going as expected.

Then it was little Lolla's turn. She is just so adorable and won her class so of course I was very hopeful. Well bummer she only got reserve. Oh well we have three more days and then we of course have Timonium and Beckley. Lolla is a little long coat that Niki gave to Pat. She just needs one major to finish her Championship.

We then went and met the lady who has the sire that is going to be bred to Pearl. We saw the brother of the sire and that was really a nice long coat. Nice size, head and lovely movement which is just what we needed. Fingers crossed it will be a good breeding.
We also took Lacy for her to see and she just adored her. We have high hopes for Lacy but I think Snowball is also going to be a good little girl.

Friday

Well today didn't go any better really for the chi's except Trixie did move up from being fifth out of seven to first out of seven but still no points. Beginning to think this was a waste of time but there you go. We did have to bring SuSu and Pearl and visit with Niki so it was time well spent.

Now it is time to show Sarah and Grissom. I only entered Grissom so that Niki could see him move as he is her breeding and such a lovely mover. Grissom is already a Champion. There were three females and one male and two male specials. Funnily the male pup was a tri the same as Sarah so I had high hopes.

Sarah won her class and then we went in for one point but that is o.k. as Sarah won and got Best of Opposite as well. Grissom got Best of Breed over the special which was very exciting. Niki was of course thrilled and I was so pleased that he won for her to see!!!!
After the show Niki and Barbara came back to the camper and then Barbara took Pat to Wall Mart for groceries. They were gone for about two hours which was nice for Niki and me to catch up on all the gossip. When they came back we exchanged gifts and had a drink and then Niki and Barbara left for their motel.

Pat and I were exhausted so we went to bed after letting the dogs out for one last time. The wind blew all night long and sleeping is not that easy when the wind is bashing from side to side.

Saturday

Today was again not good for the Chihuahuas but we have come to accept it. I showed Sarah again and she won which was thrilling again so another point on her collection towards being a Champion.
Didn't enter Grissom again but that is o.k. Again after the show Niki and Barbara came over to sit and chill after a long day as usual at the booth. We played with all the dogs and chatted and picked on chips and dip. Finally it was time for them to go back to the motel. Pat and I had dinner then sat and watched a movie before going to bed.

Sunday

This day Sarah got beaten by the worst dog of the bunch but that is o.k.—won't go under that judge again. Her barking is not getting any better. Don't know what else to try except to think about having her debarked as a last resort. People kept looking at me because of her barking. Nothing stops her, even covering the crates doesn't help!!!
Then it was time to show Konaor, my male Papillon puppy. Well the class as usual was huge and Konaor does not do well with so many dogs in the ring. It is time to retire him, have him fixed and move him on. He does not like to show any more. He looks like a pet when he drops his tail. He does fine in UKC because there are never as many dogs in the ring so moves much quicker. Will talk to Debbie and see what she says. The only points we came home with were on Sarah and Best of Breed on Grissom, but that is o.k. too. At least we came home with points and a lot of people don't.

It was time to pack up and say goodbye to SuSu who has been with me for over a year and two breeding's and of course say goodbye to Pearl, who was Eric's first introduction to Chihuahua's and he fell in love with her. We took SuSu and Pearl over to Niki's set up inside the building. SuSu started to fret so we put her and Pearl in the crate together and then she was fine. Time to say goodbye to Niki and Barbara and that is always hard when leaving friends yet again. Of course we all cried as usual.

Now time to take down and get on the road as we would really like to do at least 200 miles or more before we stop for the night. The weather is good, no wind so we keep driving and then Pat goes on to Lolla and finds us another State Park to stop at. It was a nice place and yes we have cell phone coverage here. Pat and I are really exhausted but I think it is from the wind all the time blowing the camper from side to side. Again we watch a movie and then chat and go to bed. Let's hope we get a good nights sleep as it will be a long day of driving tomorrow.

Monday

We woke after a really good nights sleep, no wind and what a difference. Got all packed up and on the road about 9:30a.m. and driving is good

so we keep going till about 4:30p.m. when suddenly it started to snow. Within minutes it was a complete whiteout but we saw a sign for a State Park so Pat rang them up and they were open. Man again it was at the top of a mountain. Twisty and curvy but at least the road wasn't falling away on either side. Again I just drove in the middle and of course very slow praying that another vehicle doesn't come towards us!!!!
When we finally parked it had stopped snowing and the sun came out, but better to be safe than sorry. Again a super park and we didn't have to worry about the dogs barking. Sarah is really getting worse rather than better. She even runs the fence barking. Very annoying.

Tuesday

We filled up with water and dumped the tanks. In the morning Pat decided to go and read a sign on the parking space on the other side of the road. As she walked round the RV a big Mule deer was standing there and they were nose to nose. The deer snorted all over Pat's face and then turned and ran away. Phew she was lucky as deer can be very dangerous to people. We were on the road by about 8:30a.m. which was good. Again we drove till it was about 6:30p.m. because we wanted to be home on Wednesday which was Pat's birthday. Of course I had forgotten to bring her birthday present.

Wednesday

Finally we got home about 3p.m. Everyone as usual is so happy for us to be home!!! We infact used $150 less in buying petrol coming home than we had done getting there. No wind coming home. Of course we are both tired and no sense in killing ourselves by taking everything out of the camper. It was fun chatting about our trip and of course the dogs were excited to see each other.

Thursday

Pat came over today to get all her stuff out of the camper and we chatted a bit and she went home. Seems funny not having SuSu any more but there you go. One leaves and another one comes. Can't be bothered to clean the Motor Home out, will do it at the weekend. Pat has all her stuff so mine is just fine in there till I have the energy to climb those steps again LOL. Well today is another day and have to clean the Motor Home. Well gee there must be enough dog food on the floor to fill another bag. Now I have to find stuff to take to Pat for our trip to Timonium and Beckley. Don't forget the grooming table and arm and of course the trolley. I am a list writer so sure I won't forget anything.

April

Well now it is time for Timonium and then on to Beckley West Virginia. As usual they have parked us up on the top car park and this is the same place as last year where we got bogged down by the mud. Please don't let it rain again this year!!!!! This is a nice show and we have always done well here even though it is classed as a Handler circuit which means usually only professional handlers get the wins.

Thursday

Our first day at Timonium is the Chihuahua Specialty. Fingers crossed for Lolla as she needs two points to finish.

Well it was a good day for Rhett in the Specialty. He was the only male pup so of course won his class. He ended up with about four rosettes and two dog beds as we were the only people that entered the sweepstakes so we won all the prizes!!! Yeah great fun!!!! Polly won two rosettes and a chi mug. Rhett then got Best of Winners which gave him his first two points. Pat is pleased but she doesn't like the mouth on Rhett but the judge says he is a lovely pup, not to worry about it!! Polly got excused because she will not stand on the table. Going to have that little cow standing if it is the last thing I do, she is really pulling my chain but I will win!!!!
Then Lolla won her class. She looks so cute and is in lovely condition after being bred.

Oh my we are all standing in line and I am on the end and the judge points to me!! Well that is lovely but then Lolla has to go back in for Breed and I know there will be dogs behind me!!!!

We go in for Best of Breed and of course it is me and on the end of the line so that is good but she pulls Lolla up for Best of Winners but then of course we have the other dogs behind us and Lolla just drags round the ring with her tail on the ground but the judge forgives it and in fact the girl behind me did apologize. Lolla finished with a FIVE POINT MAJOR!!!!! That is a wonderful achievement because when Niki gave Lolla to Pat she said "she is no show dog but should make nice puppies and be a good addition to your kennel". Sorry Niki but Lolla is a natural show dog and just loves it but still nervous coming back to the judge. A lot of judges forgave that which is why she is now a Champion.

Sayuri, my Papillon puppy out of SuSu, had a complete meltdown. Pat had to show her as I was in the other ring with Sarah. She will just have to get used to it as too nice of a dog to let it go not being shown.

Sarah didn't get anything except first in her class. Yes she is still barking.

Friday

Now let's hope we have a better day. The weather is lovely but of course we have to remember we always have rain in Timonium. Today is the day that I need Trixie to win as it is a four point major. Rhett and Polly both got Reserve and Trixie won her class again but no major!!! Yes Polly was much better on the table. More training. Bummer but still another day tomorrow. Sayuri is no better even with me showing her. I will have to think long and hard about this girl.

Sarah does her usual and just wins her class. This is getting boring perhaps I will have to pull her till she matures a bit more.

We go back to the camper not happy but at least Polly didn't get excused this time so that is very pleasing. Always have to find something good about the days showing.

We have lunch and then go back to the building to look round the trade stands. All the usual stuff but that is to be expected. We stop and chat with Sue Whaley on the way of course as have to go right by her set up to get to the building.

Didn't do much in the evening again except watch a movie and eat and drink LOL.

Saturday

Rhett wins his class and then gets Best of Winners again so picked up two points and Polly won two points and also Best of Opposite and Trixie ended up with Reserve. Yes I was thrilled.

At least we can celebrate this evening with a drink as going back to the Motor Home with points on two dogs!!!! A good day of showing with Sarah actually getting Reserve today, one step up from nothing LOL.

We had a good dinner and even though it was cold it was nice to have the dogs outside. We are parked so close to the next camper that we can't have our awning out at all nor our chairs which is annoying but too cold to sit outside. I really don't want to come here again!!!!!

Sunday

Sunday was again a good day for Trixie, she won two points and Best of Winners but only one male so no extra points. Rhett got Winners Dog but no points today as he didn't go Best of Winners to pick up the points from the females. There were no other males showing. Polly was a good girl and got Reserve. Had a picture done which was nice and the judge said he just loved Trixie's head!!! Showed Lolla again but she didn't win. Seems odd the first day she gets a five point major then nothing the rest of the weekend. LOL

Time to celebrate again with points on Trixie and a Reserve on Polly and a good girl for not getting kicked out of the ring again LOL. Sayuri did in fact not have such a melt down but near enough. Sarah won her class but that was it. It seems so stupid to keep showing her. The barking is just getting unreal with Sarah she never shuts up even when the crate is covered.

By the time we got back to the Motor Home it was just pouring with rain so we end up putting the dogs out for a bit and then going and taking a nap. No point in going back to the building in this weather. Good sleeping weather LOL. Pat reads her book and I take a nap. Hopefully it will stop raining tomorrow as we have to drag to the building again for the last day of showing.

It is nice sleeping with the rain pitter pattering on the roof and eventually it lulls you to sleep.

Monday

Guess what, no it hasn't stopped raining so we have to trudge to the building in the rain and it is just pouring. We have a towel so at least if they dogs get wet I can towel them down and brush them enough so they are not wet to the touch. Of course Sarah is the one that will need to be dried and yes I have bought the hair dryer with us as well. There is always somewhere that I can plug into. Wow they aren't that wet at all. Guess putting the tarp over the trolley worked well. Didn't look very pretty but kept the dogs dry!!!

Rhett gets the win but no points as again no other males. Polly is good standing on the table so I am thrilled with that and she gets Reserve. Trixie again goes Winners Bitch for another point and then Best of Winners but no extra point as Rhett is the only male.
Sarah is the only class dog today so she gets a purple ribbon and a blue ribbon but no points of course. Don't know why the other dogs didn't show up!!!!
We have had a real good time here even though I hate the muddy parking. We came to finish Lolla and make her into a Champion and that is what we did. Plus we got points on the other dogs as well so we are well happy.

It is still raining and we hang the mat over the back of Pat's camper so I can hose it down. Hopefully if it stops raining during the night it will dry so we can use it at Beckley.

Tuesday

Tuesday morning comes and yes it has stopped raining but very muddy underfoot. We packed up and the mud as usual was just awful. We have to put a pee pee pad down at the top of the steps so as not to track in the mud on the carpet. Poor Pat insisted on getting everything up so as we both didn't get covered in mud but I did help her put the x-pens on the rack and tie them down. Course now it is time to move!!! Yeah right!!! I got in and started it up and of course stuck in the mud. Poor Pat had to put the orange blocks in front of the wheels so we could get traction. We have to drive forward three feet on the blocks and then Pat has to move them again and again. Man it takes nearly an hour and she had to use a screwdriver to lever the blocks out of the mud. Sure hope we don't need them in Beckley as they are just covered in mud!!! Pat was just covered in mud as well and her coat was just awful. She changed her clothes and I wiped as much mud off her coat as possible. Thank the Lord for the wet wipes!!!

On to Beckley . . .

We need to stop at Wal-Mart and get supplies. We need water of course and creamer and a few other things, just small stuff.

The traffic is good. Oh my, the traffic has come to a stop, I spoke too soon!!!! I ring Zena and my phone isn't working. Oh I forgot that there was an update but I did that and it still didn't work, makes me so cross. Electronics again which I have such a hard time with. Oh well ring Zena on Pat's phone and see what she can make of it. I tell her we are sitting in traffic on I-81 and she pulled it up on the computer and there is a bad accident. She gives me the number for Alltel and they finally get my phone to work. So stupid.

Rang Zena back to tell her and she said there is a 7 mile back up where we are. Well we sat for two hours and moved about a quarter of a mile. Ugh oh we can't move. The transmission has gone on Pat's Motor Home. We coast to the grass verge as we were in fact facing downhill and beside the metal guard rail so there is no way we can park there.

As we stop on the grass verge the security patrol man comes and asks us what we are doing. Well Pat is trying to call Roadside Assistance so I tell him we have no forward motion. He says to try and pull over so I start it up but it will not move at all. He isn't happy but he spoke to the Roadside Assistance and told them that the tow truck could drive down the side lane with his lights on and that would be o.k. to get us towed!!!! We gave him a doughnut and he kept coming back to check on us.

Then a cute little State Trooper came to ask us why we were there so we went through the whole story again. Man he didn't look old enough to carry a gun!!! Let alone drive a car!!!!
We decided to ring Max and tell him as if the transmission is gone we have to get home and of course have 14 dogs with us.

We sit there for another hour and a half but the traffic is suddenly moving. Apparently there was an accident the night before and two people were beheaded and then a chemical spill which caught on fire. Oh how awful.

The tow truck finally comes and he tells us to start the engine. Well it is dead from opening and closing the windows every time someone came. Then the smart ass tells us to start the generator and we try to explain the generator will not start if the front battery is dead. We get the usual lecture but then he decides he will just tow us. Pat and I had already laid all the crates on the floor as I knew they would probably have to tow us. It was terrifying seeing the RV in the rear view mirror lifted off the ground and being towed. Luckily we didn't have but ten miles to go so it wasn't too bad.

Well gee how long does it take three men to buy three gallons of transmission fluid??????????
We took the dogs out on leads but of course it is raining so they won't do anything. We give them all a handful of dry dog food and they are good. Even Twister isn't barking which is wonderful. Guess he knows I am not happy so he won't bark. LOL
Well it takes them four hours to the tune of $224 just unreal. They put the transmission fluid in and then take it for a spin and we are on the road again.
Course all this waiting and Max arrived. No he wasn't happy but he went off to find windscreen wiper blades for the van and he came back with a rose each for me and Pat. How sweet is that???
Pat and I did go over to the gas station and buy a couple of gallons of water, tissues and milk for our coffee.
It is now 7:30p.m. and we still have about four hours to drive to Beckley, no way do we have time to stop now!!!!
Max follows us until the road divides for Rte 64 and then he goes home. Wow we are really moving now and the Motor Home is driving really well. Guess it might have needed transmission fluid for a long time LOL. Poor Pat is so tired with all that moving of bricks this morning and now the time is getting on and it is getting dark. We have to get to Beckley.

Finally we turn off and it says five miles and we are going up this winding road which I really don't think is right. We finally decided it is time to turn around because this isn't right. Gee there is the gate!!!! Guess we missed it in the dark!!!!!
We finally arrive and man it looks different to before when we were here. Well of course we came in a different gate. We can't find power anywhere. I am using the hair dryer and plugging it in every post but no

power. Pat had rung them and told them we were going to be there a day early and they said that would be fine.

Oh well turn on the generator and we will sort it out in the morning. It is now 12:30a.m and we are both very tired.

Ugh Oh we can't turn the generator on as Pat tells me we have no petrol. Oh my we have to find gas and it is past midnight but we did see one open as we were trying to find the right gate LOL Wow they are charging $2.15 but we need it!!!

We get back to the show site and stop in front of the building and there is power on this pole. No water but what the hell we are tired and the dogs have been in here since 9:30a.m. this morning. They need to be fed and we need to get to bed!!!!! Oh how nice to sleep with the electric blankets as it is so cold. Sure hope Pat sleeps good as she really deserves a good night's sleep after all this trauma!!!!

Wednesday

Morning comes and Pat lets the dogs out. I get up and oh my, it is a complete white out and the snow is coming down in large chunks! Oh this is going to be lovely as I have five dogs to bath and no water hook up.

Pat went over to the office building and the man comes and hooks us up to water and tells us the snow will stop about lunch time. Crap he took our screwdriver!!!!!

I looked at Pat and said "don't know about you but I think it is bed time again" We went back to bed and got up about 1:30p.m.

Wow the sun is shining and it is a bit warmer so we have our usual coffee and a quick lunch and then I have to start bathing dogs. At least the wind isn't blowing so we can have the awning out so at least if it does shower I won't get wet drying the dogs. No way can I dry them in the Motor Home as it just blows hair everywhere. We are both so happy to have clean dogs, now we need some points here. We are still exhausted from yesterday's stint!!!

We had dinner and then sat and watched a movie but we still went to bed early. It has been a long few days. We have so much dirty laundry with all the mud from Timonium!!! Pat and I sit and laugh about yesterday. She said "when you said we have to let the dogs out again, I thought I was going to kill you!" I know she was so tired. We laughed and I apologized for upsetting her.

At least with the wind not blowing we could let the dogs out to run and they didn't get very wet or dirty at all. They sure liked being out of the crates to run. We crate most of them but let Twister and Grissom stay out of crates while we watch a movie. Of course we could have given the muddy dirty laundry to Max but neither of us thought about that one. LOL. We just wanted to get on the road and finally get to Beckley before it got dark but of course that didn't happen,

Thursday

Thursday comes bright and early and the sun is shining Yeah. Time to show dogs.

Lolla is first and going to show her as Pat paid the entry and no point in moving her up. Wow today she gets one more point and Best of Opposite sex.

Rhett wins his class but that is it.

Polly gets excused again. She is getting worse so when finished she is going to stand and have everyone touching her.

Trixie's turn and she wins Winners Dog and Best of Winners and then Best of Breed but it is only 1 point.

Time for Sayuri. Well she isn't quite as bad but still not good. She is the only one in the ring. Don't know whether that is a good or bad thing. Oh my, Bert is showing so why did I enter Twister and Mio if he is here. Typical eh?

Sarah is the only female and then one special so she gets a blue ribbon and a purple ribbon. What a waste of money today was.

Still we have one dog with points and that is an excuse to have a glass of wine which of course we do with dinner!!!!!

We sit and watch the sky and there is obviously a storm coming and the people next to us have put up two of those fold up tent things and gone off to dinner. The wind starts blowing and of course lifts up the canopies of the tents and bends the legs. Nothing we can do and if they couldn't tell a storm was coming then there is something wrong with them. I know they would not help us if the roles were reversed so we just sat and watched and drank our wine!!! We watched another movie and then went to bed.

Another day tomorrow.

Friday

We show Lolla again as there is no point in moving her up to Best of
Breed class, and she wins a point and Best of Opposite. Funny she wins
here but didn't in Timonium. Strange but that's dog showing for you.
Rhett gets Reserve today and Polly actually stands on the table and ends
up with Reserve. I am thrilled that she at least is behaving. Guess all that
standing on tables is finally working. I think it really helps to walk her
round outside as well before she goes in the ring.
Trixie wins again Winners Bitch and Best of Opposite. Now we need majors
here guys so where are the entries for smooth coat Chihuahua's?????????
Yes we had a picture done.
The same for Sarah as again the entry is the same, Sarah and a special
so no points for her!!!!! She isn't going to win over a special as she is still
a puppy!! Oh well there you go, never know what the entries are till you
get the premium back!!!! Still two dogs with points today so we can go
back and have a drink. Pat has left two beers in the freezer and they are
just ready to drink. It makes them taste like vanilla ice cream when they
are nearly frozen.

Saturday

Same again with Lolla which is thrilling, she is hard work to show as you
have to work her to keep her tail up but she is just so appealing to the
eye. The judges either love her or hate her!!!
Wow today there are four males and Rhett wins again, for two points.
He is just racking up on the points. He is so cute cute cute!!! It is such a
shame about his mouth but a lot of judges just don't seem to care as he
has everything else going for him.
Polly's turn and of course will she stand on the table. Wow she wasn't too
bad at all. I am thrilled. Wow she got Winners Bitch and Best of Winners
and Best of Opposite for her first two points. I AM THRILLED AND YES
WE HAVE TO HAVE PICTURES DONE.

The judge was Barbara Alderman Dempsey and when having the pictures
done she says that Polly and Rhett are the best two balanced pups she
has seen in a long long time. Of course Pat and I are thrilled and yes we
will have wine tonight. This judge will be judging in Roanoke!!!!!

Oh Trixie gets Reserve LOL
Sarah got the same blue ribbon and purple ribbon. Wonder what I could do creatively with all these ribbons!
I showed Twister but he didn't win. A blow for Bert though because the judge gave it to a 6-9 month puppy, Best of Breed. It was a nice puppy though. If I had known he was going to be here with his Special I wouldn't have bothered to show Twister and Mio, but I paid the entry fee so might as well show them. Hey they had baths for this LOL. We go back to the Motor Home and of course can celebrate this evening. Wow Polly and Rhett both got two points each today so you bet I am thrilled. Finally Polly can stand on the table and be touched so guess it pays to walk her before taking her in the ring.
We have a great evening eating and watching a movie. We should both sleep real well tonight.

Sunday

Sunday and the dogs are not doing well as we have run out of bottled water so mixing the two but not good, just need to keep them going for today and then home after we show. Now today, if Trixie goes Best of Winners she could pick up the three point major that she needs as still only has one major.
Both Rhett and Polly only get second in their class but she gives Winners Bitch to Trixie for two points. Now give me Best of Winners to pick up the major from the boys!
NO she gives me Best of Opposite. Damn Damn, still only two points. Won't bother to go under this judge again.

Not a bad trip as we have had a win every day with one dog or another!!!!!
We are really on a roll here and it is exciting to be on the road and winning. I have spent many years not winning so I have paid my dues in this sport!!!
Yes we have Sayuri with us but I only showed her the one day in Beckley again for a complete melt down so we decided not to show her the rest of the time. Not fair on the dog.
Oh my now we can go home.

This is the best trip we have had yet.
We are going home with a total of 21 points. And two Best of Breeds and of course a new Champion—Miss Lolla. It has been a really good trip.

Points on both our puppies and they are only 6 months and two weeks old. Can only get better from here!!!!!

We finally get all packed up and start on the road for home. Now let's hope that the camper is going to do well. Of course we check the transmission fluid and it seems to be fine. Hopefully we will be fine driving home.

Finally get home about 3:30p.m. and I ring Zena and she meets us at the car park to unload my dogs. Can go and get my stuff from Pat's house tomorrow or Tuesday. No panic on that.

Well nice having all these ribbons but it has taken me four hours to match the ribbons with each dog. Even had to ring Pat and offer to do hers as for some reason I have ribbons left over. Course I forgot Sayuri and forgot to print out hers from infodog. Once that was done all the ribbons and pictures are with the right dog. Phew. But I can't see us getting that many points again. This really was a fun trip and so nice to have so many points.

Now just have to wait for the pictures for Trixie and the one of Polly. The first picture to come of Trixie is not good and don't think Mike will like it at all. Looks like she has testicles because my hand is on her behind and you can see a finger between her legs. Too funny but of course Mike was not amused LOL. The next picture is really nice and of course it was her Best of Breed win so have to keep that one. I did make a copy of the one picture that I sent back just to keep LOL

The third one has never arrived. Guess he lost my address directions as they printed Mike with his Canadian address. I printed my name and address on each number and gave it to the photographer. There is no excuse. Well the third picture they decided not to charge me saying it was not a good picture. Seemed fine to me but I will take a free bee any time.

I rang Debbie and she said that she has someone that will want Konaor so at the weekend I am taking him to Debbie in Roanoke. She is a dear friend and it only costs $114 in Roanoke to get him fixed and then the following weekend he can go to his new home. He had the surgery and recovered real well. Didn't seem to bother him at all which is good. Just a good vet.

He settled in real well at Debbie's home and with the other dogs. I didn't get to meet Mike who Debbie said was very interested in Konaor. Oh well I know Debbie will do the best for him.

May

Friday

Now it is time for Manassas. At least this is a short trip only two days. Man we won't know ourselves. I am showing Trixie, Sarah, Polly, Sayuri, Rhett and Kim is coming for me to show Maverick. Maverick is a SuSu and Mio breeding. I have shown him in UKC and made him a Champion at the first four shows. He is a lovely boy but I haven't seen him in a while and it will be interesting to see how he shows as showing in AKC is completely different to UKC.

We finally got to the show site. Took an extra 45 minutes as there was of course an accident on I—95 which is nothing unusual.

We set up and decided to take Sayuri and Sarah over to see Sue Whaley as I had to return her flexi lead so we took that and a bottle of wine as well. We put the prong collar on Sarah hoping it will help control the barking. There was another lady visiting with Sue and of course she offered to hold Sayuri which is just great for her. Sarah is still doing the barking and low and behold she slipped out of the prong collar but luckily didn't go far so I could just grab her again. Hopefully the collar will remind her not to bark tomorrow. No I won't hold my breath!!!

We then went back to the Motor Home and take a nap. Kim rang and said that she wasn't going to get here till Saturday morning.

We had a good evening and watched a movie, The General's Daughter with John Travolta. It was an enjoyable evening as usual. The weather is nice and the sun is shining.

Saturday

Saturday morning comes and Kim arrived. Hey the sun is shining. I trimmed Maverick up and he looks good. We have to be over at the building by 9:30a.m. to show the Papillons. Maverick is just lovely but going round the ring looking for his muma. Tomorrow I will ask Kim to leave him with me and her go over to the building and find a place to hide so she can watch. He got third out of three but moves so well he could have won the class!! Oh well.

Now it's Sayuri's turn. Well at least she is walking round the ring and holding her tail up better than in Timonium but still not perfect. She is so pretty it is such a shame she is so scared but repetition is what it will take. If not then I will breed her and hope that helps after having pups.

Well we have to go back to the Motor Home to get the chi's for 1:15p.m. then Sarah at 2:30p.m.

Oh my they are running behind over an hour so we have to wait for the chi's to show!!!!!

Rhett is first and there is only one other open dog. It is a Dazzle dog which is the same lines as Henry and man he looks and acts just like Henry. Rhett wins the point again and Best of Opposite, cool boy, he really is so much fun to show as he really is so cute.

Now it is Polly's turn and I am in the ring with a professional handler and a puppy as well. Wow Polly is being so good, even standing on the table. The other puppy won't stand on the table and doesn't walk either. Oh my, she gets first and I get second. Bummer!!!

Now it is Trixie's turn. As usual Trixie goes round the ring like she owns it and looks so good even though she has such a long neck. Time for the pup to come in and we go for points. Oh my, he gives the points to the pup which is high in the rear and sway backed and can't walk but wow has a lovely head!!!!

Oh well another day tomorrow!!!! We have time to take the chi's over to the motor home and then take Sarah and Grissom and I think we will take Sayuri as well. Be good for her to be out and about as much as possible.

Oh, another long wait to show Sarah. There are 15 dogs in front of us. Sarah is still barking up a storm. Doesn't matter if she is out of the crate or in the crate still barking!! I keep getting glances because she won't shut up!!!! One way to get attention I suppose!!! Still don't like it!

Time for us and we are in the ring with another tri girl. Sarah gets first place, blue ribbon but then when we go back in for points. She doesn't get anything. Oh well. Another day tomorrow!!!!

We went back to the Motor Home and Pat decided to take a nap so I take Kim round the trade stands and we had a good time. Gee the sun was really hot. Kim bought me a gorgeous red and white papillon pin made of pewter. It is a really a well done example of the papillon. She also bought one for herself and a red and white Chihuahua for Pat. Really pretty and very nice of Kim to buy them for us. Kim also had a name tag made for Maverick's crate which is so nice.

Kim left and we had dinner and then did the dogs and it started to rain. We didn't put the TV on as sitting in a tin can is not good as I just don't like the thought of thunder and lightning when we have the TV on. We sat and watched the lightning all around us. So pretty as we sat and drunk our wine, and talked about the day. I don't think Kim will come tomorrow.

Sunday

Sunday morning comes all too soon of course but at least it has stopped raining. There was a message on my phone and I rang Kim back and she said that Maverick wasn't feeling good so she was going to go on home. Oh well, hate that he felt bad but a shame that he didn't show as with only 3 males I am sure he could have done better today.

Sayuri was the first to show today and rather than drag her over in a crate I just walked her and then sat with her on my lap. Well she did so much better today I was just thrilled with her. She stood on the table without me holding her at all and let the judge go over her. I was behind Peggy Quartro who was showing a real cute little girl for Anita. Of course Peggy won but Sayuri walked round the ring happy as a clam so I am thrilled with her.

Then it was the turn of the chi's.

Today Rhett won again but no points as he didn't get Best of Winners.

Polly was just lovely. She stood on the table so well and walked round like a pro. Man has the light bulb finally gone on??? Well gee she got second again behind a dog that didn't walk round the ring either!! This is so stupid. Trixie won and got Best of Winners and Best of Breed.

Three people came up and told me I had been robbed as Polly was just so good walking round the ring!! Oh well such is dog showing but at least Trixie won even though it was only two points. Mike will be pleased.

Then we have to shlep over to the outside rings to show Sarah again. Once again I got told to keep her quiet. Do you know how hard it is to stop her from barking??? Going to ring Debbie about getting Sarah debarked!! Nothing else I can do!!!! No points for Sarah, just a blue ribbon for winning her class.

Time to pack up and get home. At least again we came home with points on Rhett and on Trixie but no major on Trixie which is now what she needs!!!!

It was a good trip home.

Well we came home from the show and I rang Debbie to tell her about Sarah and she gives me the phone number in Roanoke, the vet that fixed Konaor. I rang him and had a long talk with him about the procedure and he will do the surgery for me on Thursday so I will leave here on Wednesday and come home on Friday.

It was so nice to see Debbie as hadn't seen her since January when she came to Williamsburg for my birthday.
We had a great evening going out for Mexican which I love.
We get up on Thursday morning and head off to the vet with Sarah. I feel real bad about doing the surgery but she just keeps barking when we are at a show and it is getting real annoying.

We picked Sarah up at about 5:30p.m. Thursday. She was fine but we kept her in a crate for most of the evening. We fed her some plain yoghurt which she just lapped up and about an hour later we gave her some dog food again which she just inhaled. We took them out and then she came in and chomped down on dry dog food. Guess her throat wasn't that sore!!! We didn't go out to eat but Debbie cooked steak and shrimp and made salad and it was just yummy and nice to be able to sit and chat. Such a fun evening. I then helped her trim all her dogs and do claws and blimey then it was time for bed.

At the same time as dropping off Sarah Debbie had decided that it was now time for Pooh Bear to go to Rainbow Bridge so we took him with us. It was so hard to let him go but Debbie had given Pooh seven wonderful years. Pooh had terrible thunder phobia and it had got to the stage where even the TV would set him off into a panic attack. None of the medications worked any more and he was not happy around the other dogs either.
We took him home wrapped in a pee pee pad and in a box and then put him in the freezer. I bought him home with me to be buried in the back yard with the other dogs that have in the past gone to Rainbow Bridge plus of course other puppies that we have lost.
Jolene, Tammy, Tyche, Macho Man, Rosie, Soise and now Pooh Bear. They all have a plaque on the fence so they will always be remembered. They are all buried facing the house so they can see me and of course when the girls are in the back yard in season so they can all talk to each other. Just me and my stupid ways!!!
Hey even Mike saved Soise's ashes so that she could be buried here with all my dogs which I feel is an honor.

I finally leave Debbie's house about ll.0a.m. and head home. Sarah and Sayuri sleep all the way home. They were both happy to be home of course.

May

Friday

Well now it is time for the Charlottesville AKC show.
It was a good trip to Charlottesville and Vince gave us a great parking space just across from ring 6 where we are showing so we didn't have to drag all across the site like most years. Debbie is also coming to visit and for me to show her Papillon, Raye.
Debbie finally arrived about 4p.m. which was nice. The weather is really nice and we sit outside talking and laughing. For dinner we had the usual steak and salad which Debbie likes. She also bought us some chocolate dipped strawberries which of course we inhaled!!!! They are great with wine too. We sat talking and decided to go to bed around 10:30p.m. Debbie is sharing the bed with me and Pat is sleeping on the sofa as usual. About 4a.m. Pat comes running into the bedroom because Grissom has set of the smoke alarm with his foot sticking out of the crate!!! It makes a terrible noise but Debbie and I were just snoring away!! Just too funny. Have to keep his crate away from the button.

Saturday

Well Saturday wasn't a good day really. Rhett and Polly both got reserve. Never mind being beaten by a good dog but when the dog doesn't walk then it is pretty upsetting. Oh well there you go. Trixie didn't get looked at again but I wasn't going to pull her because then it would have meant only one point.
Well Sarah is still barking while running the fence so will have to send her back with Debbie to be redone. Not good!

I showed Maverick again and this time Kim dropped him off and then left to go and watch from the other side of the ring which was great. Well Maverick really is something. He is a good looking dog and has wonderful movement. He ended up third out of four but the dog that won the class then took Winners Dog. It was a Belgian dog and really nice nice nice. The Belgian dog deserved the win but he didn't take breed as Anita's dog Parker took breed with Bert on the lead. He is also another nice sable boy. Of course Kim wasn't pleased that Maverick didn't do better but I had to explain in AKC it is a bit harder to win than in UKC.

I then showed Raye for Debbie in American Bred. She is a lovely mover and has lovely attitude but her coat definitely needs some work. I am hoping with the vitamins that Debbie has her on now she will just keep improving. She only needs her two majors to finish but again you need 12 dogs for a three point major and then you have to be on your game plan!! Sarah won her class but that was it. I am thinking I will hold her out and just do one day at a show over the next few months till she matures a bit. She is still only 14 months old but still has the body of a year old pup. Especially having had the surgery she might lose some coat as well. Again we sat and had drinks and chatted until it was time for bed. We have to be up early tomorrow as the chi's show at 8:30a.m.

Sunday

Sunday comes around all too fast. I had to get up at 4:0a.m. because I heard pitter patter of rain and remembered I had left the awning out and that is not good in the rain. I have the electric type awning and you cannot tilt one end so if it rains it just gets a heave puddle in the middle and then very hard to get the electric to make the awning go up. I put the awning up and got the chairs in and watched for a few minutes the lovely lightning but then the rain stopped. Oh well back to bed. Man 7:0a.m. comes around again. We all get up and take it in turns in the bathroom to do our makeup of course and put on our clean faces and game faces LOL.

The chi's showed first at 8:30a.m. so off we went over to the ring. Well low and behold three of the people that were there yesterday didn't bother to show up! Makes me so cross that they don't show up when they have paid the entries. Must be nice to have money to waste. Well Rhett won Winners Dog as there were two males and another point. Polly got Reserve and Trixie got the one point again. Rhett got Best of Winners and Best of Breed and Trixie got Best of Opposite.

That was pleasing but of course I would have rather Polly got the one point. Next time I have to put Pat on the end of the lead of Trixie when there is only one point at stake so that hopefully Polly will get it. Polly will not walk on the lead for Pat. Perhaps it is time for Polly to go and stay with Pat and Max for a while. Will see what Pat says but it will have to be after Kalamazoo.

Kim didn't come with Maverick as she was poorly. Had a bad headache and wouldn't have been good doing the 1 1/2 hour drive to get to the show.

Then it was Sarah's turn again and of course it was the same result. She wins her class then nothing but when you are competing with top name breeders it isn't surprising.
Then it was time for Raye. We kept Raye over at the Motor Home until the Bred by Class was in the ring then she only had a few minutes till it was her turn as she is tearing bad with the sun. She did good and won her class but that was it. Again needs more coat to compete with these dogs.
Well not too bad a weekend as we did come home with two points and a Best of Breed. Some people go home with nothing.
We sat for a while and drank a cup of coffee and then it was time to pack up and head back for home. While we were sitting there I noticed that our plastic bag which we hang on the fence and put the poo in had disappeared!! They had left the hooks but taken the bag. What a surprise when they find it is just poo in the bag and tissues. Oh how funny. Never had anything stolen before but now they steal the poo bag!!!!

Sarah went home with Debbie to have her debark redone. Sure hope it works this time. I am so grateful to Debbie for taking her home again.
Konaor also goes to his new home on Monday, Mike didn't work out, so he is going to live with a lovely family, a lawyer and a Church Minister and they have a son and daughter. The daughter wants to do agility and obedience with Konaor. Will be interesting to see how they do. Konaor needs to be in a home of his own where he can shine and be the only dog.

Our next trip is Harrisonburg and then on to Michigan Kalamazoo for the Top Ten in UKC. We are taking Twister, not Konaor, Mio, Grissom, Sarah, Polly, Rhett, Evie, Henry and Lolla, and Trixie but she will not be showing as not registered with the UKC. We will be showing Rhett and Polly in the classes on Friday Saturday and Sunday. Yes Twister, Grissom and Sarah are also showing those days as well. We will pick Sarah up in Harrisonburg as I am showing Raye again for Debbie.

June

It is Wednesday and I am taking the Motor Home over to Pat for her to put her stuff in and then fill up with water etc. It is much easier than bringing it over in Pat's van as we tend to forget stuff when we do it that way.

Pat comes out and I nearly died when I saw her face. Her right eye is swollen and she says she has a sty on her eye. Man it looks real bad and sore. We get all the stuff stored away and I go home. Hope Pat's eye gets better!!

Well Pat rang me this morning and had to take Hunter to the eye doctor so got him to have a look at her eye. She had a tick in her eye lid between her eye lashes. He of course took the tick off and gave her antibiotics and a cream for the eye. Hope she will be o.k. but it sure looks sore.

Well today is Thursday and time to bath the dogs ready for the show in Harrisonburg.

First one is Polly and I find a lump on her neck the size of your thumb nail. It was a tick. We took it of but it has left a huge lump. Hope the judges don't see it but I will just tell them it was a tick. Nasty little buggers!!! Now Twister and Sarah, will save Grissom and Mio for last. Everybody is clean so we are ready to go. Nearly kills me all that standing to bath the dogs but it has to be done and I do like them all done on the same day!!!

Friday

I get my dogs loaded and am out of the driveway by 9:30a.m. so will be over to Pat by 10.0a.m. when I have filled up with petrol at the 7-Eleven on the way. Get over to Pat's and we load up her dogs and off we go. Her eye is black and blue and swollen nearly shut. Good job I am driving.

Debbie is meeting us there for me to show her Papillon Raye and bring back Sarah.

We get a really good parking spot just across from the ring that we are showing in.

Kim shows up with Maverick on Saturday morning as I am showing him as well.

Haven't entered Trixie as it wasn't majors last year and Mike said not to enter unless there were majors last year.

Oh the first day we are parked some lady drove over my plastic box that holds the electric cables. What is wrong with these people that they can't see a big white plastic box on the grass!!! Debbie bought Sarah and now she cannot bark at all. Makes me feel real bad but it had to be done. Will be interesting to see how she does when on the trolley!!

When we parked and I put down the mat there were mushrooms on the ground so I picked them and threw them away as don't want the dogs touching them. We all sit in the sun chatting and laughing as usual. Got to decide what we are going to have for dinner. Lots of people are starting to arrive, but we really have a good spot!

Saturday

Pat goes and gets a catalogue and yes I have entered Trixie. Oh well there you go.

We trek over to the ring and Rhett wins but no points as only male, and Trixie wins Winners Bitch and Best of Breed another point and Polly gets Reserve!!! Mike was not amused that I showed Trixie but there you go!!! Think I will have Reserve Queen tattooed on my forehead!!!!

I showed Maverick and he showed impeccably. Ended up third out of four but he looked fantastic and it was the Belgian dog that won the class again and then Best of Breed. Showed Raye and she did real well but doesn't really have the coat to compete with these dogs just yet. Hope with the supplements I have given Debbie she will improve.

Sarah did her usual winning her class but that is it. She is still a puppy and needs to fill out some more. Hey she doesn't bark any more. She is still running the x-pen but only a small squeak can be heard. Oh so much better. In the evening we sat around eating our usual steak and salad dinner and Pat mixed up cocktails. We saw another friend and invited her over if she could bring some ice. She came over with a bag of ice and we all sat drinking and laughing and telling the usual RV stories. A fun evening.

Later that night Grissom set off the carbon monoxide detector again. Pat heard it and ran into the bedroom where Debbie and I were snoring our heads off. She had visions of dragging our dead bodies out of the door and was horrified to see us still sleeping. Must have had too much to drink LOL!! We put four crates in the hallway where the carbon monoxide detector is and when Grissom rolls over onto his back his foot goes through the crate and hits the button. Too funny. We just pull the crate away from the wall and then all go back to bed LOL.

When we went to bed I told Pat to try taking a Benadryl for her eye and see if it helped at all, obviously she was still awake enough the hear the alarm LOL.

Sunday

Well Sunday came around and Kim rang to say she wouldn't be coming as she was sick. Too much sun and I think she works so hard during the week that being in the sun takes a toll on her. Oh well perhaps I will get to show Maverick some other time. He is really a nice dog.

Pat's eye looks so much better it is unreal. Her face below her eye isn't as swollen as it was before so guess the Benadryl worked. I will get her to take another one tonight.

Well good little Rhett won another point today and this time Polly won the point over Trixie as I asked Debbie to show Trixie because Pat had to show Sarah as they both showed at 8:0a.m. in the morning!!! Well I was thrilled because Polly won another point, Best of Opposite and Best of Winners, so will have a picture done. Very nice, gives her three points now but she won over Trixie which is nice. I didn't pull Trixie because then it would have broken the points for either Trixie or Polly winning!!!! A good job I didn't enter Sayuri because she was in season, so she stayed home. I then showed Raye, the papillon, but again not enough coat so handed her to Debbie and ran round to the other ring to see how Pat was doing with Sarah. Both the chi's and the Papillons, Tibetan Spaniel's were all set to show at 8:0a.m.

As I got round the corner I saw Pat in the ring with Sarah and two specials. Man I was so upset thinking that the other people hadn't bothered to show up but there they were sitting outside the ring. Sarah won another point which was thrilling. She now has three points the same as Polly. I had pictures done of both dogs and the judge for Sarah told me she saw Sarah when I first got her in Roanoke last year and thought she was a lovely girl then. Wow that really made me feel good so have to go under that judge again!!! The pictures came out very nice.

We got back to the motor home all excited and had a drink and lunch and then packed up ready to leave for Kalamazoo. Well gee someone has driven over the second plastic box holding my electric cables. Now both of them are broken so let's hope we don't need them in Kalamazoo.

Kalamazoo is where the Top Ten UKC Premier show which Twister, Grissom, Sarah, Lolla and Evie have all qualified for.

During the drive to Kalamazoo Pat proceeds to tell me she had to use the port-a-potty and there was no loo paper so she had to use the $1 bill she had in her pocket. Oh my, usually we have all sorts of paper towels but all she had was a $1 and a $10 bill in her pocket. Would have loved to see the face on the next person that used the pot and saw the $1 bill floating around LOL LOL

We are hoping to do at least a couple of hundred miles before we stop for the night so as to finish the trip on Tuesday to get to Kalamazoo. Smooth driving and the dogs are all doing well. Except Twister. He keeps winging like he needs to go out so we pull off the road at an exit and while I am walking him Pat goes and gets Subway.
Well what a rip of—$26 for two sandwiches and 6 cookies. Won't be going there again. I walked Twister for about 15 minutes but he was still winging after being on the road for another 30 minutes. We pull off again and I walk him and he finally poops but the size of bunny rabbit droppings. Oh well off we go again. He must have an upset tummy. Oh my, he starts winging again and this time I am not stopping. We put him on a flexi lead and have him sitting between us up the front and he lay's down and goes to sleep. Pat even dosed him with Kaopectate while we are driving along. Man she doesn't even get any on him LOL.

Yes we drive 250 miles and find a State Park to stay in for the night. Wow not as cheap as when we went to Kansas because now is open season time. Oh well such is life.
Twister seems a bit better this evening so don't know what was going on with him. We passed Dave and Jolene twice. They are having a hard time towing the trailer with a car in it!!!! They are towing one of those box trailers with her car in it so they have wheels and they also have a funeral to attend during the trip!!!!!

Nice State Park but of course we really don't have the energy to go trekking around to see what they have LOL. Bedtime comes around by

9:30p.m. as we are just tired. Don't know why you get so tired when you are just sitting and driving and talking!!!!

Monday

We had a good night and we are back on the road again by 9:0a.m. and have about 300 miles left to go. Twister seems fine and is sleeping in his crate. Now we are on the Pennsylvania Turnpike. I like these roads even though they are a bit windy. Well Twister must be feeling better, just hate it when he squeaks all the time.

Pat decided she needed to use the pot so she climbed to the back. You just can't stop just to use the pot unless I have to go of course LOL. All of a sudden I hear her scream and then start laughing!! Man she has slid off the pot as I went round a corner. Her little legs don't touch the floor. She is sandwiched between the shower and the wall and is having a hard time getting up because of her gammy leg!! Oh how funny. Rang Eric and told him he has to make her a seat belt or some sort of handle for her to hang on when she uses the pot LOL. Feel so bad for short people LOL

We stop at a fast food place and get chicken wings, yummy and some fries of course. Yes coffee to drink as I am not a soda person.

We drive on and finally find another State Park where we can park. Again it is a nice place and we still can get a parking place not too close to any people so don't have to worry so much about the dogs barking.

It was a nice relaxing evening, watching a movie and just chatting about the upcoming show.

Finally time for bed. We did put up the awning as I hate having to get up when I hear it raining. We also get the chairs in as not nice to sit on wet chairs in the morning. Not that we do much of that as usually busy packing up. Just easier to get them up so they don't get damp.

Tuesday

We finally arrive at the show site in Kalamazoo, Michigan and our little golf cart is sitting there waiting for us. This year they have parked them down in the parking area so Pat doesn't have to walk up to the building as it must be a mile up there. Hence renting the golf cart!!!!

We have a good parking spot and today we can rest and tomorrow I start bathing dogs again LOL.

Get all set up and let the dogs out. They have been crated for a while so time for them to run around and have some fun. At least the weather is nice and we can have a nap!!! Not many people here yet but that will change of course.

Dave and Jolene are here, they arrived about 2:30a.m. in the morning last night. A long drive!!!!

We watch another movie and sit and drink some beers of course. Nice to see the sun shining again. Finally went to bed at 10:30p.m. and that is late for us but then we have a rest day tomorrow apart from bathing dogs.

Wednesday

Wednesday morning and it is time to bath dogs. We have breakfast and tidy up a bit.

Will start with Twister, do the two tibbies and then the chi's. Can blow dry Lolla now but with the small dryer. It is so much easier now that I bought two table arms and can leave one round by the shower and then have one under the awning for drying. Twister is so easy to do and always looks so nice after he is done. Sarah as usual is a handful but then she is a puppy and really likes to try my patience. Grissom is good but as usual only wants me to dry one side of him, little shit!!!! Lolla looks so cute when she is blown dry and all fluffy. They are all done now we can sit and have a drink and eat dinner and rest some. Guess we need sort out what we are wearing tomorrow and jewelry of course has to match!!!!! We have a good dinner of salad and steak again. So nice to have a spare day to just chill.

Thursday

Thursday morning comes round all too soon as usual and we have to be over to the rings for 8:30a.m. We have to show the chi's first so we will take them over on the golf cart as it is just raining a fine mist!!! Pat has put the waterproof blanket up on the back of the golf cart with clips and we can just take the two crates for Evie and Lolla as we are outside so can park by the rings, don't need the trolley.

The weather really doesn't look too cool. Looks like it is going to rain or thunder!!!! Sure hope it waits till after we show. I am wearing my pink suit with the black flowery skirt. At least it has pockets so don't have to worry about bait. Pat is wearing her brown and white spotted outfit which is real cute. Just got dressed and I went to the fridge to get the bait and the bottom button comes off my jacket!!! Oh my do I panic, yes!!! Good job we have a repair kit and of course, Pat fixes the button for me and as usual she is cool as a cucumber as I panic.

Off we go, tummies twirling with nerves but hey it is just another dog show right!!!!!

The results of today's shows determine if we will be in the Top Ten show on Friday evening so yes there is a lot on the line with today and of course it is going to rain!!!!!
Evie and Lolla go in the ring together as there is no distinction in UKC between smooth coat and long coat!!! Four long coats and one smooth coat Evie. We all go round and then my turn to put Evie on the table and wow she stands really good. I am well pleased. We do our up and back and she is just lovely going out in front on the lead like her mum Pearl used to do.
We all line up and the judge pulls me out as 1st which is the Top Ten Best of Breed. Wow, now we are onto group.
One lady with a long coat came all the way from California for this show!!!!
We are both thrilled and now time to go and get Twister, we leave Evie and Lolla in the motor home as now it is raining really hard!!! We take Twister back without his crate so he doesn't get stressed and wet as now it is raining but not really heavy!!!!! At least we have time to let the other dogs out to run a bit.
Twister is looking good and feeling good so fingers crossed. There are four of us and of course the No.1 dog is Carrie Lovell's dog. She had two chi's in as well!! She won't be happy if she doesn't win this one. We all go round and do our piece. Twister is just lovely on the table as always and moves like floating on air. Yeah I am first getting Best of Breed again. Wow now we have Twister and Evie going to group. Pat will have to show Twister as she will panic if she has to put Evie on the table.
Funny how I am always thinking of the next thing instead of enjoying the win!!!!

Now we go back to the motor home and leave Twister and get Grissom and Sarah. We load them up on the golf cart and off we go. So far two for two so we are doing well. Mind you what am I going to do if Grissom wins, then we will have three for group!!!!! Deal with it when the time comes.

Time to take Grissom and Sarah in the ring. Pat has to show Sarah and I show Grissom. Man he looks good going round the ring and so does Sarah but we have Dave and Jolene in there with three dogs.

Well there you go, end of the winning streak. Dave and Jolene win with their Eagle Crest Kachine Doll and Grissom gets an award of Excellence. Phew I don't have to worry about showing three in group. Well done Jolene.

We take them both back to the motor home as now we will have to bring Evie and Twister back.

Oh my they are doing group different. Each ring will have group instead of them doing it all together. That means I will be in one ring with Twister and Pat in another ring with Evie. Oh the rain is coming down now!!!! Let's hope that my group runs faster than Pat's class and then I can run over and show Evie for Pat. I know she is standing there just dying in case she has to go in the ring.

Well Twister doesn't get picked in the top four but he gave his best now I can run down and show Evie as looks like she is standing by the side.

Oh this judge did it different, she is judging groups of nine and Pat is still standing on the side. Yeah!!!!! I still have to stand for about ten minutes but then it's my turn. It is now pouring with rain but we have to go outside. Evie is just lovely, doesn't seem to bother about the rain at all. She is the only smooth coat dog out here LOL Nice for me!!!

We all line up and the judge pulls out the Australian Shepherd first and then me!!!!!!!!!! I can't even remember who was third and fourth but we will meet again Friday night for the Finals.

Wow what a coo. Evie is the first Chihuahua to get through to the Top Ten Finals. They have never had a toy companion dog in the Top Ten!!!!! We went and had pictures done of Evie and Twister because he got Best of Breed as well. They will look terrible as I am drowned.

When we got back to the motor home Pat informs me that because my jacket is so wet you can see my underwear through it. Oh my, hope it doesn't show up in the pictures. Friday night will be some sort of exciting. At least Evie will be in the ring on her own.

Pat washed my jacket as being wet the ham in my pocket had stained the fabric. It came out and looked good.

We sat outside and let the dogs all run for a while. Nice to have them out of crates and running. They really do well considering they spend so much time in crates. Of course we have to ring home and Niki as well as Debbie and tell them how excited we are with our wins. Now the sun comes out which is just typical eh!!!! Oh well nice for the dogs to be outside.

We finally get to bed after drinking a lot but that is o.k. too.

Friday

Friday morning comes and the sun is finally shining. We are showing Rhett, Polly, Lolla, Twister, Grissom and Sarah today. It's their turn to shine LOL.

Rhett and Polly go in separately as they are puppies and then they go back in together for best of winners. Polly wins Best of Winners so that is her first win towards being a UKC Champion. Need two more wins.

The judge said that because of Rhett's mouth she just couldn't give him the win. Funny he has done all this winning in AKC but will never be a UKC Champion. Yes of course we know his mouth is bad but he has everything else going for him. Have to say though his mouth is worse than Twister's. Twister is overshot whereas Rhett is undershot and it is going wry!!! Oh well we had fun showing him. So many AKC judges told us just to push on and wait and see what happens. We both know it isn't going to get any better. Both Pat and I know that but we would like to get him finished as a Champion.

Lolla goes in with the other long coat but she wins! Then she has to go in with Polly and of course Lolla wins as she is just so cute!!! Lolla gets Best of Breed.

Now you don't get any more points in UKC for getting Best of breed so not a let down for Polly.

Now we have to go back and get Twister again. Much easier having the golf cart but we have to let the other dogs out as they automatically think it is time to go out and after leaving them yesterday and Mio pooing in his crate, we will let them out!!! Nice really as we can have a cup of coffee!!!!

We take Twister back sitting on my lap as he really likes to travel like that. He is a spoilt mummies boy!!! Just love riding in this golf cart!!!!

Well gee there are only three and I am in the ring on my own as Twister is the only Grand Champion.

Last year there we 8 Papillons and this year there are only 4, just amazing!!!!

We go back in for breed and Twister wins Best of breed. Wow two days in a row he has won Best of Breed. Way to go Twister. Now it is time to go and get the tibbies. Phew good job we have the golf cart as no way could we do this without it. Pat and I put the trolley on the back of the golf cart and then the crates on top. We lift it off when we get to the building. Not easy but much easier than dragging it behind the golf cart as last year I wore out the wheels on the trolley LOL

Wow would you believe there are 13 Tibetan Spaniels going for Best of Breed

Pat has to show Sarah as I have to show Grissom. She does a lovely job of showing Sarah but of course she is the youngest here and she acts it too!!! Well Dave and Jolene win again and Grissom gets reserve!!!! Oh well now we have to go and get Lolla and Twister as they are going back in for group. At least today we are all inside. Pat takes Lolla and I take Twister. Pat is fine showing Lolla and she does a good job. Oh well neither of us get any placing in group. Oh well there you go. Bad isn't it when you are upset about not getting placed in Group? Hey there are a lot of dogs and remember companion group is not as popular as all the big working dogs.

Now we have to go back to the motor home and think about the evening show. I have to wash my hair as it just looks awful after being in all that rain. So easy with the outside shower and doesn't take but ten minutes as my hair is so short. Need to nibble on something before we go to keep the butterflies not twirling quite as much!!!!! Won't have time for a nap either LOL.

We both put on our evening outfits. Mine is purple with glass beads round the neck and on the skirt. Pat is wearing a lovely black top with gold and silver embroidered flowers and a long black skirt. Pat gave me a gorgeous butterfly necklace some time ago and it is purple and matches real nice and has earring to match. Feel good. Let's go!!!!

Evie of course doesn't really have a posh outfit so let's hope she does well. Pat gave Evie a good brushing as she is shedding as usual!! Looks good and nice and soft and shiny!!! Trimmed her whiskers again just incase I had missed one before.

We struggled to eat a couple of crisp breads so my tummy wouldn't be grumbling all the time but then I am so full of nerves don't think it will matter.

Pat and I find a table over in the corner and a couple of chairs. Like I can sit!!!!!!! Oh my look who's here, none other than the judge that told me to retire Evie last year after he traumatized her on the table. Oh his wife wants to sit next to us!!! Nothing wrong with that but I have to be careful what I say LOL

Well I go over to line up and they put me in between a Standard Poodle and a Golden Retriever. Oh my poor Evie is just terrified and is trying to climb up my skirt. Oh well this is not going to be good but nothing I can do about it. We all go round the ring and of course Evie is not happy and neither am I. This isn't fair at all!!!! Will have to say something if they do this again!!!!
Oh well I have to wait till it is my turn and put her back in the crate. She is best in the crate resting although she is so happy to be looking around. At least I get time to eat a bit of the buffet that they have supplied. Just want the lemonade as my throat is so dry with nerves.
Oh quick it is my turn to go back to the ring.
They are not very organized with this so I just have to keep watching as I am in after the Poodle.

For the Top Ten, there are three judges and each dog is examined by each judge but you only have the one dog in the ring and an escort to each ring. The escort gives the judge the envelope and then she takes the envelope back after judging to give it to the next judge then they tally the results at the end. They have 20 dogs to judge but only 10 will qualify as being Top Ten Winners. At least the steward told me I can carry Evie in between rings. He knew that I was not happy being between the two big dogs.

Of we go to the first judge.
Wow Evie is just amazing. She is out on the end of the lead with her tail wagging and ears working. I have no idea where Pat is but hope she can see it. I put Evie on the table and she stands like a rock, lifts up one paw but that is o.k., at least she isn't attempting to eat the judge LOL. Way to go and on to the next judge. Again Evie goes round the ring with her tail up wagging and just having a blast. Oh my this is such fun. Sure hope Pat is watching. Again put her on the table and she is good as gold. The crowd is clapping for Evie.
Onto the third judge and lets hope she holds it together. This is a judge that doesn't usually like my dogs. Oh well what the hell, Evie has done all I wanted her to do and if she does bad now it doesn't matter.

Oh my, Evie stands like a rock on the table for the third time. I thought she would be getting tired by now but no, she is having fun. As I go round the ring I can hear someone shout "Way to go Evie" and of course it is Pat but it doesn't bother Evie at all, she just keeps going, twitches her ears as she hears Pat. Just love her. She moves just like her mother, Pearl.

Phew it is over and I am thrilled with Evie. Pat is just as thrilled and man we need a beer now!!!!!!! It doesn't matter if we don't get in the Top Ten because Evie did all I wanted her to do. She has forgotten all the bad things that happened last year and is now a true Grand Champion in her own right!! Just love her.
It has been a pleasure to show Evie and I feel honored that Pat has let me take her this far.
We put Evie back in the crate after lots of hugs and kisses, and now we have to wait for them to tally the results and then we will all go back in the ring!!!! I feed her some ham and Pat got some chicken for her as well, I think Pat is more nervous than me!!!!!

Wow they are calling us again to line up. Now this time I am going on the end of the lineup. The steward puts me again in between the Standard Poodle and the Golden Retriever. I told him "NO I want to be on the end as I have the smallest dog here." He says no way you have to stay where you are!!! I didn't agree and told him "I am English and I want to go on the end" He says this is America. "Well yes I am an American Citizen and English and I want to be on the end. If you don't agree we will ask all these people where they think I should be in the line up!" He was not happy but in the end he agreed and put me on the end with the Toy Fox Terrier and French Bulldog in front of me. Yeah where I wanted to be, but he tells me not to take all night walking round!!!! Cheek of him!!!!

We all get to go in one at a time as they call out the name of the dog and owner. Fun but of course I can't hear it. Everyone is clapping and cheering and finally after 19 dogs it is my turn to go. Evie struts her stuff and tail wagging all the way round. She is such a charmer.
We are all standing in line as the announcer says they will do No.10 first and then No.9 and so on till No.1.
The room is deathly quiet as he calls No.10 first "NO.10 IS THE "CHIHUAHUA"

The room erupted and everyone was cheering and clapping as I stepped forward to shake the hand of the President of the show and he hands me a silver engraved plate and a large red and white rosette. Oh my heart is pounding and I am so thrilled for Evie and of course for Pat!!!!!

It ended up with the No.1. dog being the Australian Shepherd and he was also from Virginia. Four of the Top Ten dogs were from Virginia. Total of 425 dogs and 147 breeds!!! The UKC has never had a Chihuahua in the Top Ten finals!!!!

A thrilling evening and now it is time for pictures. All three judges and the President and of course Pat are in the picture. Well do you think there is some room for me LOL and Evie of course.

Amazing how many judges came up to us and congratulated us on our win, all the judges being so complimentary about Evie of course. I kept her in my arms because then she doesn't have to protect me like she would Pat!!!!

We get to have our picture in the Bloodlines magazine which is good and free which is even better.

Now time to go back and change clothes and let the dogs out and have a drink and of course get on the phone and tell everyone how well we did. We had in fact a magnum of Champagne and you better believe we drank most of it. We ordered Pizza and they deliver it up at the front of the building so Pat took the golf cart off up there to get it. A fun evening ringing everyone, Pat would have rung the President if she had his number!!!! I was so thrilled for Pat. And this is a dog that I was told never to show again!! Just goes to show she could do it under constant training and good handling!!!!

It really has been an honor to show Evie and have all the success that she has had. I thank Pat for the honor of showing Evie and having such a fun time doing it!!!! She is a lovely dog. And did I mention that her mum is of course Pearl who we have left with Niki to be bred again. Evie is also Polly's mum!!!

We have had a dam good day and so far a great weekend, doesn't matter if we don't win any more after this coo eh!!!!!!!!

We were so excited and of course had to ring everyone and tell them, made it hard to sleep!!

Hopefully the picture will be with us by the end of the next week.

Saturday

Well Saturday comes around and yeah the sun is shining. We can take over the chi's first and then come back for Twister and Sarah and Grissom.

The chi's show first and Rhett gets beaten again for Best of Winners by Polly.
Then I show Evie against the lady from California with her long coat.
Well surprise but Evie wins again!!! Now Evie has to go to Group so I will have to show her as Pat gets so nervous about putting Evie on the table. Hey I stand the chance of getting a group placement at least.
Time to go and get Twister and of course let the dogs out but we have time for another cup of coffee!!! Going to be swimming in the stuff soon LOL
Nice to be able to let the dogs out though!!! They really get upset if we leave them in the crates and just swop dogs out!!!!
We don't need to take a crate for Twister as he can just sit on my lap. The weather is lovely so don't have to worry about getting wet!!! Still only the four Papillons but Twister comes through and wins Best of Breed again. He really is stunning and I think he must have been talking to Evie as now he wants to run on the end of the lead. Too funny!!!
Now we have two for Group so Pat will take Twister.
Back to the motor home again to get Sarah and Grissom and we will take them back and come back again to the building for Group as they won't do Group till about 1:30p.m. after lunch.
Well bummer Grissom gets Reserve again but with 13 Tibetan Spaniels in the ring what can I say!!!! Only two of them are mine!!!! All the rest are Dave and Jolene's dogs!!!

Well good in one respect now I don't have to worry about having three dogs going to Group as that would have been difficult.

Back to the motor home and lunch. As usual Pat makes a killer sandwich out of the wraps and ham and cheese and potato salad. Yummy!!! Yes, another cup of coffee. Still too early for a glass of wine LOL. I am sure it is Happy Hour somewhere!!!!
We load up the golf cart again with Evie and Twister in crates to go back for Group.

There are 27 dogs in the ring and of course Evie Twister and a Pomeranian are the smallest dogs here so we are the three on the end. I am in front of Pat with Twister so he will behave for her.

Strange, Twister is hacking as he comes back to the judge, I have never seen him do that before.

We all do our go round and time to stand and wait for the judge to pull out the top four placings.

She pulls out the Pomeranian first and then me with Evie for Group 2. Sorry Twister doesn't get anything but that is o.k. He did good for Pat.

Man it was a good day for us showing today.

Last year Evie got a Group three and this year a Group 2. Way to go Evie

Now we can go back to the motor home, change clothes and of course ring home. Evie got a lovely Red and white rosette again with Group 2 on it, just a bit smaller than her Top Ten rosette.

We decided to drive round the trade stands as probably most of them will be going home tomorrow. Pat bought me a lovely necklace and earrings and a watch with Chihuahua's on it that look just like Evie. Also bought a lovely leather lead for Rhett.

Now we can go back to the motor home and of course ring home and tell everyone how well we have done today.

By the evening all the dogs seem to be coughing up white foamy phlegm. The only ones that aren't, so far is Grissom and Mio. Have to be real careful with the small chi puppies, Lacy and Snowball.

I ring Debbie and all her dogs are doing the same thing. This isn't kennel cough but a real hacking reaching from the lungs sort of cough. Not good. We were with Debbie in Harrisonburg so I wanted to know if her dogs were sick as well.

Now I wonder if that is what was wrong with Twister yesterday!!!!

Debbie has rung Niki and she has told us to dose them with a broad acting antibiotic such as Doxycyline which we have of course. The dosage is very important not to overdose the pups so we divide a pill between six dogs and then another pill between the other six dogs. Gave it to them in about a tablespoon of food and then in two hours will give them liquid Benadryl as that will loosen anything in the lungs.

Gee a real bad night. Poor Pat was up with the little ones coughing nearly all night long. Poor Trixie took her blanket and went under the crate bed so as to get away from the noise.

Let's hope they are better in the morning. So far we have gone through 9 crate pads and two rolls of paper towels. Not good.

Sunday

Well Sunday morning comes and of course Pat is wiped out with worry about the little puppy chi's as they have not had a good night. I don't know how she dealt with them and didn't even wake me up!!!!!
Pat decided not to show Lolla as she is also hacking and wouldn't look good.
Polly isn't doing it hardly at all and neither are Sarah, Twister and Grissom so we are going to show them. It is the last day so have to go for it!!!!

Would be nice for Twister to win today as that will make him five Best of Breeds out of five days!!!!!! Yeah right I should be so lucky, this is a dog show remember!!!!!!!!!!
Well Polly wins again and also gets Best of Breed over the long coat chi from California. Hey now she is a UKC Champion because she has had three wins over Rhett which gives her 105 points.

I am thrilled and Pat said Polly was so good, she could have even beaten Lolla but of course I don't agree as Lolla is so cute. Decided to use the new leather lead on Polly and oh my, what a difference a lead can make. Now she is running with her head up and not sniffing the ground.
I will have to give Pat the money for this lead as it is real nice for Polly but did nothing for Rhett.
Well gee, Twister doesn't win today although he acted real good and didn't seem sick at all. Well that is how it goes, just a dog show but he won four days out of five so will have his picture done as well as Polly of course with New Champion on it!!!!

Now it is time for Sarah and Grissom. Well gee this judge is really strange. Thought he was going for movement but not with the tibbies. Gives it to the biggest tibby in the ring, must go 20 pounds. Oh well there you go, just a dog show and we have done well so shouldn't be disappointed but of course we are LOL. I don't think that some of the judges read the standard before they enter the ring LOL.

Well now it is time to get back to the motor home and start packing up as we need to do a couple of hundred miles so as to be home for Tuesday.

While packing up I notice that there are black patches under the mat and it is fungus. I am now wondering if this is what is making the dogs sick. It seems to be affecting their lungs in some way and making them cough up foamy liquid.

It is the same as poisoning when they mouth a frog. I will have to remember to ask Debbie about it.

Debbie rang and said that Raye was choking up this foam and coughing. Well I am sure glad they did this on the way home and not on the way there. Would have been awful to go all that way and not be able to show. Again we have to dose the dogs before we get on the road. Doesn't take us long to pack up at all and of course change our clothes and make a cup of coffee for while we are driving.

We drove about 150 miles and decided to stop before too late. I rang Niki and she said to dose the dogs with Doxycycline and yes we already have. She says Doxy is a more wide based antibiotic other than Amoxicillin but we only have 5 pills left. We have to divide one pill between six dogs and then after two hours give them all a dose of Benadryl liquid which of course we have as well and have already done. It really does seem to be helping with the coughing as now they are resting.

We decided that as we can empty the tanks we can have showers in the Motor Home. I just hate going over to a shower house and worry about getting my feet wet and there being bugs.

We keep driving till about 4:0p.m. and decide to stop. We found a State Park on Lake Erie and it looks pretty good but of course have to drive about 20 miles to find the place. Man they put these State Parks in the middle of no where. The name of the State Park is Sterling State Park Monroe on Lake Erie.

Wow this is lovely and after dinner we plan to take Twister to the lake and take some pictures. Make sure we spray for bugs LOL.

We had a good dinner of shrimp and salad and a bottle of wine and now we are going over to the lake.

Such a lovely evening and of course we did spray for bugs as they eat me alive. Twister stops about half way and goes flat on the floor trying to catch his breath. This bug has really got a hold on their lungs. I picked him up and after about five minutes he seems fine so over we went to the lake. Twister does not like the water but he will walk in it just a little bit if I go with him. Pat took some pictures.

When we got back to the Motor Home it was covered in huge flying bugs. Pat called them hematite's or something like that but they got in Pat's hair and are all over the side of the Motor Home. Oh I don't like bugs LOL Time for showers and then bed!! I turned on the water heater.

All of a sudden I hear the pump making a funny noise. We go round and water was pouring out of the water heater. Guess the stupid thing is broken. The water is coming out of the overflow valve on the water heater. We turned off the pump and tried to close the overflow valve but it wouldn't. We ring Max and he said to tap it with a hammer and low and behold it worked. I was too frightened to try that so gave Pat the hammer LOL. The water stopped running so we could at least use the pump for dishes etc. Reckon that the thermostat has gone which is why it is overheating which opens the release valve. I will have to fix it when we get home. Oh well when we camp tomorrow we will use their showers.

Pat spent most of the night up and wiping the mouth of Lacy and Henry from the foam. Used up a roll of paper towels. Twister seems to be better but now Grissom, Sarah, Henry, Evie and Lacy are doing the coughing and foaming thing. Poor little Lacy is just so small that this could kill her so we have to be real careful.

We have finally put it down to the mushrooms as there were mushrooms in Harrisonburg and Debbie was there with us. I picked the mushrooms before putting the mat down and that was the worst thing you could do. By picking them the spores just spread. Even Pat and I are coughing and Pat had to use her inhaler to open her lungs up and she had been fine up till now.

With this being an air born bug we have to change all the beds in the crates when they are wet and bag it and put it in the storage hole at the back of the Motor Home. Wash all the dog bowls so we are not cross contaminating anything. They only have water in their crates so they are not drinking from the same water bowl. This is going to be a hard trip home. At least we will be on the road for all of Monday and hopefully by the time we get home on Tuesday the worst will be over so we won't contaminate the dogs at home.

Monday

We got up and were on the road by about 9:0a.m. and hope to do at least 450 miles today and that will give us just about 200-300 miles on Tuesday.

The dogs travelled real well and so far no one is coughing. Guess the medication is doing well and they are all sleeping. Wish Pat could sleep as well but she won't.

Good driving but we have done about 300 miles and both Pat and I hear a flapping noise. Oh my, this sounds like a tire shredding. We pull over in a lay by and both get out and look round the wheels. Can't see anything except the mat thing on the step is flapping because a spring has gone. Oh my, what a relief. Let's keep going!!!!! We wrap a bungee round it and off we go again!!!

We didn't find a State Park so found a camp ground. Not really as nice as the State Parks and we are parked under trees and on dirt. We ate dinner, had showers and went to bed, after dosing the dogs of course. There were a lot of bugs under the trees but the bug zapper and candle we had did work real well. The dogs were still a bit sick but doing much better. At least they are all eating well. Pat and I are so tired and she should be from not having any sleep last night. We just chill and tidy up and go right to bed. Pat needs a better night tonight.

Tuesday

We got up and packed up and were on the road by 8:30a.m. The tanks are all empty and ready to get home. The dogs had a much better night and Pat finally got some sleep. Divided our last Doxy pill between them all and gave them Benadryl and hit the road. At least they all sleep while on the road.

We have to decide what we are going to do when we get home. None of the stuff in the Motor Home will go in the house. All the bedding has to be washed and all the crates have to be bleached. I will have to spray all the inside of the Motor Home with disinfectant and hopefully that will clean all the spores out. This is the first time that we have had any sickness in the dogs when on the road apart from having to give one of them the odd Metro pill because of loose stools. Needs to be the last as well, can't go through this again!!!

It is nice to be home but takes me two days to get it all clean and bleached. It has taken me four days to wash all the dog beds and the bedding, etc.

I have bleached the mat and crates so they should all be o.k. now. Just didn't want to bring the germs in the house to the other dogs.

Well our next trip is Bell Alton and West Friendship at the end of June. DeeDee, Pat's grand daughter is coming with us on this trip.

June

Won't show Trixie in Bell Alton as never had majors there. You watch there will be majors this year!!!! Going in Pat's Motor Home because she has the slide out and we need the extra room because of taking Dee Dee.

Time to take my stuff over to Pat's to put in her Motor Home. Much easier as I cannot get my stuff and the crates in my car all at the same time. Plus this way if I forget anything I just put it on the kitchen table with my purse and it goes in the car with the dogs!!!

Wednesday

We got all loaded up after meeting Pat in the Blooms car park. It is so much easier than trumping through the grass and over the bricks in Pat's front yard. Eric just takes my car home for me.
Pat can't get up and down our driveway so easier to meet in the car park.
We stopped at Wall Mart as usual to get groceries. Not bad as we spent $93 and will probably spend that again when we leave Bell Alton which isn't bad for feeding us for 5 days. Course we have lots of snacks for DeeDee but then need snacks for us too LOL.

On the road but we didn't turn Lolla (navigational system) on as we are going on Rte I-17 and then I-301 which means we don't have to do I-495 and I-95 which I just hate. Would rather do the traffic lights on I-301 and take an extra 30 minutes to get there than fight with the traffic on I-495!!!!! Good that Pat knows where she is going as I have no idea!!
We finally turn Lolla on when on I-301 and eventually after telling us to turn round five times she agrees that I-301 is a better route LOL.

It is a good drive and we arrive at Bell Alton about 1:15p.m. and man it is hot but that is o.k. we turn on the generator and the ac will do good for the dogs. They won't let us park till about 4:0p.m. but that is fine as the generator is running.

Oh no the ac wont work. Pat and I spend the next hour changing fuses by taking out one that is working and then changing them out one at a time. Nope the ac will still not work and none of the lights or plug outlets are working. What is the deal here!!

Well we have the extractor fan working and at least that is drawing out the hot air in the Motor Home. We opened all the windows and there is a slight breeze blowing through. I am sure when we get plugged in it will all work again.

We will just have to sit here and wait our turn to park. Vince came down and we told him and he says tomorrow he will get a mechanic here to see what the problem is.

Well it gets round to 4:0p.m. and the line starts to move so we close up and start the engine!!!! NOPE the engine is dead which means the battery is dead, which also means the generator wasn't running the ceiling extractor fan but the front battery was!!! Oh well Vince comes and says he will get us a mechanic to come get us going. He sent John to jump start us but it won't work. Man he has huge truck but I guess with the fan running for four hours it has just drained the battery completely.

Oh well time for another cup of coffee. At this rate we will have used all our drinking water and creamer LOL

Poor Pat is so upset but just another thing to deal with. We sat there waiting and then decided that we could coast down the hill and get close enough to the fence to plug in and then the battery charger under the sink which should put enough power in the battery to be able to start it. Great that she has so much cable. We coasted down the hill and I went round the fence and she threw the cable over and we plugged in. Hey the air conditioner is working and all the lights!!! It shouldn't take more than an hour for it to charge up the battery.

I finally get back and then the mechanic shows up. Well that is typical. He says that in the time we have been plugged in the batteries under the step are hot and if he can't jump it then will change the batteries. John comes back and they hook up the cables and wow it starts!!!!

Man we had the generator running all that time and it didn't charge anything!!! What is the deal with this???????????

But we still have to sit in line to get parked and it is 8:0p.m. by the time we are parked and all set up and we still have to eat and do the dogs!! It has been a very long day. Good job that Twister was so quiet else I might have murdered him!!!

We let all the dogs out and then feed them and do dinner and by then it is time for bed LOL.

At least we aren't showing tomorrow so have a day of rest, just need to bath the dogs that are showing.

DeeDee is happy running around finding little people to play with!!! We finally get her to come in so we can go to bed.

Thursday

Morning comes and the sun is shining and of course Dee Dee is off playing with her friends.

Pat can sit and rest while I bath the dogs.

We bathed the chi's but didn't bath Sarah, just gave her the waterless shampoo stuff and made her smell nice.

Dee Dee has found a new friend to play with so that is good.

We took the dogs down for a walk to the building, Polly and Sarah. Gee they haven't even got the rings up yet as we don't start showing till Friday. Thursday is the day for the hounds so we take our chairs over to sit and watch. The English Foxhounds are so nice and really Pat just loves them. Oh my, it sure is hot out here so time to go and get cool again.

At least we have a nice parking spot but being by the barns there are a lot of flies and man they are eating my legs up. When I was bathing the dogs, Pat said there was blood running down my legs from the bites. I must remember to spray before I come outside.

We had dinner and then sat and watched a movie. Gee we didn't get to bed till 10:30p.m. which is late for us and we have to be in the show ring for 8:30a.m.

Pat is starting her training tomorrow for being a ring steward. They pay and it will help keep Pat on the road. But this means that she isn't going to help me show so I have to get help from Dee Dee. Just need to be cool calm and collected and it will be fine LOL.

Friday

We go over to the ring and have to take Sarah as well because she is being shown at 9:30a.m. after the chi's. Rhett is shown first and he gets Winners Dog over another dog so gets another point. He is racking up the points. Now he has 10 points. For a dog that has a bad mouth he sure has everything else going for him. Polly gets Reserve again. Should have Reserve Queen tattooed on my forehead LOL. Dee Dee had to take Snowball back in the ring for me and she did a grand job.

Not showing Trixie as it has never been majors here before.

Now time for Sarah and yes again we get Reserve!! There goes the Queen again LOL. Perhaps having a t-shirt with Reserve Queen on it would be cheaper than a tattoo and tattoos are permanent LOL.

Dee Dee comes back with me to the Motor Home and helps me get all the dogs inside. I changed my clothes and helped Dee Dee change hers and then we go over to see Pat and get some French Fries and ice cream. It was good but as usual it is hot out here. I don't know how Dee Dee manages with her long hair.

Pat is doing a grand job and was thrilled that Rhett won but again sorry she did not see him win.

Dee Dee went off with her friend and I went back to the Motor Home and the dogs.

One of the ladies that also shows chi's came over and we chatted some. She is a nice lady, Kim and has some nice dogs.

Pat finally came back at about 2:0p.m. and was exhausted of course. We sat and she told me all the funny stories about being ring steward.

We have dinner and Dee Dee comes back and said that at 7:0p.m. they are doing a Karaoke thing and of course she wants to compete. Yes there is a trophy for first place. We go over and take water of course. Dee Dee finally finds a song to sing and she does real well. It sure was fun sitting there listening to people sing. The weather starts to change so we go back to the Motor Home to put up the awning. It looks like we are in for a storm. Pat and I sat and watched a movie waiting for Dee Dee but in the end Pat went and got her as it was getting late. Dee Dee had a fun time and they did give her a ribbon which was nice. Now time for bed.

Saturday

Rhett wins his class and then goes in for points but doesn't win today!!!
Only gets Reserve.
I showed Polly and Snowball. Now Snowball and Polly have won their
classes so they both go back in the ring for points and Polly gets Reserve
again!!! Dee Dee did a grand job showing Snowball and I am very pleased
with her.
I think Polly now has 10 Reserve ribbons LOL
Time for Sarah and she gets Reserve too. Think this is going to be the
results for the rest of the week LOL
Pat just doesn't understand why Polly is only getting Reserve. Well I
think it is because she needs to lose some weight. Have to start walking
her again. She gets a bit porky!!!

We decided after Pat got back to go over and have a look at the trade
stands. Oh Mrs Brown has the small buckets and they are only $3.75
so will have to ring Debbie and tell her as that is a cheap price. I went
back and bought 10 buckets for Debbie and two for Kim. Will take the
buckets with us to Roanoke for Debbie and I will mail them to Kim
when we get home.
Was good to celebrate this evening even though we only got Reserves
LOL.
We watch a movie and of course Dee Dee is off playing but she has to be
back by the time it is dark and she is very good at doing that.
Pat is tired after stewarding all day so we are off to bed!!!

Sunday

Now it is Sunday and time for a change eh!!! Pat has to be over at the
building for 7:30a.m.
Dee Dee is already dressed and I get dressed. Think I will wear my animal
shirt as the last time I wore it I won. It does look good though. So off we
go again.
Dee Dee helps me load them all up on the trolley and off we go again.
She is getting good at this and carries the dog bag for me.

I show Rhett first and he wins but he is the only male so unless he gets Best of Winners he won't get any points.

Oh and guess what, Pat is in the next ring being steward so she can watch to some degree.

Snowball just goes round the ring as though she is having a good time but she did growl at the judge for some unknown reason but he was a huge guy.

Now it is Polly's turn and she stands on the table like a rock considering he is so tall I am amazed. Well done Polly and of course I just had to tell her.

We went back in the ring and Polly wins Reserve again!!!

Well Rhett has to go back in for Best of Breed and he ends up getting Best of Winners which means he picked up a 3 POINT MAJOR from the females!!!! Yeah and Pat was in the ring next to us showing so she got to see!!!! Of course we will have a picture done.

We went outside for the pictures and I was talking to the judge about Rhett. He said it was such a shame as he just is such a nice boy but with that mouth he felt he couldn't go any further. He was amazed when I told him Rhett only needs a major to finish.

Now I have to go over and get Sarah.

Pat comes back after she had lunch so she could sit in the cool and rest a bit.

I take Sarah over on the lead as no point in taking the crate. Oh there is my earring on the table. It must have come out when I took the lead from round my neck. Glad I found it as it is one of my gold butterfly ear rings. Would hate to lose it!!!!!

Sarah does good, gets Winners Bitch and then Best of Winners but only one point. I don't care, all those single points add up. Gee been a good day!! Yes I am thrilled to bits.

We have a picture done as she probably won't win in West Friendship, back to my Reserve ribbons and Reserve Queen LOL.

Pat comes back and we talked. She has been stewarding with Clayton Mooney and he said that Polly needs to take off about half a pound as she is looking barrel chested. She has a great front on her and it makes her look too round carrying that much weight. Guess we will start walking her LOL.

We take a nap while Dee Dee is off playing with her friends again. These flies are awful and we will have to buy some more bug spray when we leave here!!! Pat and I take the dogs walking as everyone is packing up to leave for the evening. Nice walking with a cooler breeze!!!

At least it is not quite as hot today and with the breeze blowing it makes it nice and cool under the awning. The dogs are happy to be outside playing again and with Sarah not barking any more it is just great!!!

Monday

Monday comes and again Pat is off Stewarding but this will be her last day. Dee Dee is not happy about helping me again but it is the last day of showing.

Pat and I have talked about Dee Dee doing juniors and we think Twister is really the only dog that she will be able to handle but I will have to put her name on his papers but that is no big deal. Just have to train her and the dog as he isn't used to other people but I know he will do well for her if she can do the training.

Oh my, Rhett wins again Winners Dog. He now has 13 points. Well done him. Just needs that last major to finish.

Polly wins her class today, now Dee Dee will have to take Snowball in again as she is the only entry. We go in and Polly gets Best of Winners and one more point. Then we go back in the ring for Best of Breed and the judge gives it to Polly. I am thrilled of course and yes will have a picture done with this one. Dee Dee does a wonderful job showing Snowball and of course I tell her so. Yes Polly does need to lose some weight.

Sarah has to go in just after the chi's and she gets Winners Bitch for one point again. Man I am thrilled. I don't bother to have another picture done as it is getting expensive for one point. I can put the purple ribbon on the picture I had done yesterday.

Well this was a good set of shows. Two points, a 3 point major on Rhett, 1 point and Best of Breed on Polly and two points on Sarah so we did well. There are a lot of people that go home with nothing from these shows. Yes I don't like not winning.

Fingers crossed for Trixie at West Friendship as she also only needs that major to finish.

Well, we are all relaxed and sitting outside after dinner and Sue Whaley comes over to chat and have a drink. Pat mixes up some good slushies and we sit nattering for about an hour and then Sue goes off back with Vince. Sue was very complimentary about our wins and so thrilled that we are doing so well. She is a nice friend. She also bought over a check for Pat. Her first pay check for working as a steward. We didn't think you got paid when you are training but that is fine. Pat is thrilled and Sue said that a lot of people were impressed with how quickly she learned. That is good.

We decided to take the mat over to the fence and spray it off as it was a bit nasty from the dust and dirt underfoot and nice to have it clean for West Friendship and it will dry in this heat nicely.
We just hung it over the fence and spray washed it.

Pat and I then decide that we are going to have showers outside by attaching a quilt to the barn wall. Most of the people have left and there are just a couple of old guys driving round on a tractor picking up all the trash cans and putting them in the barn beside us.

Of course first I have to get the shower to work as the flow of water is non existent. Don't understand as Pat put on a new shower head. We take it apart and nothing so Pat goes inside and turns off the pump so I can take the hose off at the tap connection. I look and can see something black and immediately think that Pat must have put the washer in and it turned. I get my head in the hole to see inside. Wow it isn't a washer but a black piece of plastic as thick as a piece of paper and the size of my thumbnail. Gee another cheap and easy fix LOL.

I clipped the shower head to the strap on the outside window and Pat clips a quilt across from the motor home to the barn wall. We put a mat down so we are not standing on the dirt as I have to be so careful of my feet and we don't need to track mud into the motor Home.

Of course Dee Dee has to be first guinea pig so to speak LOL. Pat takes her round and she has a lovely shower. Of course you have to turn the water off in-between soaping up and rinsing off but this time we are hooked into water so it doesn't matter and of course we aren't taking 45 min showers like one can do at home. Just get wet and soaped and rinse off LOL.
Dee Dee is thrilled but of course wants to then go biking but she is now in pajamas so it will be bed when Pat and I have finished.
Pat goes round the back and I keep an eye out for the guys with the tractor.
She comes round with her usual turban wrapped round her head which the dogs just do not like. Too funny that they all bark at her!!!!!

I wait for the water to heat up and it is my turn. Well I just get my hair all soaped up and Pat shouts that the men are coming back. I stand up and they have pulled up almost along by the motor home and as I stand up with soap in my hair the little man looks right at me!!! Pat forgets she is short and has put the quilt only high enough to hide her LOL LOL. Poor man didn't know where to put his face. He just smiled and said we are leaving you a clean trash can!!!!
Bet he will be talking about the soapy lady he saw for the next few evening when they have a brew or two LOL LOL

We had a good laugh and decided to sit and watch the movie "RV" with Robin Williams which we all enjoy and sit and laugh our heads off. Good job no one was around to hear us. We know the movie word for word!!! There is a part in the movie where the wife puts a cherry with stalk in her mouth and ties the stalk into a knot and says "this is what you learn when at Harvard University". Well Pat once had to put the snake down the toilet yet again and it tied itself into a knot the same way and when she pulled it out of the toilet it went twang with liquid manure everywhere!!! Just another event when travelling in a motor home!!!!

We had been watching the movie for about 10 minutes when a man bangs on the window and he is the Fair Ground keeper and of course wants money from us. He tells us that the people that have parked opposite us are carnival people and if we want we can move. He apologized if they cause any noise in the evening coming and going. We decided it was too much hassle to move but we did put the bikes round the back and chain them up and we went over and bought back the mat which we had washed so it was clean for West Friendship.
There is no way we are packing up this lot at this time of the day so we will just stay where we are. We took the dogs out and couldn't see anyone around so we just did the dogs and went to bed.

Tuesday

The morning came all too quickly of course but time to pack up and move on to West Friendship. We have to stop and get groceries so we have decided that Pat will stay in the motor home with the engine running while I run in and get the stuff on our list. Doesn't take me long to get everything and Pat of course helped put it all away. I bought some doughnuts so we could eat them while on the road. Just didn't want to not be able to crank the engine again and I can sure shop quick when it's necessary.

It is only about 77 miles but seemed to take forever going on I-301 and all the traffic lights but much nicer than travelling on I-495 round Washington.
We finally arrive and get a nice parking space after we drove round about 10 times to find the right spot. The usual parking guy wasn't around so we just had to go where we thought we would be o.k. Didn't want to have to move once set up. While we were sitting looking we had the doors open and Pat's disabled sticker went flying out the door. Took us ten minutes to find it and it was way up the field. Too funny. We parked at the back of the building so only had about a five minute walk to the show ring. We are in the shade but have no water connection. Just have to deal with it. The dogs will just have to have dry shampoo which is really very good and makes them silky.

Once again Dee Dee has found two little friends to bike with so she is happy. So nice that she is such a social child. Their mother also shows Chihuahua's so of course when we walk Sarah and Polly we have to go over and say high. She has some nice long coat chi's as well.
We talked for a bit and told her when she was tired of Dee Dee to send her home.
Pat and I chose another movie to watch and Dee Dee came back so she got undressed and ready for bed. It is another day of rest tomorrow which is nice as we don't show again till Thursday.
Oh my, the man came around for more money. We had to pay $25 for the night and another $25 because we came a day early. Man what a rip off. They sure know how to get money from you but then it would have cost at least that to stay at a camp ground and we are here in a good spot with electric!!! Needed to be set up before the crowd move in, didn't want to park on the tarmac in this heat. At least not as many flies here which is good. Sure hope it doesn't rain though as we are in a bit of a hollow part of the ground here!!!!

Wednesday

We won't bath the dogs as we are not hooked up to water. A nice restful day and we take our bikes and bike round the place. Not a bad ride if you do it so you don't have to go up hill all the way LOL. The weather is

good and we can rest up some before showing again tomorrow. Nice for the dogs not to have to show today as I know they get as tired as us!!!!
A good day and Dee Dee enjoys playing with her friends.
We cook up this chicken dish and it is just awful but of course we make Dee Dee eat it, even if just the chicken!! Won't bother to do this again!!!

Thursday

Thursday morning and we are off to the show. We aren't going to show Trixie today because it isn't a major and Mike said not to show if it wasn't a major. Oh well there you go. Rhett gets another point and Best of Opposite but Polly only wins her class. Oh well I keep forgetting that they are only 10 months old but with Rhett winning I just feel she should too. Still getting the weight off might help.
Time to show Sarah and man there are only two females. Oh, I recognize the other female from Charlottesville and I beat her so fingers crossed. The judge is Randy Garren and I have only showed Papillons to him before but have always won with him. He used to love my Papillon girl called Zella.
Oh my, he gives the win to Sarah and Best of Breed. Yeah. Only one point but better than none eh!!! Will have a picture done after Group LOL just incase we get placed LOL LOL Wow I am thrilled out of my gourd!!!!!!

Mike, our friendly handler is there and he says I have to go to Group and show Sarah. Oh man I hate going to Group because I never win. There goes that wanting to win streak again!!!!!
We went back to the motor home to celebrate with coffee and something to eat but the good news is the Non-Sporting class is the first class in Group so we shouldn't be there long LOL. We took Sarah over in the crate on the trolley with Evie as she really was pissed about not being shown. We took them outside and as we walked in they were taking the people in for the Group so I was just there in time. Sarah behaved very well and around we went. No didn't get placed LOL. I did have a picture with Randy Garren and it was outside so very hot. The photographer didn't like that I couldn't get Sarah to keep her tongue in and stop her tail wagging. Oh well there you go, she is a hot happy dog!!!

While we have been away Eric said that the RV Store, Dixie rang to say they have the thermostat in for my water heater. Hopefully he will go and get it but I doubt it. We will fix it when we get home. He is thrilled that Sarah won.

We go over and look at the trade stands but nothing that we can't live without. Bought the buckets in Bell Alton so can't see anything that we need.

We have dinner and then take Sarah and Polly walking round. It is nice here as there are some nice gentle slopes and good footage on tarmac and as it is early evening the sun is not baking hot on the dog's feet. We walked all the way round which is about a mile and that is about all my back can take LOL Yes I can see that Polly is getting trimmer, not quite so stodgy!!!!

We sit outside for a bit as it is really nice with a bit of a breeze blowing. Time for bed again. Dee Dee has been having fun with her friends. Oh it looks like rain so we better put the awning up just incase.

Friday

Friday comes and we show Rhett first of course. Well gee the judge tells us that she is going to with hold the ribbons as she doesn't like Rhetts mouth and she doesn't like the mouth nor the build on the other dog!! Well this is a first but I can understand.

Snowball shows real well and she ends up with Reserve. Polly wins her class but that is all. Oh well there you go. Glad I didn't show Trixie else she would have said something about her mouth as well. Not one of the best mouths but there you go. She just has one tooth that sticks out a bit!! Can't have it all!!!!!

Well a disappointing time with the chi's so let's hope Sarah pulls it out of the bag!!!!

Today there is one male and three females and one female special. Oh they are Santera dogs. Nice dogs and she is a nice lady. She is the judge that gave Sarah the point in Timonimum!! Sarah does good and no she doesn't bark going round the ring. She gets Winners Bitch so we have to go back in the ring up against the special and of course the male. Oh my, he gives me Best of Breed. Wow, just lovely but of course still only one point. I am thrilled and of course Pat says I have to go to Group again. Oh well might just as well. I will have a picture done after Group of course. Supposed to be bad luck if you have it done before Group but I don't have luck like that LOL. How thrilling to go to Group two days in a row!!!!

Well the Non-Sporting class will be third so we have time as it is only 9:30a.m. We went back to the motor home and have coffee and will have a sandwich before we go back over for Group.

Dee Dee is off playing with her friends of course. Must be nice to be so young and have no worries but to play hard. She is bringing her friends over and they are going to eat lunch at the picnic table which is outside the x-pen. That will be interesting!!!!!

We leave to go back for Group and this time I just take Sarah on the lead. We only had to wait about 30 minuets, timed that good and in we go. Sarah is being real good even laying down and wagging her tail. Pat even came over to give me more bait as I have to keep her focus by feeding her.

Well we didn't get placed and time to go and have a picture done as she did win over a Special and that is an achievement. Nice judge too, he even went down on one knee because I went down on my knees. Again Sarah is panting as it is almost 90 degrees out here. Had a good laugh with the photographer as he said I should give her ice and then she would keep her tongue in LOL.

Well so far West Friendship has only been good to us with the Tibbie so let's hope we do better with the chi's tomorrow as showing Trixie because it is a major.
Pat decides that she is going to bike down to the store and bring back a bag of ice!!! She is going to go into the Pizza store and get them to deliver so by the time she gets back the Pizza should be here!!! I hate it when she goes off biking but what can I say.

While she is gone I tidy up a bit and do dishes and make the kitchen all nice and clean. We only do dishes once a day when we are not hooked up to water as there is only so much in the tanks so can't waste it!!!!! Pat comes back carrying the Pizza as they don't deliver!!!! I felt so bad for her carrying the Pizza and a bag of ice!! But it was yummy and we all enjoyed it. Thanks Pat.

We sit and watch another movie and then go to bed.

Saturday

Saturday comes and lets hope Trixie does well. Please, she only needs one major to finish and can then go home to Mike in California.

Show Rhett first and he gets Winners Dog again for another point. This is great seeing as yesterday the judge with held ribbons. Just too funny. Snowball gets second in her class and so does Polly. Oh well here we go with Trixie. She is the only one in her class and the judge says "My, this is a big girl, I could pull the scale on you" so I told him to "go ahead as the dog hasn't eaten any food for the last five days we have been on the road". He smiled and picked up Trixie and looked at me and nodded as much as to say he agreed. Trixie doesn't carry weight very well and she is all loose and floppy when she hasn't eaten. Oh well a blue ribbon for her and that is all. This isn't going as planned LOL.
Oh well lets hope for Sarah to be good for us.
Pat and I go back to the motor home and recount what has happened today. Yes I am upset that neither Trixie nor Polly won, remember I hate to loose LOL.

Time for Sarah again and I just can't believe that again she takes Best of Breed over the special. Wow I am thrilled but again only one point, that is fine. All those single points add up. If she gets another point tomorrow she will have 9 points and then only need her majors which I expect might take me a while as have to find 8 females for a major now!!!!
Might be nice if there are majors in Roanoke but then there will be the usual, top class breeders and they all have very nice dogs. Oh well such is the fun of showing dogs!!!! I never thought I had a chance of beating Santera dogs. It is so nice to be showing Sarah without her doing the usual barking, just a squeak now.

Oh my we have to go to Group again LOL.

Again we take Sarah over on the lead and I put her on the chair which Pat carried over but man we seem to be waiting a long long time!!!! Sarah seems to be dealing with it well but it will show when I take her in the ring.
I take her outside to pee which is a good thing as she needed to go.
Finally go in the ring and Sarah is just awful. When we enter the ring, I don't think her four feet were on the ground more than two seconds. She is jumping and lunging and barking, well squeaking, all the way

round. She is doing back flips etc just awful. I don't know what has got into her except I won't be bringing her on a lead again she will have to wait in the crate as I think all the time and other dogs have just wound her up like a ticking bomb. Well at least it gives everyone a good laugh. Pat said that people were all oohing and aahing over Sarah's moves LOL. Glad someone liked it as I felt very embarrassed. At least she is good on the table and when it is my turn to walk round. No rosette but that is o.k. we gave everyone a good laugh LOL

Didn't have a picture done as this is getting expensive at $35 a pop and as it is only one point don't think I will have any more done. I can always put two ribbons on each picture.

We go back to the motor home and take a nap. All this running and jumping with Sarah just about wore me out LOL. I know Pat is tired. Hopefully Dee Dee will sit and watch a movie or go to sleep herself.
We had a good nap and yes Pat did rest. Now time to feed the dogs and do dinner and watch a movie, enjoy a glass of wine and go to bed.

Tomorrow we show and then go home. Been a long hard trip but we have got good wins.

Sunday

Again we have early showing but that is good because then we can pack up and get on the road home.

Show Rhett first and he gets reserve again.
Then I show Snowball and she ends up third out of four!!! Well that is good as she is still a puppy and wasn't that good on the table. She really goes round the ring well though.
Next is Polly and she does win her class of two which is nice. Fingers crossed she gets the points eh!!!
Next is Trixie and again she wins her class of two so this means Pat will have to take Polly back in the ring for points as I really want this major on Trixie.
Well best laid plans, Trixie ends up with reserve and nothing for Polly.
Well this really hasn't been a good set of shows for the chi's. Oh well lets hope there are majors in Roanoke as I know Trixie is due in season and then she will have to be bred. Can't miss this one so will just have to finish her after she has puppies.

Now is time for Sarah and let's hope she does well.

I left Pat and went over to show Sarah and I can't see the other people that were here the other three days. It is time to go in the ring and no one else shows up. Just me. Man if they didn't like me beating them they could have shown up today and perhaps they would have won. What is the point of entering and paying the entry fee which was $34 today and then not showing.
Sarah goes round very well, and stands on the table wagging her tail as usual. Wow I won!! Have to stand there while the steward calls the other competitors and then she gives me Best of Breed again which is a nice rosette this time. We joked and laughed saying how hard it was for the judge to give me the win. She was very nice. We will go under again even though there wasn't anyone else to compete with.

Well Sarah has been our saving grace at this set of shows. Yes, keep having to remind myself that a lot of people go home without any wins so I should be very happy. Yes I am thrilled with Sarah because I was beginning to think she was never going to win!!!! Pat reminds me that it was good for me to be seen in Group as all the other judges sit there and watch Group. O.K. I will agree to that. They also see me making a fool of myself when she doesn't walk nicely LOL.

Now time to pack up and head home. Again we are going down I-301 as even though there are traffic lights with it being a holiday weekend, after July 4th the traffic on I-495 will be awful. Need to get home!!!
Not a bad trip and we stopped at Blooms and met Zena to pick me and the kids up. Will go over next week and get all my stuff!! Pat and I always have a hard time saying goodbye to each other because we do have a fun time on the road. We discuss all our wins and losses and decide which strategy will be good for the next show.

The RV store rang while I was away and they have the new thermostat for the heater so I will pick it up and Pat will help me put it on. She is good as I read the directions and she puts it together. Anyone can do these things real easy if you read the directions.
Yeah it works. We can now use the water heater again! Way to go Pat.

Well gee now we have Lolla, Evie and Gracie all in season and yes going to breed them all.

Gracie is bred to Henry and of course they have no trouble.

This is Thursday and Lolla is on day 9 and we try to breed her with Rhett but he doesn't think she is ready. We will try again tomorrow.

Now time to try and breed Evie. Really need her and Henry to do this naturally as we really don't want her to have a c-section again. Well gee Henry doesn't think she is ready either so we will try again tomorrow. Perhaps Pat hasn't counted her days quite right.

We are on Friday and this time Rhett and Lolla get a tie for 44 minutes. Yeah, way to go Rhett. Let's hope we have more than one pup and I can get it out this time. Don't want to lose this litter.

Still Evie doesn't want to breed with Henry so we will AI her tomorrow as I didn't bring the kit with me. Don't think we will miss it as still think she isn't quite ready today.

Saturday and today if Evie doesn't breed with Henry then I will AI her as don't want to miss. Not going to happen so we AI Evie. At least Lolla and Gracie were bred properly.

Sunday and we A I'd Evie again and will do it again tomorrow so that is three times so hopefully we will have pups. Evie seems such a hard dog to breed naturally, don't know why!! Still to A I her is nice and quick and at least you know it is done!!!!

August

Monday

Today is Monday and I go over to Pat's to pick her up on our way to Roanoke dog show. It is about a four hour drive so we should be there by about 2:30p.m. Well that is what our "Lolla" says and she is never wrong!!!! We always enjoy the Roanoke show because my dear friend Debbie lives there and she is a member of the club and always looks out for us when it comes to the parking.

All loaded and off we go. We arrived like we said at 2:30p.m. and Debbie has a nice parking place for us. We have electric, water and sewage even though it cost $125.00 for the five nights. Still that is only $25 per night and we have electric, water and sewage so a good deal really. Much better than running on the generator for five days!!!! There are three people hooked onto the water spicket and I don't have an attachment but the

Pomeranian guys lend us one and we will give it back. I will try and buy one when we go shopping with Debbie.

The weather is lovely but they are talking storms of course in the evenings. Always run the risks of storms being so close to the mountains!!!

We let all the dogs out and of course we have Evie and Lolla with us. We never leave them at home and especially as they are supposed to be making babies!!!!

Oh my Twister thinks that Evie is very interesting and this is day 23 so she should be over and done with!! Luckily I have the small x-pen with us so we put that up at the end and put Lolla and Evie in there. Amazing how Twister can lift up the x-pen but hasn't got the sense to figure out how to get under it at the same time LOL, LOL. Well I didn't bring the AI kit so let's hope Henry can perform as we will try him with Evie this evening just to see. Perhaps Pat did have the dates wrong and she just wasn't ready to be bred!!!

We have dinner and then start to play with Evie and Henry. Man Henry can squirt that sperm everywhere except where we want it to go. Pat gets it squirted in her eye and her eye swells up. She has contact lenses in and it is burning her eye and makes the contact lens edge curl up. Wouldn't think that sperm was that potent would you???? Her eye is swollen and we put Henry and Evie in a crate hoping they will tie. Pat has to go and clean out her eye but can't get the contact lens out. She took a dose of Benadryl and hopefully that will take down the swelling. Don't want another episode like the tick she had on her eye.

Well Henry and Evie have messed around for an hour and a half and Henry is just exhausted. Yes we will try again tomorrow.

Now time to watch a movie and then go to bed. Pat can't see very well but at least the swelling has gone down enough to get the contact lens out!!!

Tuesday

Tuesday today and we have to bath Sarah and the chi's ready to show tomorrow. Debbie is coming to pick us up about mid day to go shopping and to the Chinese Restaurant for lunch or brunch. Yes have to remember to buy a water attachment so I can return the one I borrowed.

Sarah is very good and I have her all done by 10:30a.m. and the chi's only take a few minutes as we don't have to blow dry them. They can just air dry and it is nice and warm so they will be fine. Wow it is ll:0a.m. and Debbie has rung and said she is on her way. She got finished early.

Went shopping with Debbie but Hamricks (Department store) was very disappointing this time. I only bought one t-shirt. Oh well there you go. Guess they aren't having such a large inventory now!!! Lunch was good though at the Chinese Restaurant and we met a friend of Debbie's, Sandy. Nice gal.

Pat and I had decided that we would only show Wednesday, Thursday, Friday and Saturday and then go home as didn't care for the judges on Sunday plus would have to pay for another day's parking.
Going to show Polly all four days but not Sarah. She will only be shown Wednesday, Thursday and Saturday. Been under the judges the other two days and didn't win so no point in wasting more money!!!!

Well it is time to try and breed Evie again with Henry. This time Pat will have to hold her still so hopefully we don't have any more accidents with Henry missing.
Wow they tie for 45 minutes and Pat has to hold Henry so that he can't turn round as the last time he tried to turn he slipped out!! Not going to loose this breeding. We were beginning to wonder if Henry was ever going to stop. Better get some nice puppies from this breeding as it might be the last time for Evie and hopefully no c-section!!!! Poor Pat's arms are aching from holding Henry still all that time. It wasn't as bad for me because Evie just stood there. Have to write the date down because we will forget by the time we get home!

The next one to come in season will be Trixie and she will be bred to one of Junko's dogs, a nice red and white, Champion Guichon's Jackpot. Junko has lovely dogs and she usually beats me LOL.

Pat's eye is looking better so the Benadryl is the way to go if this ever happens again!! Hopefully NOT.

Wednesday

As usual we show the chi's first. I am still showing Polly in Bred By Exhibitor because then I can show Trixie in the open class. Rhett goes in first and there are only four males which is two points, and only four females which again is two points so even if Rhett gets Best of Winners he still won't get the major!!!! Yes Rhett gets the two points but not the BOW. Oh well there you go.

Polly wins her class but she is the only one and so does Trixie. Trixie ends up getting reserve. Oh well she didn't really need the points and Polly doesn't get anything!!!

Now it is time to show Sarah. Well gee there are only two males and two females, one of course being Sarah so she could get another point but even if she gets Best of Winners it will still only be one point. We just don't seem to be able to find shows with any more entries for a major!!!!

Well Sarah wins and gets Best of Winners again but only one point. Really not worth having another picture done as this is getting expensive for one point!!!Of course I am thrilled and will have a drink tonight LOL!!! She really is looking good and without the barking so much nicer to handle LOL.

Fitting Sarah gets a win here when she came into our life at this show last year!!!! Course now she is debarked so what can I say.

We had another good day showing even though of course I am disappointed that Polly didn't win. Sarah now has 9 points so not bad for this season.

We are still thinking about doing the weekend in Raleigh which is in September. That will be our last show as Trixie is due in season and she is to be bred this time. Always thinking one step ahead.

We went back to the motor home and had some lunch and then took a nap!!!! Don't like these early morning starts LOL

We had a good dinner of steak and salad. We opened a bottle of wine to celebrate the win on Rhett and on Sarah. Watched a movie and then went to bed.

Thursday

Thursday comes around and the sun is shining, which is usual here in Roanoke, but never think it won't storm as it can in a heartbeat!!! So close to the mountains.

The chi's show first and fingers crossed for Trixie again.

There are only 3 males today as we pulled Rhett. He has 18 points now so really not worth showing him. There are three females including Trixie of course.

Well Polly wins and also gets Best of Winners and Best Opposite Sex but still only 1 point!

Hey that is o.k. all those odd points add up and Polly beat Trixie who got reserve.

I could have pulled Trixie as it would still have made only one point. Oh well there you go. I never seem to be able to think about this before I go in the ring. Need to do more studying of the entries but hey you have paid the entry fee so why not show!!!! Yes will have a picture done!!!!

A very pleasing morning and we can take the chi's back and pick up Sarah. It is just easier to have her in the crate rather than walking her as seem to have to wait so long and she is just not good having been out of the crate.

This is Judge Frank Sabella and he did in fact give me the first points on Sarah in Kansas so this might be interesting.

Only two males again 4 females so only one point again!!!

Yeah Sarah wins the one point again. Wow she actually beat some good dogs too. That makes me feel good. No won't have a picture done just for one point again. There is just not enough room on the wall for all these one point pictures LOL. Oh well one day she will get more than one point.

At least the barking is no where as bad as it used to be!!!! I don't quite feel as though I want the ground to open up and swallow me any more and people are not telling me to shut the dog up!!!

Well not showing Sarah tomorrow but will on Sunday. Don't think she would win with that particular judge. Wow she now has 10 points!! And five Best of Breed ribbons. Not bad as she is only just over a year old and to think I was going to pull her the rest of the season!!!!

Will be interesting to see how she does on Saturday.

Pat and I are thrilled of course that we got points on two of our dogs today!!! Yes of course an excuse to open a bottle of wine or we might have slushies tonight!!!!

Well the water heater is still messing around so I guess that putting the new thermostat on it didn't fix it. It really needs the new valve thing which of course I already have. Debbie is going to get the guy to stop by and have a word. Debbie got him to ring and he is coming tomorrow morning to fix it but I told him we have to be out of here by 9:30a.m. and really I don't want any one here while I am trying to get ready to show. Pat and I had tried to put the new valve thing on but we couldn't get the old one off. Guess they have a special tool or take something off to get to it!!!

Only showing the chi's tomorrow and they don't take much grooming. Of course whiskers have to be done as they seem to grow overnight, just like a man LOL.

We decided tonight as we won with two dogs that we would order Chinese. The slush puppy lady gave us the phone number of a local place that delivers so we ordered Duck and Sesame Chicken and of course fried rice with everything in it!!!

It was very good and very filling. Yet again there is enough for lunch tomorrow!!!

Now time for a movie again, and then off to bed!!!!

Friday

Morning comes and the guy to fix the water heater isn't here yet so that is good we can eat breakfast and get dressed. He rang to say he was on his way and of course we have to leave. He said to go ahead and lock the door as he didn't need to get inside the motor home and I will run back as soon as I finish showing.

Nice man and he was there waiting for me to pay him. Worth every penny as I already had the part and that is always the expense. So much easier to have these things fixed when you are at a show rather than dragging the motor home to the repair shop at home and leaving it of course. He did tell me that you have to take the chimney cowling off to get the part out which of course makes sense when you look at it.

Well today is Friday and we are only showing the chi's, Sarah doesn't get to play today!!!!

Rhett wins his class but only one in it!!!

Polly wins her class!!

Now for Trixie, if she wins her class and oh hell only 5 females but if Trixie gets Breed over the specials she will pick up the major!!!!

Well geez she wins Winners Bitch but only two points and Best of Opposite sex again!!! Just so frustrating when you can't get that stupid major and Polly gets reserve again LOL.

Well at least I wasn't showing Sarah so we have had a really easy day of it!!!! Now time to go and look round the trade stands. We need to buy some more cow hooves as this is the only place that we have found them to be of a good price. Here you can buy 24 hooves for $12.99 whereas most places charge $1.50 each. Pat and I bought two bags each and that is enough to keep us going till next year LOL. My dogs love the cow hooves and it is the only thing they don't really fight over. Rawhide or anything like that is real bad as they will fight till the death.

I am so amazed that really all the trade stands have the same old stuff as at the beginning of the season!!! They need some new life in here!!!! Wish I could think of something that we could make and sell but there you go!!

Time to go back to the motor home and take a nap!!!!

Saturday

Saturday and it is our last day of showing. Think we will have to do the weekend in Raleigh just to see if we can finish Trixie.

It is a major today so need Trixie on top form!!!!

Rhett wins his class but that was all. There are some nice males here so not surprising he didn't win today. Polly wins her class but of course she is the only one in Bred By but that is fine, at least I get to run her twice. Pat has to be on the end of the lead to go back in as I need to show my heart out on Trixie. Come on it is a major today!!!! Well just lost it as Trixie gets second in her class of two. Oh well I will show Polly and see if she can win the major!!!!!!!!!!!!!! I really shouldn't ever be nervous about this having done it so many times but NO Polly gets Reserve yet again!!!!!!!!!!!!

I think I will have Reserve Queen tattooed across my forehead or across my chest for every judge to see LOL LOL. Oh well there you go. Such is the fun of showing dogs.

Raleigh here we come LOL. Yes we made the decision to do just the weekend with Trixie Polly and Sarah of course.

O.K. now it is time to take the chi's back and get Sarah. She just needs a bit of combing out and a spraying and she is ready to go. She has a lovely black coat and it shines real nice in the sun.

Today is not a major for the tibbies so as usual going in with fingers crossed for Sarah as it is two points. Oh well there you go she only gets to win her class and that is all. So that makes the decision to do Raleigh so let's hope for majors there.

Sarah now has ten points and no majors!!!!

Debbie came back to the motor home and we sat and drank coffee and chatted before Pat and I started to pack up. It is a shame that we aren't staying for the dinner dance but as we aren't showing on Sunday it would just be a waste of money paying for the parking. We didn't like the judges on Sunday and silly to waste the money to enter when you know you haven't won under the judges before!!!!

Debbie left after hugs and tears as usual. Always sad to say goodbye to friends after a dog show but we have to pack up and get home.

Pat and I can pack this up in about 20 minutes. We both know where everything goes and can read the other persons mind as to what happens next. We work as a team and should be home by about 6.0p.m.

It was a good drive home and I ring Zena and tell her when I am leaving Pat's house to put the other dogs up. Just easier getting these out when the other dogs are up in crates!!!

Don't have to worry about emptying the tanks so can park the motor home the right way round. It is so much easier when we can empty the tanks before we come home.

So now we have to do the entries for Raleigh and have fingers crossed it will be a major in the Chihuahua's and Tibetan Spaniels and hope that after I do the entries Trixie doesn't come into season.

Raleigh

Well Sarah comes into season on August the 17th and she is just over 18 months old now so I am going to breed her to Grissom. I know she isn't finished but Grissom isn't getting any younger. Sarah does have 10 points and five Best of Breed ribbons so she is over half finished!!!! Can still show Sarah as she will only be a few days pregnant!!! Gee might calm her down a bit LOL.

We decided to do Raleigh just the Friday Saturday and Sunday so have sent entries in for Sarah, Trixie and Polly.

Well gee Trixie comes into season so we have to make arrangements to get her to Junko in Maryland. August 23rd and I have sent her entries in. Typical eh!!! Oh well we have to breed her as she is 3 1/2 years old now and not getting any younger.

Pat and I decide to take her as she is to be bred on Monday the 27th August to Junko's dog in Maryland. Mike chose the dog out of two that Junko has.

Now Sarah is on day 8 so I really must put her out as she is beginning to flag to Twister and don't want that!!!! Oh my just as I bent to pick her up the phone rang which of course I answered and with that Twister was on Sarah and they were tied! Oh man I am so upset, screaming and crying as I was saving Sarah for Grissom and he is just sitting and watching!!!!! Oh I am so cross, what am I going to do!!!

Well you better believe I put Sarah out as soon as Twister had finished, can't believe he only tied for less than a minute but guess he knew I was very very angry with him. I put her out and of course rang Niki immediately.

There is heating out in the laundry room when it is cold and we have fans blowing when it is hot. They have their own fenced in yard which I love and of course it is dog proof. Plus three doors to go through so if one of my boys does get through the first door there is no way he can get through all three without being seen!!!!

Niki told me to breed her to Grissom this evening and hopefully his sperm will interact with Twister and at least we will have a split litter which of course means I have to DNA Sarah, Twister and Grissom and then the puppies. Going to be expensive!! All this is because I answered the phone. You better believe I won't do that again eh!!!!!!!!!!!! No because next time Sarah goes out in the laundry room the day I see she is in season!

We tried to breed her to Grissom but he is not interested so I have to AI her.

Well not very good looking liquid and I don't think it has sperm in it. Oh well put it in anyway!! Perhaps it will kill Twister sperm!!!!!!!!!

I AI'd her again on Tuesday and again Grissom wasn't interested and I had Trixie who is in season sitting on his nose!!! What is the deal with these tibbies that they don't want to breed!! Niki warned me and man she was right!!!!

Well Wednesday and don't think Grissom is up to being AI'd again. He has thrown up in his crate and just acting sick. Perhaps he doesn't like being AI'd but it is his fault and not mine as I don't like having to do it either.

Debbie rang and suggested that tomorrow I take Sarah for a progesterone test, to see if she is still dropping eggs. Well Thursday is the day we leave for Junko so will have to get Sarah to the vet early. They will have to ring me when we are on the road so gave them my cell number!! What a bloody mess eh!!!

Seems funny going to Raleigh without Trixie but makes a difference not having to worry about her climbing the fence.

Thursday is the 27th August and we take Trixie to Junko for breeding before we go to Raleigh next Thursday and won't be able to pick her up till after Raleigh. Oh well she will not be a Champion when she is bred. Let's hope she gets her figure back ready for the spring. Would really like to finish her myself but if she has to go back to Mike for that last major then so be it!!!

We had been on the road about an hour and the vet rings to say that yes go ahead and breed Sarah as she is ready now!!!!!! Yeah way to go Sarah so lets hope we can get at least one or two tibbies right!!!!!!!!

We have a good trip to Junko and find it right away. She has a lovely place and of course we sit on the patio and have a drink and chat about dogs and showing etc. We could have stayed all day but have to leave as it is a three hour drive home.

We talked all the way home about what a lovely set up Junko has. Sure hope Trixie behaves herself and I did tell her that Trixie is a fence climber so she is aware of that!! Her set up is cinderblock and chain link fencing six foot high where Trixie will be staying. Such a lovely set up and Junko gives me some pipettes to try using for Sarah. Have to get home so I can breed her again.

We stopped before getting on the main road and had lunch in a little country restaurant and it was good. We had onion rings and a sandwich each. It was very cheap too. That is good.

We got home about 6.0p.m. and we didn't hit too much traffic so a good trip home.

It is time to try and breed Sarah again. Let's hope it is good. Well not good as having a hard time twisting the tube in Sarah so perhaps she is already taken. Oh I will be so upset if they are all Twister pups. No point

in dwelling on it eh!!!!! Will try one more time tomorrow and see what happens. Then will let it go as she is on day 12 tomorrow.
Well day 12 and we AI again but this seems to be the best breeding of her yet. The tube just slid on in which is good. Fingers crossed eh!!!! I have done all I can do to try and get a Tibetan spaniel pup!!!

Tomorrow is Saturday and we are going to have a chocolate fountain evening. Pat is coming over with her family so we should have a good time. It is such a fun evening dipping fruit etc into the chocolate fountain. Dee Dee had the best time and it was nice to share an evening with Patrick and Michelle

September

Well now we are off for the Raleigh shows. September 4th 5th and 6th we will show. Can't pick Trixie up till after this week.

Thursday

Was a good trip, Raleigh is an easy drive if you don't get stopped with traffic. We get a good parking space and just have to pull the trolley with the crates on, up the hill to the doors. Not far at all. Better than going all the way round the front. In fact I think we were parked nearly the same spot in the spring.
Doesn't take us long to set up and then we took Polly and Rhett over to the building for a look to see who is here and what they have on the trade stands of course LOL
Now time for a nap, our favorite part of the day!!
Of course we buy a catalogue so as to see what the entry is and gee it is not a major on Friday but is on Saturday and Sunday. Sorry Trixie isn't here but she had to be bred.

Friday

Friday comes round and I take Rhett in first again but he only gets reserve this time. Well there were four males and with Rhett's mouth not getting much better we are not surprised he doesn't win. Snowball is in next but she is the only one in the class so of course wins LOL. Next is Polly and again the only one in the ring. Well that is good as now Pat can take Snowball back in and I take Polly in. It is nice not having Trixie really as then Polly doesn't have to go on the lead with Pat. Well again Polly gets Reserve. I am sure getting a lot of reserve ribbons but there you go. We have another day tomorrow and of course Sunday.

We went back to the motor home to get Sarah. Still only 6 females but that is two points this time so fingers crossed!
Well low and behold Sarah doesn't even win her class. We won't go under this judge again.
I keep all this written down in a book under judges!!! I record what judge gives what ribbons so that we know if to go under that judge again!!! With money being short you can't afford to go under a judge that you know won't give you a win!!!

Yet another day tomorrow, all the fun of dog showing. We went and walked round the trade stands again but still the same old stuff. We don't need to buy anything but we will have to go and have lunch in the restaurant as they cook the best fried chicken we have ever eaten. While we were waiting to show a girl came round and gave us two tickets for the restaurant so lunch will only cost us for the drink!!!!! Well gee can only find one ticket but that is o.k. as this is my treat to Pat as it is always hard to do this show because the kids go back to school on the day after we get home!!! As usual the chicken is out of this world. We have to pick it right down to the bones. Yummy.
We go back to the motor home to commiserate as usual LOL. We are much better at commiserating with ourselves rather than staying over at the building talking to people who just talk about us behind our backs!!!! It is time for a movie and a drink and then to bed.

Saturday

Saturday comes around and today is majors for males and females. Fingers crossed for Rhett and Polly, let's hope she can shine today.

A lot of good dogs here today and people that we have met in the past. Rhett wins his class again but with all these good dogs can't see him picking up the major. I think Pat will think about re-homing him after this but we will see how he does. Rhett gets reserve which is good but really still needs that last major. The lady is here that is thinking of buying him. He does have 18 points and one major so really is a champion even though he doesn't have that last major. Snowball goes in and is the only one in her class so if Polly wins her class Pat will take her in. Wow Polly wins her class out of two so let's go for the win Yeah right!!!!!!

While we are waiting Kim comes up and says that Polly is going to win this and another girl who we have seen before but not in a long time, Sandra Clarke tells me that I am going to win. LOL LOL Knock me over with a feather if I do!!!!! This is a dog show and anything can happen!!!!

WOW POLLY WINS A 3 POINT MAJOR AND BEST OF WINNERS, where is the feather??? Doesn't get an extra point for BOW because there were the same amount of males so no extra point. Hey I am just so thrilled, we have to go and have fried chicken again to celebrate LOL. Pat kept telling me Polly is a good dog but when you own it you can't see it. I am thrilled with her, and another day tomorrow. Yes this time I do have a picture done as this is exciting, a 3 point major and Polly isn't a year old yet!!!! Way to go Polly. Eric will be thrilled. Yes I do have a picture done as this is her first major and it should be very nice.

We show Sarah and of course get only second in her class again. I am going to have to lay her off now that she is pregnant anyway!! Hopefully she will mature after having pups!!! Yeah who am I kidding, myself LOL.

We go over and change our clothes and then went to the restaurant. This is the only place that we really lash out and spend money as the fried chicken is oh so good, can almost taste it. Fun to sit and chat with people that you know, all enjoying the fried chicken like us.
Back to the motor home for a nap and of course have to call Eric and tell him that his girl got her first Major. She now has 8 points with one major. Hopefully will finish her next season oh and it might be here as this is usually the first show we do!!!
It was nice to sit and chat and of course celebrate Polly's win. Am I biased or what LOL. We watch a movie and do some sewing and then time for bed.

Sunday

Sunday comes around and we load up the trolley and don't take Sarah as she isn't showing till 2:30p.m. so that means we won't be out of here till about 3:30p.m. if we are lucky!!!!!

So can we get a coo and another major on Polly or on Rhett would be nice. Well gee there are only 5 male chi's because the girl, Sandra Clark has left and gone home. Apparently her long coat Chihuahua didn't win under this judge so she just packed up and left. Well that breaks the major!!! Oh well this is what has happened all season which is why we didn't finish Trixie.
Rhett only wins his class and Polly ends up with Reserve. There you go Reserve Queen again. Hey can't complain when you won yesterday eh!!!

We decided to go back to the motor home and do a bit of sewing as it is daylight and we have a lot of time to spend sitting!!! There really isn't anything we can put away on the inside and can't pack up outside because the dogs have to go out when we get back from showing Sarah. Of course I change my clothes so as not to get any food down the front and it is more comfortable sitting in non show clothes!!!
So we go off to show Sarah and she gets second in her class but the dog that won the class ended up winning the points and he gives Sarah the Reserve!
Well we are coming home with a major on Polly and five reserves!!!!!!!!!!!!
Still some people don't win anything so we are lucky to have won at least one major when only it is only a three day show!!!!

Now it is time to pack up and be on the road again. We should be home about 6:0p.m. providing we don't hit too much traffic.
Well that is our last show of the year as we now need to concentrate of delivering pups. Gracie, Lolla, Evie and of course Sarah!!!!

It was a fun trip home as usual with Pat and me celebrating and laughing and discussing the pros and cons as usual. We have such a fun time chatting that we sometimes have missed our exit which is why we love "Lolla" as she talks to us and tells us the next exit LOL. I think we have more or less decided that Rhett has to be re homed. Don't want to use him with a bad mouth in our breeding program.

I drop Pat off and Max is home to help unload the dogs and congratulate me on my win which was so nice of him.

Pat will come over Monday or Tuesday to get her stuff. No rush as this is the last show of the season so we just clean up the motor home ready for winter.

We picked up Trixie on the 10th September and she should be due 1st November. Yes I will have her x-rayed so we know as she has never been bred before.

Sarah is due the 25th October and Evie is due the 27th September and Gracie is due 17th September and we don't think that Lolla took which is a shame but there you go. We were either too early or too late when we bred her!!! The next time Pat is going to try Henry as he is a proven stud. Perhaps Rhett didn't have good enough sperm, too young who knows these things!!! Oh well he is going to a pet home so will be fixed anyway!!!

Well I am at work and get a phone call from Pat saying that she thinks Gracie is having contractions and when can I get there. I had already taken the whelping bag over there so that Pat can have everything together. I finish work and head off to Pat's.

This isn't the usual easy go delivery for Gracie. Usually she whelps without any problem but this is long going and I think this will be her last breeding. She is telling us she doesn't want to do this any more.

She had four pups but the last one took a long time and doesn't look too good. Pat works on it and she gets it going but it is very tiny. Only time will tell.

We thought there might be another one but it might just be the uterus so we decide to put her up with the pups. She had enough oxytocin to have pushed out an elephant so she should be good to go.

Pat rings the next morning saying that Gracie had another pup in the night which did not survive and the last born did not survive either.

Guess she won't be having any more pups but she has been a real good mother every time we have bred her. Well done Gracie.

Gracie is now five so time for her to be spayed and just be a house dog now. Gracie was Pat's first show dog in Chihuahua's and Pat and Heather learnt a lot showing her. She has done Pat proud and given her some nice pet pups which have lovely homes.

Well Friday the 25th September comes around and I get a phone call from Pat that Evie has started to have contractions. Well it is 3:0p.m. and we are all supposed to be going to Cracker Barrel for dinner as it is Eric's birthday.

Hopefully Evie will be over by 6:0p.m. and we can make dinner.

Well the first one comes with one foot out and it is blue so of course we ring the vet and pile into the van with the crate and heating pad and flannels of course!!! Luckily it is only about 10 minutes away but in the meantime Evie pushes out the pup and I get it squeaking and it is doing well. Good news as the last time Evie had a c-section and then would not look after the pups so we don't want that as can't give these pups to Gracie this time.

They put us in another room and low and behold Evie has another pup, male this time so that is good. We hang around for about another 30 minutes and they say she is doing well so did we just want to go home which of course we do. No charge so that is nice.

I did ask the vet technician that Dr Lessinger was on call and of course she said yes. I asked the girls out the front as we were leaving and they also said yes Dr Lessinger was on call.

Well at this rate we won't make dinner and when we get back to Pat's house Max wasn't even dressed. He said he wouldn't go and stay with us but of course we both told him to go as Eric would be disappointed, bad enough that I couldn't be there eh!!!

They had a fun evening and everyone in the restaurant sang happy birthday to him. Sad that Pat and I couldn't be there but our dogs come first and of course Eric understands that.

Well gee we wait and we wait and after two hours decide to give her a dose of oxy and help things move along!!!! Pat ordered Pizza for us and of course more coffee!! It was a good pizza

It is now ll:0p.m. and still no puppy. We keep walking her and walking her but nothing. Finally at ll:30p.m. we decided to ring the vet and tell her that Evie (Dr. Lessinger) is still having a problem with two in there. When we had Evie x-rayed the girls told me that Meryl was on call and of course we get to find out that she isn't so I am very sorry. Still Meryl meets us at the surgery just as I deliver another pup which is huge. Meryl gave Evie another shot and the last pup comes out but doesn't look good and is very tiny!!!! We leave there and go home. I am so sorry that we upset Meryl and will keep her informed with Sarah. Wish the girls in the front would get their information up to date!!!!!

Pat worked on the puppies all the way home but they are not going to make it I feel sure. Yes been in the canal too long but it is the choice Pat made rather than have a c-section.
Go to the vet and have a c-section and risk her rejecting the pups like she did last time or just end up with two dead pups and two live pups!!!!! Well Pat made the decision that no c-section this time and have two live pups!!!!!!!!!!!!!! Evie is doing fine and nursing the pups well. It was a good decision which we had to make.

Let's hope that the next time we breed her she will have a normal delivery!! So hard with these little guys to know which way to go. Evie loves the pups and is feeding them and cleaning them and that is not what she did with the last litter and we had to give them to Gracie to look after which she did well.

We are sorry we missed Erics birthday party at Cracker Barrel but it sounds as though they had a great time so we weren't missed that much!!!

I finally got home to bed at 2:0a.m. in the morning. Phew long day!!!!

Now we have to wait for Sarah and Trixie. Let's hope they have an easier time than Evie.

Well the 21st October is here and I am taking Sarah in to be x-rayed. Let's hope she has four and two of them are Tibetan spaniels. Fingers crossed.
Meryl comes out and says there are six and tried to pull it up on the computer but nothing so we go back to the x-ray room and there on the screen six puppies and they all look to be a good weight!!!!! Unreal but there you go. Tibetans usually have three to four pups and she has to have six!!!!

On the way home I rang Niki and she said there would be six and two will be Tibetan spaniels so fingers crossed. They will have to be DNA'd and I have already sent in the DNA for Grissom and Twister.

I get up on Friday the 23rd and look at Sarah and she seems to be panting and shuddering. Well guess I will be spending the day watching and waiting. I ring Meryl and tell her and she says the first four will probably not be a problem but she will probably be tired by the last two so keep her informed.

Well gee I wait all day and nothing. Pat came over and we sat and watched and again Pat said ring me when she starts. Spend all evening watching and waiting which is what you do when waiting on pups coming and finally decide to go to bed at ll:45p.m.

Zena had just come home and she of course was tired and has another show to go to tomorrow so she really doesn't want to help me whelp puppies.

I started to get undressed and was watching Sarah and saw a distinctive shudder and contraction!!! I went and got Zena and we both watch and decide yes she is having contractions. Zena needs to go to bed as an early start in the morning so I get dressed and we ring Pat of course!! My faithful friend.

Dear Pat says she will come over and be here to help. Pat arrives with all her makeup on and looking real spiffy. I asked her if she was going on a date and her reply was "if we have to go to the vet I am ready LOL" Well gee you will have to wait for me to put on my bra and makeup as I just threw a t-shirt on to deal with this LOL.

The first pup comes out at 12:10a.m. as Pat walks in the door just as we are getting the pup going!!! I did ring Meryl at 10:00p.m. and tell her still nothing so not to worry but she told me she had girls on call just incase. It pays to have a wonderful vet who is willing to come out in the middle of the night. Yes she did tell me she was on call so got it from the "horses" mouth so to speak LOL.

Well the first born was at 12:10a.m. so now we wait. And wait and wait. Drink another cup of coffee of course. This puppy is a female and weighs 6 ounces!!!

The next one is born at 1:45a.m. so at this rate with four more to go it is going to be a long night!! This one is a boy and is really nice. They both look like Tibetans now!!!! Pat gets the puppy going and I go into the kitchen and make another cup of coffee and Pat yells that she is pushing again!!!!

The next one is born at 2:00a.m. and it is another boy but this one is black and white!! Ugh oh is this going to be a papillon????????????

Well that was nice and quick and we have three to go. Usually come in pairs so I am sure we will have a long wait for the next one.

It is 2:15a.m and she is contracting again and out comes another one, girl this time and red and white!!!!!!!!!!!!!!!! My heart is sinking but this could be a tibbie as Grissom's father is a red and white!! Yes of course it could be a tibbie!

So have I got time to go and finish making another cup of coffee. Wow all these pups are weighing in at 6 ounces. Huge as we are so used to the tiny chi's who usually weigh 4 ounces on a good day when delivering!!!! I have the coffee made and low and behold she is pushing again and out pops number five puppy. It is another male and again weighing in at 6 1/2 ounces. This is 2:30a.m. and so far we have not had to give her a shot of oxy at all. I really think Sarah read the book on delivering puppies!!!!

All so healthy and wanting to nurse and Sarah is being so good letting them nurse and still has another one in there. Well I expect this one is going to take a long time to come but we are doing well so far so not to get too excited. She is doing well and under no stress so if she hasn't had the last one in another hour then we will give her a shot!!! And still haven't had to ring the vet. Yeah way to go Sarah!!!

Blimey it is 2:45a.m. and Sarah is pushing out the last puppy. Well I am just amazed. Six puppies and it hasn't even been three hours and not one dose of oxy but I will give her a dose now as she did retain two placentas and this will also help clean her out and shrink the uterus.
We take her outside to let her pee and poo but she pees and wants to be right back with the pups. I already have the crate and everything set up in the bathroom so Pat helps me carry the pups and Sarah in to settle them down for the night. The heating pad has already been on so just need to get her some water and food. Think she deserves it.

She has delivered 36 ounces of puppies and all without oxy and no stress to her at all. Now let's see if she can be a good mum and look after them. I will have to go up in the attic and get out the big whelping box as the crate is going to be too small for her within a few days with this gang of puppies!!! The DNA kits have already arrived and we will do them on Monday. Give them a couple of days before we do it as have to put the brush in their mouths. Will have to write descriptions for each pup and number them real well as hard to tell the brown ones apart except of course the female. She is red just like Grissom so I have high hopes for her. All the mouths look just like Sarah.
We get them all DNA'd and now have to wait about six weeks before we will know.

Sarah is a good mum and it really will be fun watching them grow. I could spend hours sitting on the toilet watching them suck and listen to them squeaking. Sarah is so good. I am just amazed as I did worry about her looking after them.

O.K. now we have to wait for Trixie. Let's hope she has an easy time of it. I have to ring up and get her x-rayed. She is due the 1st November so will have her done on 28th October which is 4 days early so that should be good.

I went to work Tuesday as Sarah is doing well and can be left.
Need to be home the rest of the week as waiting on Trixie. She is not my dog so no way will I be away from the house while waiting for her to deliver.

Well today is Monday and time to do the DNA on all the pups. We line up all the paperwork so that nothing gets messed up . . . Zena brings in all the pups and we write a description and number for each pup. Oh please let the little red girl be a Tibetan Spaniel but of course I have my doubts deep down in my stomach.
If they are not Tibetans then I sure hope that I can find good and nice homes for them. All the paperwork is done so now just need to mail it and wait.

Well Tuesday morning I get up and Trixie is acting like she is going to go into labor but seems funny and I haven't had her x-rayed. I rang the vet and told them and asked if I could bring her in as need to know that all is o.k. as this is 6 days early. She isn't due till Sunday. Rang Pat and she said she would go with me which is good as better take Trixie in the Crate and heating pad just incase as Evie had two on the way to the vet. Seems the car ride shakes them up. Have her x-rayed and there are three pups.
Way to go Trixie seeing as she has not really been eating the last few weeks. She would only eat chicken if it was fresh cooked, wouldn't eat the chicken livers any more nor the dog food of course. She would munch on a bit of dry kibble but blimey not enough to keep a bird alive. Let's hope that the pups are good weights. They look good on the x-ray!!!

We get home and set her up on the dining room table but every time she has a contraction she is trying to stop it so I get the crate from the bedroom and put her in the crate and covered her with her blanket. As soon as we see a bubble we put her on the table to deliver the pup. She just doesn't seem to be swelling enough to pass these pups!!! The first one seems to be on the way, but taking a long time so we give her a shot of oxytocin to help push this one out then the next should be o.k.

The first one is born at 12:30p.m. and weighing 4 1/8 ounces. See small compared to the tibbies. Wow the first one is a girl, way to go Trixie, now let's have at least one more girl!!!! This pup is having trouble breathing, fluid on her lungs but Pat is working hard with her. We have learnt that if you fold up a flannel and lay the pup head down over the rolled up flannel, usually they stop aspirating. We put flannels in the microwave to warm up the pups. A cold pup will never nurse which is why we have the heating pad on so high!!! Not to cook them but to keep them warm and when nursing in between whelping we always cover them with a warm flannel again so no drafts etc. which can chill them so fast!!!!
You know I have to have the ceiling fan going as I get so hot delivering pups. You would think I was giving birth!!!

Trixie will have nothing to do with the pup so we put her back in her crate and cover her with her blanket. She seems much happier like that and no need on stressing her out any more. That will come when she has finished and has them to look after!!!!

Wow 1:10p.m. and she is pushing again. At least she doesn't panic when we put her in the crate on the table as the contractions just take over. Man this is hard to get out and of course coming back feet first!! Not good as it means the head is going to be the largest body part to come out!!! Oh this is hard and she really isn't swelling up like she should. Looks like she might tear but nothing I can do now. If she tears we will have to take her to Meryl and get her stitched up. Wow another girl and this one is larger at 4 5/8 ounces. Again we put Trixie back in the crate on the floor with her blanket over her!!! This one is much easier to get going.

When we picked her up from Junko she was squeaking in the car and I told Pat to give her the blanket which Junko had washed and put in the bag. As soon as Trixie had the blanket she laid down and went to sleep all the way home!! Needs the security!!!
Pat is doing a good job getting them going and the first born one is now doing well. Touch and go there for a bit but I know Pat can work on them. Great putting the flannels in the microwave to warm up a pup. I got that tip from Niki of course.

I offered Trixie some milk which at least she drank. Wonder how long for the last one. We will give her about an hour and then another shot if she hasn't had it by 2:15p.m. Better to give her a shot and move it faster than let it sit in the birth canal.

Guess she will have to have the blanket when she is done but I worry she might cover the pups and not let them nurse. Will just have to play it by ear!!!

Wow the last one is born at 1:55p.m. and again it is a girl. Way to go Trixie and this one weighs in at 5 ounces!!!! Well the first two are brown in colour and this last one is a bit lighter with a white muzzle and blaze whereas the other two have dark muzzles like their mum. Can't tell anything as they are just blobs but all seem to be doing well and at least she is letting them nurse.

Can't put them in the bathroom as Sarah is in there so they will go in my bedroom in the crate with a quilt wrapped round them and of course the heating pad underneath!!!! Got her all settled in now have to find something that she will eat!!!!

At least they were all born during the day and no c-section necessary but I suggest that she is bred again next time else I don't think she will have another litter. Don't think she got tore but it wasn't what I call an easy birth. Hope Mike is pleased with them.

Well she won't eat dog food and the only thing she will eat is raw ground beef. Oh and I have to hand feed her. She has to eat so as to produce milk for the pups and not going to lose any pups now!!!

I give her some plain yoghurt as she seems to like that but will only eat the raw ground beef if I hand feed her. Oh well just see how she does.

Took all the dogs out and Sarah and Trixie and all are now down for the night. Hadn't been in bed an hour and Trixie is kicking up a fuss so I get up and take her out. She was underneath the crate pad and digging up the pee pee pad over the top of the heating pad. Get it all straight and put her back, let's hope now she sleeps. I did put each pup on a tit just incase.

The morning comes round fast and the pups are still alive but Trixie is under the crate pad yet again. Well better weigh them and see what she has been doing all night. Wow they have all gained 1/4 to 1/2 an ounce each so I am thrilled as they usually lose the first night. She still doesn't seem over keen on them but she will just be kept in the crate till she gets used to them. At least she is real keen to get back to them after being outside. Hey at least I don't have to worry about her going over the fence with pups in the bedroom LOL.

Sarah's pups have all gained and are doing very very well. She really is such a good mum. Have to get the large green whelping box out of the attic as they are just too big for this little crate!!! Oh they are so cute. Sure hope at least one is a Tibetan Spaniel.

Trixie is doing better even though she has me up at least once every night to go out. Still hand feeding her but using the fresh ground beef and wrapping it round dog food as the only way she will eat!!!! This has been a week and it is getting old. Hey at least the pups are gaining every day so that is good. She must be feeding them even though every time I check on her the pups seem to be one end of the crate and her at the other.

Last night was bad, had to get up to her and she had squirted crap out of every hole in the crate.
Will have to take the wire crate out and disinfect the whole thing. I will put the pups and Trixie in another crate while I do this. Luckily I had a quilt wrapped all round it so it didn't go on my bed quilt as that is not an easy quilt to wash!!! Have to get her and the pups out and then find another quilt to wrap round the crate!! Oh the fun of having pups!!!! Sure hope Mike appreciates all my hard work and the laundry of course LOL.

Well the pups are now 8 days old and doing well. Trixie is at least eating the dog food and of course is hungry now!!! Yeah I think the light bulb has gone on and she knows she is stuck in that crate with those pups till I take her out.
Three lovely girl pups and I have to choose one as my payment for whelping the litter and looking after Trixie.
We took pictures and sent them to Junko and she says that the one girl that is a darker red is a long coat!!! Well doesn't look like it to me so will have to get Pat to come over and look at them. I thought if it was a long coat it was from birth but guess I don't know anything about Chihuahua pups LOL.

Sarah pups are doing well and trying to get their eyes open. Went up in the attic and got out the large green whelping box as the red crates are just too small for all these kids. Oh they are so cute, just pudgy furry balls. Of course they are all gaining so I am not even bothering to weigh them every day. You can tell when you pick them up if one of them isn't doing well.
Pat comes over to see all the kids and yes she says that the red girl of Trixie's is a long coat.

Wow hopefully Mike will let me keep her. At the moment we call them Ugly Betty No.1. No.2 and No.3. I think both Pat and I are a bit disappointed as we really thought these were going to be such lovely pups.

Pat's pups out of Evie are just so much nicer in the head but then we are of course used to seeing Evie and Henry pups so more or less you know what you are going to get. Remember Polly is out of Evie and Henry.

It would be good for me to keep the long coat because I have the two Evie pups to show that are both smooth coat and of course Polly to finish and then Trixie to finish. She will only be here for the first part of the spring season as then Mike will come and get her and the two pups so I have to try hard to finish her at our first show which will probably be Raleigh again. The long coats are shown in a separate class except for UKC and there they all go in together.

Well Sarah pups are six weeks old and the DNA results have come back. I have put up a small x-pen in the dining room and all the pups, Sarah's and Trixie's in the same pen. Have to put in two litter trays as it is hard for them to get to the litter tray with so many bodies in the way.

I have no idea how to read the results of the DNA so I ring Pat and she agrees to come over and help me with them. We laid it all out on the table and go through them one at a time. Obviously we can count out Sarah's DNA as she is the mother and then we have Grissom's DNA and Twister's DNA to compare the puppies to.
Puppy No.1. is compared first as easier to do it in numerical order even though my stomach is turning as I really want puppy No.1., a lovely dark red sable girl to be a Grissom pup.
"Sorry Shirley this is a Twister pup" comes from Pat and my heart just sinks. O.K. on to the next one and yet again a Twister pup, we go on from one to another and finally all six are Twister pups!!!
Of course I don't believe it so we start it all over again writing it down so I can see it on paper for myself. I just can't see all the numbers and letters lining up to be Twister pups without writing it down. Oh man I just don't believe it. We AI'd Grissom four times and none of his sperm made one Tibetan spaniel puppy. Man that Twister is a fertile son of a gun isn't he!!!

Well there is nothing I can do about it except cry with Pat. We will have to find great homes for these guys as obviously they have stolen my heart already. Tomorrow I will email my friend Linda and ask her if any of her friends are interested in a puppy. Linda knows many many people and will also ring Debbie and tell her.

Well the pups are nine weeks old today and Linda is coming to see them and then I am taking them to visit with Debbie as she has some friends interested as well. We are two weeks away from Christmas so let's hope we can find nice homes for them.

Linda emailed me and said that she is coming tomorrow at mid day with two friends as I told her I was taking the pups to Debbie and of course she had to have her puppy fix before I took them. Zena and I gave them their first shot and also wormed them. I then printed out each puppy its paperwork ready to take to Debbie. Obviously didn't have to do any pedigrees just a contract stating that this was a breeding from two well bred dogs, one being a Champion of course and Sarah is a UKC Champion and that the pup has to be spayed or neutered by the time it is six months old. I have that in all my contracts and don't give the registration papers to the new owner till the pup has been fixed. We finally go to bed even though I am so upset over it just have to go on and think ahead!! Sarah will be bred again but to Grissom next time.

Pat comes over to help me bath the pups as I have just two hours before Linda arrives and of course you know me, had to clean the house first LOL.
Pat and I have a production line going, I bath one and hand it to her and she dries it. I bath another and dry it and so on till we have all six done. Silly as they are not dirty but when ever I pick up a pup I always snuggle it and nothing is nastier than a smelly pup.
With nine puppies in an x-pen and two litter trays they are bound to smell doggy LOL. They all did well with their baths and are running around in the x-pen with the Chihuahua pups. Glad no one got sick from it.
It is funny watching Sarah feeding all nine pups and then Trixie trying to feed them all. They even lift Trixie's back legs off the floor. Just too funny to watch.

Linda comes with two friends and they think the pups are just lovely and take the boy that has the most coat and the red and white girl. Two gone, four to go, so I load them all in the car and head off to meet Debbie in Charlottesville as that is half way for the both of us. Debbie is thrilled with the pups and so happy that she can have a puppy fix. Debbie hasn't had any pups for about two years and once you have had a litter of pups there is nothing like it. We stand and oooh and aagh over the pups, everyone does their business in the litter tray in the back of my car and we load them all up in Debbie's van for her to take them home. Of course I give Debbie a bag of litter and enough food for at least a couple of weeks, plus all the paper work of course which I worked so hard on. Didn't want to forget that eh!!!

Yes I cry a few tears on the way home but that is just me. Now I just have the chi pups to deal with and they are doing great so just go from there.
Debbie emails me in the evening to say she has sent pictures to some people and that two ladies are coming tomorrow to see them. She is just so good at this sort of thing!!
She finds homes for all the four pups with the last one leaving on Christmas Eve. I am so thrilled that they all have nice homes.

Mike and I finally decided that I will keep the long coat and I am naming her Diva, her registered name will be Daggot's Queen of Pure Delight. We have used the Queen word as Trixie has Queen in her registered name. Nice don't you think?
The other two are Daggot's Ice Queen, which is Sasha and Daggot's The Swan Queen, which is Ugly Betty because she is not an ugly Betty any more.

Pat and I have decided to do the York Pennsylvania show in March and then go on to the show in Raleigh and from there we will go on to Hickory North Carolina and also visit with her mum while we are there!!! Should be a nice trip being away for 20 days.

The plan is for Mike to pick up Trixie while we are in N.C. to take her and the two pup's home.

March

Pat and I are busy sorting out our stuff for our trip and doing our entries for the shows.
I decided to weigh both Polly and Trixie. The top show weight for Chihuahua's is six pounds so they both have to be under.
Oh my both Polly and Trixie weigh six pounds two ounces so I had to ring Pat and ask her what to do!!!! We decide that they must not spend

as much time in the crates, I usually put them up every morning but that is going to stop. They both need more exercise. Yes we have to cut down on the amount of food and I will have to walk them every day. Their diet now consists of ¼ of a cup of dry food and a good helping of canned green beans. Well it's a good job they are so hungry and they eat it as I don't think I could LOL. Plus of course Eric is on strict instructions that the girls are not to have any cookies, dog biscuits etc. Only food I say!!!

We have been walking and of course very little food and the weight is coming off, Polly and Trixie are both at six pounds so that is good. Well now Polly has come into season so she has to go out in the laundry room with Sayuri and Katey who are also in season. I have bred Sayuri to Mio and Katey to Grissom to see if he can produce puppies at all. Katey didn't take the last time I tried to breed her so it will be interesting to see. I bring Katey in but Sayuri needs to stay out there till Polly finishes. We will still keep walking them as they both still need to lose weight. Pat and I walked the girls and when I got home I weighed them. Yeah Polly is down to 5.8 ounces and Trixie is down to 6 pounds. Hey the green beans are working. Wonder if it would work for me but I hate canned green beans. Still need to get more off.

Oh just wonderful, today is Thursday a week before we leave and Trixie has decided to also come into season. Just wonderful she will be real exciting when we are away and of course I have to take Twister as I never leave him at home. We will have a fun time of it LOL. Not too bad as it means she goes out with Polly and Sayuri but can't leave them out in the yard like I usually do because remember Trixie is a fence climber and that is all I need for her go over the fence after deer or a rabbit!!!! I will still keep walking them so it should be o.k.

Today is Sunday and I am going over to Pat to clean out the water tanks and load her stuff and of course the bikes. Oh I am so excited. Before I left I weighed the girls and Polly is at 5.2 ounces and Trixie is 5.6 ounces. Way to go girls. Pat will be thrilled. I haven't lost much weight with all the walking but it sure has worked on the girls!!!!

I arrived at Pat's and the first trauma of the day is my new bike is broken! Max tried to fix the gears because they were not working, just bought it right, well two months ago, so that means a trip back to Target for another one, hope they still have the same bike!!!!

Oh well that is after flushing the tanks to get all the antifreeze out of the pipes. Mind you a good job we did winterize them as we have had a bad winter and a lot of snow!!! Last thing you need is broken pipes in a motor home. Well that has gone smoothly now down to Target.

Just my luck we took it back to Target and of course they don't have the same bike. Oh well just get another Schwimm brand bike and pay the difference!!! I end up with a lovely Schwimm, Pink bike. Yes it is Barbie pink, Zena will love it. Get them on the bike rack that I had put on the back of the motor home and it works real well. Just another one of those problems to deal with!!!

Tuesday

Tuesday morning is here and I am off over to pick up Pat. Yes have the right dogs with me, Sarah, Twister, Polly, Trixie, and the three pups. We get all loaded with Pat's dogs, Henry, Evie, Snowball, Lolla, McGee and Abby. McGee and Abby are the Evie pups we delivered at the vets. Gee the first time we have all three breeds of dogs, the Tibetan Spaniel and one Papillon and the Chihuahuas. We have a good trip and arrive at the show site at 2:30p.m. but then of course have to wait to be parked till 3:30p.m. We have a good parking space, just about 50 feet from the building so not far to pull the trolley with the crates on. York is a nice show and we haven't been here before so will be interesting to see the different trade stands and see if they have anything that we haven't seen before!!!

We decide to take a nap and then we will take the pups over to the building and see what is going on. Well gee they haven't even got the rings up yet.
Went back and fed the dogs and ate dinner, it was quiche and very good. We decided to go to bed about 10p.m. as really tired.

Wednesday

I got up at about 7:30p.m. and Pat told me that she has been cleaning crates and carpet. I just stood with my mouth open. Poor Miss Snowball had a real upset tummy and squirted liquid shit out of her crate and all over Sarah underneath and all over the carpet and also into the crate of

Abby. Oh what a mess to clean up. Yes we dosed Snowball and hopefully she will do better. She will not eat the plain yoghurt and that would really help her. Oh well they can be stubborn.

Pat left and went over to the building as she is stewarding for this show. Wow it is 8:45a.m. and Pat has come back saying she can stay with me till after I finish showing the chi's.

I decided to wear an animal print top and black pants as I think that will be a good contrast for Trixie's colouring, which it is, time to go over to the ring.

Today the judge is from New Zealand and I am hoping Trixie will win as yes it is a major at last.
I take Snowball in first and she really isn't very good. Mind you she probably doesn't feel good so that doesn't help. Oh well she gets second place. Next is Polly and she looks so trim I am thrilled with her and she goes round the ring nicely. Stands on the table nicely and wins her class of two.
That means Pat will have to take her back in as Trixie is the only open dog. Of course Trixie wins and we go back in for the points. YEAH TRIXIE WINS AND IT IS A FOUR POINT MAJOR!!!!!!!!!!! She is now an American and New Zealand Champion. We went back in for Best of Breed and Trixie gets Best of Opposite.
I am thrilled and of course have a picture done. The judge was very complimentary and said he new the breeder and liked her dogs. Man I don't care, Trixie is now finished and can go home with Mike. He still has to decide what he wants to do about breeding her. Not my problem this time. Pat and I go back to the motor home very happy and of course have to ring everyone at home and tell them.
Oh dear before I start getting too excited I have to groom up Sarah and take her to the other building to be shown. Oh my, this is a trek!! It is nearly half a mile to pull the trolley with Sarah and carry a chair. When I get there they have already started the class so I get Sarah out of the crate and go straight in the ring. Well there are fifteen dogs in the ring and of course I didn't get any placement. Oh well I would never have entered had I realized it was a Specialty and there are 147 dogs in all. Still Sarah showed good so I am happy with that. I load her up and trek back to the motor home. At least the sun is shining which makes it a better walk back.

I rang Mike to tell him of our win and of course he is thrilled. He wants me to give Trixie to Junko so that she can breed her again to Jackpot, the same sire as these pups!!! Will give her Trixie on Friday as that is when I think she will be ready to be bred. All the dogs are having fun playing with her and she just loves all the attention since she has had the puppies. She even plays with toys now which she never did before.

We decided to have a quick dinner as Pat entered three puppies for the puppy match. McGee, Diva and Betty but we will also take Sasha as she needs the ring time as well and also to be in the building is good for all of them.
We arrive at the building at 6:30p.m. for the puppy match but it starts with the working group first and there must be 50 dogs, well puppies. We sit and sit and at 8:00p.m. I suggested to Pat that we take our pups over to another ring and work with them and then go back to the camper as we still haven't fed the dogs!!
We took the kids over and walked them in a different ring of course. They did very well and after about 30 minutes both Pat and I had enough bending down enticing them with food and decided enough was enough LOL. We were pleased they did what we wanted so that is enough.

Of course it was also time for a drink to celebrate our win and sit and chat and laugh over the happenings of the day. We finally went to bed at 10:00p.m.

Thursday

Today is Thursday and I have moved Trixie up to the Best of Breed class for the rest of the week. That means she will go in last with the other Best of Breed dogs and also the two winners.
Pat is stewarding but comes back to help me load up the dogs and get over to the ring.

Snowball shows first and as usual not very good. Don't think this little girl is ever going to get the idea of showing but we will see. Next, Polly and she wins her class of three dogs which I am very pleased with. Pat hands me Trixie and of course I march in the ring and then remember that she is in Best of Breed. Well never had to take a dog in Best of Breed class before so I got confused LOL.
Everyone had a good laugh at my expense LOL. Well we all go back in for Winners Bitch but I didn't win nor get reserve. Oh well there you go. Not my day today.

Now it is time for Trixie and in we go. I am third in line so keep Trixie motivated with food so she doesn't think about going for the dog behind me. She goes round real nice and I walk her at a slower pace so that she doesn't paddle with her front legs which she will do if you walk real fast. The judge picked another special for Best of Breed but did give Trixie Best of Opposite Sex so that is pleasing.

A good day and now I have to get Sarah over to the other building.

Pat helped me take the dogs back to the Motor Home but I have time for a sandwich and a cup of coffee of course. Well its 1:30p.m. so I have to get over to the building. Man it is nearly half a mile but this time I am walking Sarah on the lead and pulling the trolley. Much easier and gets some of the spitfire out of Sarah so hopefully she wont bark quite as much. Yeah who am I kidding, only myself, at least it is just a squeak now.

I get there just as they are finishing the Bred By Exhibitor class so only a few minutes to wait.

There are ten in the class and I am fourth in line. We all go round and Sarah is being good even though she is barking a little bit but at least it is just a squeak. We all lineup and he pulls out first, second, third and then points to me for fourth. I am thrilled to even get in the line up at a Specialty. Of course no points but I am happy.

I load up Sarah and start the trek back. Oh I can see Pat walking towards me. She is thrilled when I tell her about my placing. We get back to the Motor Home and go to take Sarah of the trolley and she has crapped all over the crate. Not like her at all but I guess all that shaking in the trolley upset her tummy. We will have to do laundry when we leave here as have about 20 dirty beds so far LOL.

Now it is time for a nap after taking all the dogs out and having a cup of coffee of course.

We have a good dinner and celebrate with a bottle of wine. It is Merlot but oh I just cannot drink this. Let's have beer instead!!!

We watch a movie then on to bed. Tomorrow is another day.

Friday

So today was a real burn out day!!! Snowball wasn't any better today but hopefully the light bulb will go on soon!!!

Polly won her class of three again but no points.

Trixie again didn't get placed. Well gee this isn't going according to plan but that is dog showing for you. Junko comes back to the Motor Home with us and she takes Trixie home with her to be bred again!! Mikes choice. She will bring her back tomorrow morning.

Now I have to go and get Sarah down to the building. This time I walked her and dragged the trolley. Yeah she decides to pee and poo on the way to the building. Good girl Sarah.

The usual result, Sarah doesn't get placed but remember she had puppies in October and still needs to grow hair on her back legs and fill out her tail. I really shouldn't have entered her but she didn't lose all the hair till after we did the entries LOL. Her lovely plume tail now looks like a Mohawk!!!!

I put her in the crate to take her back to the motor home and she crapped again!!!! Will have to walk her both ways from now on but need to take the trolley incase I have to wait a while before showing else she gets too wound up!!!!

Well the end to a not so good day so time for a drink and to commiserate over our losses!!!! We sat and watched a George Clooney movie, Up In the Air and it was very good.

It is certainly nice weather here and we are enjoying the sun very much as we have had such a bad winter with so much snow. It is so nice to be able to sit in the sun.

After the movie and taking the dogs out we hit the beds. Nice to have the electric blanket though as it really gets cold at night.

Saturday

The sun is shining and that makes up for the losses yet again!!!!!!!!!!!!!!!

We did take the pups over to the building again and they are doing much better walking on the leads.

Pat went over to Sue Whaley to take some chocolate cake which we hadn't eaten and while she was gone I did the dishes.

All of a sudden I hear Pat yelling at me to turn the water off. I had finished the dishes and ran outside to see what she was talking about. The water was leaking out of the dump pipe and when we opened the compartment, I had forgotten to close the valve and water was leaking out of the pipe instead of going into the tank!!!

I can't believe no one had seen it and told us as it is a $250 fine for dumping water!!!!

Pat went inside to get a towel but started handing out dogs. Then she screamed as the fence was open!! Luckily it was only Snowball, Lolla and Polly and as soon as you say their names they hit the ground as that is how we taught them for being caught when pups. Guess it helped!! I was just thrilled as if it had been Sarah we would never have caught her as she just takes off running!!!!

Yet again we couldn't get a signal on the computers so gave that up. Hopefully they will have a signal when we get to Raleigh. Instead Pat sat and did her embroidery and I sat and wrote in my book. Have to keep up to date as I can't remember what happens every day.

Again we watched a movie and then went to bed.

Sunday

Junko arrives early and luckily we are both dressed LOL.

No wins again today, we got back to the motor home about 10:30a.m. and decide to pack up and get on the road to Raleigh. We'll go as far as we can. I didn't bother to drag Sarah all the way over to the building again as I am sure she wouldn't get placed again and the class for her started at 10a.m. We are both upset over this trip and decide best to pack up and get on the road.

It is mid day by the time we get all packed up and on the road. We would like to do about 250 miles before we find a camp site.

As we are driving we see a sign for a KOA camp ground and that will do fine for just the one night. Not a bad place but we are parked on gravel and covered in leaves makes picking up after the dogs not so easy. Even with the flashlight you can't see the poo LOL.

I am setting all the crates and stuff inside and hear Pat grumbling!!! We have a problem with the jacks at the back of the camper. The lock nut has come off but luckily has dropped underneath and Pat finds it. We finally put it back together but will need to fix it because once a locking nut has come undone it will never be tight again!!!!.

It is just another thing to deal with when we get to Raleigh. I am sure there will be an RV mechanic hanging around.

There is laundry wash at this campground so we treck over with all the bags and end up doing 3 loads of laundry just for dog beds and then we did a load each of our clothes so we have clean knickers and socks for the rest of the trip LOL. Only one problem I have forgotten to bring soap powder so we wash the dog stuff with Clorox bathroom spray and wash our clothes with shampoo. Hey it works just fine. Course the dogs beds could have done with a bit more but that is fine. They smell clean at least.

I hang my t-shirts up as never put them in the dryer, my socks are still a bit damp but we just draped the stuff over the shelves and they will dry overnight.

For dinner we had chopped up pork on top of salad and it was very good. It made a change from cooking tonight. We opened a bottle of wine and we cut up an orange into slices and put it in the drink. Oh my, that was so good. Zena gave us the oranges and they are blood oranges and so juicy and sweet. Usually oranges are so dry but these are good, will have to ask her where they came from!!!!

It was a lovely evening and we sat outside with our drinks and then I went and paid the camp fee.
They gave me a brochure and it stated "Please no noise before 7a.m." Wow that means Pat will have to stay in bed till at least 6:45a.m. before letting the dogs out so they don't bark. There really isn't much for them to bark at here. Not even seen any squirrels, and not having Sarah barking all the time really helps!!!
Now it is time to shower ourselves.

You have to remember the shower stall is one of our storage places. We keep the dry dog food in there, our towel's, dog towel's, dog toys, waterproof coats, etc etc so it all has to come out and be put on the bed in the bedroom. Really don't like to put it back until of course the shower is dry again. I usually wipe it down with one of the towels.
I go first. Now you have to picture this shower is not very large and it only has a 24" glass door which is surrounded by brass trim. You have to open the door and step into the shower like stepping into a bath tub. Well I nearly fall into the shower as I missed the height, just picture this fat old lady trying to get through a 24" door is not so easy LOL. Still it is nice to stand under the running water and wash my hair. No can't shave the legs as no way can you bend down in this small space LOL.
Pat is laughing as she can hear me cursing and I start laughing too which doesn't help me trying to get into the shower. Finally done and what an effort it was LOL. Still feels good!!!!

Now Pat's turn and of course she will come out with a towel round her head like a turban and the dogs will go crazy LOL. Yes they all bark like idiots till she speaks to them.

Wow clean bodies and clean laundry, what more can you want!!!!

Now this is the first night that I have not put the chairs up inside, the embroidered chairs and I wake up to the pitter patter of rain on the roof. Oh well the chairs will dry out while we are on the road again LOL. I must make a point to get them in every night.

Monday

Morning comes and even after all the rain the sun is shining and the chairs are just damp. We start packing up and Pat finds out that the nut again has come off the jacks but is still just under the back bumper. We fix it again but will have to buy a new one or get it fixed in Raleigh. There is sure to be an RV repair man there somewhere.

The navigational system that Pat has, she has named Wonder Woman and she says we will be in Raleigh by 2:01p.m. but of course we have to stop for groceries and gas as well. That should add about an hour.

It is amazing that Wonder Woman is taking us across country to I-95 which I just love. Much rather drive the back roads than the highways any time. It is a lovely surface and good driving. Wow petrol is expensive here at $2.73 per gallon but can't go anywhere without it.

Twister keeps winging and I have stopped twice and taken him out and all he does is pee. Little shit!!!

Oh my Pat has figured out what is wrong with him. We have Abbey and Snowball in a crate between the two seats on the green box because they have such bad travel sickness and Twister isn't as close to me as they are!!! So we put him on the floor behind the crate and now he can see me much better LOL. Quiet at last.

Wonder Woman tells us to turn and there is Wall Mart right on the corner. Great.

I get the small x-pen out and we ex all the dogs but walk Twister and Sarah and of course Trixie as she will go over the x-pen in a heartbeat!!!! A car stops and asks how much the puppies cost!! Yeah right like we sell pups on the side of the road!!!!

This is a new Wall Mart but we find everything we are looking for and even find a pair of pants and a shirt for Dee Dee for only $3.00 each. Love bargains.

Finally arrive at the show site in Raleigh and we have only driven just on 200 miles which I find amazing. I thought it was much further.

Find a nice parking space at the back of the building and we have full hookup which is what we were hoping for. We could have parked closer to the building but as we are going to be here for 6 nights we really needed full hookup!!!!

We have to bath dogs etc and it pays to have full hook up so we don't have to breakdown and go and dump tanks. That is such a pain.

Oh my, the wind is blowing a gale here so can't have the awning out.

Just like I knew it would, a man comes round and said he is a RV repair man and did we need anything done! Yeah time to get the jacks fixed. We told him the size of the bolt and he went and bought it and put it on for us and no charge. Tried to give him a bottle of beer but he declined. So much nicer than having to wait untill we get home to get it fixed.

Oh it is so cold we have to put the heating on which is a bit different from Pennsylvania!!!!

We took the pups over to the building again to see who is there and they have nothing set up!!!

Of course we aren't popular so we leave. Too much going on and really people are not allowed in the building while they are setting up. I should have known that!!!!!!!!!

We have a nice restful day. I bathed Polly as she is the only one showing on Wednesday.

We finally watched the movie Old Dogs with Robin Williams and John Travolta, which we finally got to work after buying a new one in Wall Mart. It is a good movie and we laughed a lot.

Time for bed.

Wednesday

Today we are only showing Polly so she can walk over to the building and back rather than drag just one crate on the trolley over there.

There are only two males and four females which is one point for the males unless the male gets Best of Winners then he would pick up the points from the females.

I am the only Bred By Exhibitor dog so obviously Polly wins her class. We go back in for the points, Winners Bitch and he gives the points to ME!!! Yeah way to go Polly, two more points, I then go back in with the male for Winners Dog and of course the two Specials. Wow he points to me giving me Best of Winners. Bummer that there weren't more males as then it would have been a major.

That major is going to be hard to find LOL. A lovely female wins Best of Breed and such a lovely lady. Her name is Gloria Johnson and she said she loved the look of Polly and would I like some grooming tips which of course I will always accept. She tells me Polly is a lovely dog and if I ever wanted to breed her she would love to supply a stud!!! I was very impressed, not very often a fellow competitor says you have a nice dog!!! We talked about Polly's breeding and Gloria said that she knows of Henry, CH Belle Shoals Regarding Henry. I am so thrilled for Pat to finally be getting recognition for her breeding good dogs.

Great for me and yes we have a picture taken. I find out later that the dog that won Breed also got a Group One. A lovely dog.

Polly now has 10 points.

After all the excitement we get back to the Motor Home to change clothes and head over to the building for our favorite lunch, fried chicken which is the best at this restaurant. We wait all year to get here for fried chicken LOL.

We browsed round the trade stands and we both order some name tags. I ordered nine for the crates in the bedroom, just call names and then one for Diva's crate. This way we can put the right dog in the right crate LOL.

I cooked sweat and sour chicken for dinner and it is not good. No I can't eat it at all. Why doesn't it taste as good as when Zena cooks it????? Oh well there you go.

Pat bathed Abbey and McGee and we watched a movie and then went to bed. Let's hope we have as good a day as today as tomorrow we show McGee and Abbey.

Thursday

The sun is shining yet again which is nice considering how far we have to walk. I walked Polly and Pat pulled the trolley. Wow the building is very crowded today and very loud. Hope it doesn't upset McGee or Abbey. Polly is used to it so don't have to worry about her.

I am first in the ring with McGee and he just walks round the ring as though he owns it. Not bad for a six month old puppy and this is his first show. We go back in for Winners Dog but he doesn't win the points. He gets Reserve instead which isn't bad for his first show!!!!
Abbey is next and Pat takes her in as she won't walk for me just yet. She is just spastic and won't walk round the ring but the judge is very soft with her so as not to upset her in any way. Nice of the judge to do that!!!! Usually they just dismiss you!!!
Polly is next and she goes round well. I am pleased with her. We all go back in for Winners Bitch but Polly doesn't win this time. Oh well another day tomorrow. We won't show to this judge again. Not going to waste any more money LOL. Have to write down these judges in our book LOL.
On our way back to the Motor Home we stop and pick up our name tags, wow $77.72 but then there are nine tags and one for Diva. Didn't think it would be that expensive but there you go. Dog shows are the only place you can get the name tags done how you want.

It is a nice walk back to the Motor Home but now I have to bath Sarah as she is being shown tomorrow, Saturday and Sunday. I only entered her for the last three days as she only needs majors and it is a major on Saturday so fingers crossed.
We have lunch first which is the left over soup that Pat made yesterday and it is good.
I bath Sarah and she is very good for a change and looks good too! Now it is time for a nap.
Well two campers down from us there are English Cockers and Keeshond dogs and they never stop barking, can't sleep with this row going on. Sure hope they stop tonight!!
For dinner we had a nice steak and salad and opened a bottle of Merlot which neither of us could drink, it is so dry!!!! I tried this once before so why did I open it again!! Yuck!!!!

After dinner we take Abbey and Diva to the building to walk around hoping it might make Abbey a bit better tomorrow. She seems to do real well but Diva just wants to hug the concrete again. She is fine outside but doesn't like it in here with all the dogs barking etc. The noise level in the evening in here is far worse than during the day. In the evening the dogs barking seem to echo all round and it really puts the pups off!!! Oh well lets hope Abbey will be better tomorrow.

Now they walk home just fine, away from the barking I guess and always heading back to the camper the dogs seems to know where it is.

Time for a movie and we watch Taken with Liam Neeson which is a great movie. Time for crackers and cheese spread and we drink a bottle of Egg Nog from Wall Mart and it is very yummy. We finish the bottle and feel real good, time for bed.

This time we remember to put the awning in and of course the chairs. Don't want them wet again and don't know if the wind will blow so best to be safe than sorry!!!!! Pat is so drunk she wants to lay on the step and go to sleep LOL. It is a wonder she can get the right dog in the right crate!!!

Friday

Today I am going to wear my favorite animal print shirt, have many pictures on the wall in this shirt so let's hope we have luck again today.

We are showing McGee, Abbey, Snowball, Polly Trixie and Sarah today.

McGee is first and he stands on the table like a rock. The judge even says he is so good for such a young dog. This judge makes you set the dog up across the table and then you move to the front to hold the dog while he examines the dog!!!!!

We go back in for the Winners Dog but McGee doesn't get the points nor reserve. Bummer as I thought he really liked him. Oh well I do know he is famous for not giving to pups. Hey they all have to start somewhere.

Pat takes Abbey in and just as she walks through the gate a huge Siberian Husky lunges up and gets Abbey in his mouth!!!!! Pat was just traumatized but goes on in. Surprisingly Abbey walks round the ring much better today and stands on the table well. Hey perhaps last night helped her.

Now my turn with Polly and she is the only one in the ring again. Yes of course we get a blue ribbon.

As I am walking out the steward is calling Trixie's number and I tell her that she is a move up and the Judge says he will hold the class but I have to go to the Superintendents office to have it verified. Do you know how far it is for me to get to the office??? They can't find the paperwork for about 5 minutes looking and she finally finds it and comes back to the ring with me. Phew I am exhausted and have to grab Polly to go back in for Winners Bitch.

Well of course I know he isn't going to give it to me when I held up his judging. Oh my, he points to me for Winners Bitch!!! I am just amazed but thrilled as now Polly has 12 points so just needs a 3 point major to finish!!!!! Way to go Polly. Now I have to take Trixie in and Polly so I give Pat Trixie and I take Polly in. Well didn't get Best of Winners with Polly and didn't get anything with Trixie either but then there are 7 Specials and of course the same No.1 dog as it has been every day!!! The dog's name is CH Ayrwen's Star Kissed Delight and she is a delight to watch going round the ring. I didn't have a picture done as will put the ribbons on the last picture. Not enough space on the walls!!!

Now it is time to go to the next ring as it is Sarah's turn. We carted them all up to the building because we only have about 15 minutes in between ring times.

There is only one male and two females, the other dog has a professional handler so don't hold out much hope for me to win!!! Well the other female doesn't look anywhere as good as Sarah and it has lousy movement behind. Hopefully we have this in the bag. Well what a surprise I get reserve and the other female gets Winners Bitch. Oh well tomorrow there are enough dogs for a major so lets keep our fingers crossed.

I think seeing as it is a major tomorrow I am going to ask Sue Whaley to show Sarah then there will be two professional handlers in the ring giving me a better chance of the win. Sue agrees as long as she doesn't have a conflict with another dog she is showing.

Yes I am disappointed as Sarah was the better dog but again playing politics is a hard and expensive game.

Because we won again with Polly we are treating ourselves to lunch again in the restaurant, fried chicken. This time we take our bikes back to the restaurant and we also need to find a store as we are running out of coffee!!! Not good.

After lunch we go to find Sue and ask her about tomorrow and of course she agrees which is just great!!! Thank you Sue.

We ask a few people how far to the store and of course they tell us that it is about a mile but you have to go on a very busy highway and Pat is worried I might fall off and get run over LOL.

Guess we have to find a friend that will take Pat to the store. We biked all the way round the campers and finally find her, the last camper in the line. She agrees and will come and pick one of us up when she has finished with her dogs. Lanna arrives and takes Pat to the store for our coffee. When Pat comes back she is so upset that she could only get Folgers coffee which of course neither of us really like. Hey it doesn't matter, it is coffee and we have to survive LOL.

It starts raining a bit but Max says they are having snow showers at home. Better there than here as I will just die if it starts snowing!!!!!
It is now time for bed and I asked Pat why she put McGee in the puppy class instead of the Bred By Exhibitor class. She said because he was so bad on the lead she thought it best to go in the puppy class. I then reminded her that his wins have to be in the Bred By Class for him to end up with the Champion Medallion when finished. That is why I am on all the pups papers so we can put them in the Bred By Class.
Pat is just mortified and starts crying so I ring Debbie and she looks it up on the computer and the AKC web site says that you can have some wins in the puppy class and then move up to the Bred By Class if the dog has not matured, all the wins have to then be in the Bred By Class in order to get invited to the Eucanuber Dog Show.
Pat is very relieved and can now go to sleep LOL. Great news as now I don't have to put the pillow over her head.

Saturday

Pat said when she got up this morning there was frost on the grass and ice on the tables. No wonder it was cold last night but I love that electric blanket. Tonight if it is cold again we will leave the electric heater on low.
Well it is a major in males and females today and also a major for Sarah so we have all our fingers and toes crossed today!!!!
There is a bike race in town today so all the show times have been delayed for 30 minutes as they have closed a lot of the roads. Nice as it gives us more time in between showing the Chi's and then Sarah.
Hopefully it will have warmed up a bit before we trek over to the building.

Wow the building is full of people and it is hard to pull the trolley between all these people and dogs. Guess being Saturday everyone is out to visit the dog show!!!

We park the trolley by Sue's set up and she lends us a couple of chairs as they are in short supply today. Of course she is going to show Sarah as doesn't have a conflict.

I take McGee in first but we get second, gave first to a dog with no top line. Then he gives the points to a dog again with no level top line but a professional handler on the end of the lead.
Now time for Abbey and she is good but doesn't win her class either. Oh now my turn and yes Polly wins her class of two!!! Wow. We all then go back in for the points and he gives it to a dog that hasn't walked with its tail up all week, which I have beaten every day but has a professional handler on the lead, but I did get reserve so that was something. I take Trixie in and again she doesn't get anything.

Well interesting, the judge gave the points to a handler for the males and a handler for the females, at least he did chose the same dog for Best of Breed which has won every day!!
Now I am very hopeful for Sue to show Sarah. This is a political day of showing!!!

We take the chi's back to the motor home and have lunch and Pat rings her brother to talk about where we are going to park when we get there on Monday. Roger, Pat's brother is going to take Monday off work so he can visit with us and take us to visit with Pat's mum. We have to get groceries again and of course do laundry. In the evening we are all planning to go out to eat together.

Now time to groom Sarah and get back to the building. I walk her over to the building as usual and she poos, always on the lead, I guess she gets nervous too LOL!!!
Sue comes over and cuddles Sarah for a few minutes and says she will be back in time for the ring which of course she is!!!!!!
Now come on judge, keep it simple and give the win to the handler on my dog!!!!!!!!!!!!!
Only one male again but there are 8 females, 3 in the puppy class, 3 in the Bred By Class and then two in the open class being the same dog as yesterday in with Sarah. Sarah wins her class which I am thrilled with and then they go back in for Winners Bitch and he points to Sue with Sarah, yes I am thrilled!!!!! They next go back in the ring for Best of Breed and Sarah wins Best of Winners, no extra point as only one male but that is o.k. she now has her FIRST MAJOR WIN!!! Just need one more and she will be a Champion.

It really was so nice to see Sarah going round the ring as I am always on the end of the lead and never see the dogs move. Wow she really does look good. Sue was of course thrilled with her win just as much as me. I had bought a bottle of wine over for Sue and she did no more than open it and say a toast "To great friends". A nice end to the day of showing. So glad I decided to ask Sue to show Sarah, sometimes it pays to use a Professional Handler.

We are thrilled of course and go back to the Motor Home to have coffee, ring home, ring Niki of course and then we decide to visit the flea market which is always here at the weekends.
It was very hot walking round and I have a bad headache. We finally found an ice cream stand and buy ice creams, a few dog toys and a fresh pineapple which was only $2.00 a bargain.
I just have to take some pills and go and lay down. Pat goes over to watch Best In Show and the Pekinese wins today. Yesterday it was the Chihuahua, such a coo for such a small dog!!!
When Pat comes back we feed the dogs and then eat dinner.

Time to sit and write our shopping list for next week and sort out our menu's.
It was very cold last night and we have the electric blankets and the little fan heater going. Well crap one of the blankets won't work. You know they just don't make stuff to last. Yes I understand they are about four years old but they have only been used about a dozen times if that!!!!!
The last time we used it we had to wrap tape round it to make it stay on but this time it just won't work!!!! Well Pat has the little fan heater out there and I have the electric blanket so we are toasty!!!!

Sunday

We slept really well and Pat didn't get up till 6:45a.m. which is late for her LOL.
It is a major in the male Chihuahua's today but not the females. That is o.k. as if Polly were to win and then get Best of Winners it would give her the last Major that she needs because the female would then pick up the points from the males. Fingers crossed eh!!!
McGee is first and just is amazing. He really is getting better every day and stands on the table like an adult, tail up and not moving even to have his teeth inspected. I am so proud of what Pat has achieved with

him. He wins his class of two and now we have to wait till all the other males have been shown.

Time to go back in for Winners Dog and we all go round and the judge points to ME!!! I am thrilled of course. Way to go McGee.

Now is Abby's turn with Pat and she is getting better but this will be her last show. When she comes out some lady says to her "You should ask that lady (Pointing to me) about selling you a really good Chihuahua as she has good dogs"!!!! I thought Pat was going to say something but I had to go in the ring with Polly and she wins her class. Now time to go back in for Winners Bitch and Polly doesn't get the win. Oh well we have won two days here with her so I shouldn't be greedy LOL.

Now it is time for Best of Breed and McGee has to go back in and he gets Best of Winners. HE HAS WON A FIVE POINT MAJOR at six months and 3 days old. Way to go Pat and McGee.

Yes we have a picture done and the judge just says she adores McGee and we will have a lot of fun with him. Pat is thrilled. The judge is from California so I am sure we won't meet her again!!!!

Now it is time for Sarah and Sue asks if she can show Sarah again as if she goes Best of Opposite then it will be a major if all pick up their numbers!!!! Of course I agree.

Well one number doesn't get picked up so that breaks the chance of getting the major. Oh well Sarah ends up with Reserve which is better than nothing. Yes I am pleased but cross that the one person didn't show up, probably because I won yesterday!!!!

Well it was a good week here, two lots of two points on Polly, a three point major on Sarah and a five point major on McGee. A lot of people go home with nothing from shows so we did real well. At least it keeps the families at home happy when we win!!!

We trek back to the motor home to change clothes and Pat says she is buying lunch for our win to celebrate. Great news to me LOL. We bike back as it is so much easier than walking all that way.

Lunch was good and now back to the motor home and we put the bikes on the rack as that will be one less thing to do in the morning when we pack up. Pat goes back to watch Best in Show and she brings back three friends to see the Trixie pups. They were very complimentary about the pups movement, bites and temperaments etc which is pleasing.

They leave and it starts to sprinkle but nothing bad. We feed the dogs and have dinner. It wasn't very good so will have chips and dip later on. Zena had given us the dip so we mixed all three together it was really good and spicy!!!!!

We went to bed so pleased with all our wins.

During the night the dogs started barking because a storm came through and it was really loud thunder and rain on the roof. Woke us both up but after it had passed the dogs went back to sleep and so did we. When we woke up there was about 2" of standing water outside but at least it had stopped raining so we could pack up. We are both taking Benadryl at night because of all the pollen allergies. If I don't take it I start coughing and all the mucus goes down my throat and the same with Pat. Hate this time of the year!!!!

Monday

It was slushy packing up but I did inside and then helped Pat lift the x-pens into the holes.
We were on the road by 9:45a.m. and are heading now to Pat's mum's house. Pat is excited about seeing her mum as they haven't visited since just before Christmas.

Because of all the rain Pat is worried about parking behind her mum's house as it is grass and we must have had at least 2-3" of rain last night and Max calls us to tell us there were tornadoes last night in the area and there are places without power so make sure we have plenty of gas!!!!
Pat rings one of her uncles and he says to park in his yard, he has about two acres and it is all level and we can also plug in which is great. It is only about 9 miles from Pat's mum and Roger will take us over to visit with her. Our plan is to go to Roger's house to do laundry and then for him to take us to Wall Mart for our groceries!!! Then tonight we are all going out together for dinner!!!
Best laid plans, Roger arrives and Pat is so eager to leave and visit that we forget the laundry and the grocery list. We visit with her mum for about an hour and then all left to go to Roger's house.
At least we did get the dogs out and fed!!
Ended up sitting and visiting with Roger for three hours and we could have been doing laundry. Oh well we will do it when we park next!!!!

Roger's wife finally came home. She had been at the emergency room because of a bad headache which she had for three days. Gee it took them 4 hours to just tell her she had allergies and to go home and rest!!!
They didn't even give her any medication for the headache.

She changed her clothes and off we went to the Restaurant. It was called
Nick's and looked really nice. We sat in a booth which wasn't really cool
for five of us but then Pat's mum is real tiny!!!!!
The waitress came and we all ordered and also some starters called fried
green tomatoes. It was 6:45p.m. The meal including the starters didn't
arrive till 7:50p.m. and the fries on Roger's and Pat's mum's plates were
cold!!! The waitress came back and I told her that the fries were cold and
Pat had still not got her dinner, just not good enough considering the
restaurant only had about 20 customers. The manager finally came out
and apologized and said that the meal would be free and please order
desserts!!! No desserts as we have been gone for nearly four hours and
the dogs will need to get out. Pat gave the waitress a $20 tip as it wasn't
her fault that our dinner was so late in arriving.

Finally we leave and get back to the motor home. Of course Roger and
his wife and Pat's mum have to stay and see all the dogs so we let them
all out and they are good, hardly barked at all!!!
I take pictures of Pat and her family and they finally leave. They had
been gone about ten minutes when Pat's aunt comes over and invites us
over for strawberry shortcake and coffee. Of course we could not say no
so off we go to visit with them. They have a lovely house and Pat's Aunt
Josephine collects bunny rabbit ornaments. So cute, all over the house
and so tastefully done. We have a fun visit and then time to get back to
the camper. Pat's relatives have been so kind to us while here.

Finally got to bed but I was up at 2a.m. throwing up for about 30 minutes.
Guess something I ate at the restaurant as I didn't feel bad when we went
to bed. It was a good job I didn't have the electric blanket plugged in else
I would have broke my neck trying to get to the bathroom to throw up. I
will have to pack it up in the morning.
Pat gave me a pill and it settled my tummy and we all went back to bed.
At least the dogs never make a sound when I or Pat get up in the night
and that is good on my sanity LOL.

Tuesday

Pat was up early as usual and after she did the dogs she went and visited
her uncle and aunt. She came back after I was dressed and had started
packing up the inside. You have to envisage that we have 12 crates in here
and they all have to be in the right place before driving off!!! Four go up

on the bed above the driver and passenger seats. Another four go on the sofa and then we have to have Abbey and Snowball in a crate between the two front seats and then of course Twister behind them so he doesn't winge all the time we are driving. Then Trixie and Sarah are on the seats to the table. They don't need to be strapped in because they cannot slide between the table and the seat so they are relatively secure.

By the time Pat gets back we are all done except for putting the x-pens in the hole which we do together as they are heavy.

We wave good bye to her uncle and aunt and we are on the road by 9:30a.m. and our next stop is Wall Mart as have quite a list. Well gee we find a Wall Mart after only about 10 miles and off we go. I have to walk Twister again and Sarah and they both pee which is good.

We get everything we need and only spend $66.27 which is good. Pat went over to the Dollar Tree and bought some more dog toys.

We have a good drive but the ABS light comes on with the dashboard lights and that isn't good. I will have to ring Eric when we park. We only have about 15 more miles to the campsite so I am sure it will be o.k. till then. This camp site is called Thermal City Gold Mine and that is just what it is, a Mining camp site!!!! Wow we have full hook up and it is only $20 per night.

They also have a washer and dryer which of course we need to use LOL.

The sun is shining and there is no wind so nice to set up and can have and awning out so a little bit of shade for the dogs and us of course.

I ring Eric and tell him about the ABS light and he says it is a sensor so nothing to worry about. Of course if it was flashing then I would have to get to a Ford dealer but it isn't flashing so not to worry about it. Yes of course the brakes still work LOL.

We are parked on sort of a sandy base with some rocks but the dogs are having such a fun time digging in the sand and playing with the rocks.

We didn't have breakfast so Pat is making sandwiches and coffee of course. After we eat we will go and explore and of course find laundry facilities.

We have such a lovely parking space, so glad Pat found this place. There is a river running behind the camper and people are sitting in the water panning for gold. Oh what fun they are having.

We pack the dirty dog beds in a large bag which I can carry and of course we have to remember the soap powder this time LOL. We take change and some dollar bills and trek to office to find the washer and dryer. Oh the office has a gift shop as well. The washer and dryer is only $2.00 per load so we load it up. While waiting for the laundry we decide to play our hand at Gem Mining.

You buy a bucket of dirt for $60 and then sit on a bench with a sluice in front of you with running water, you put a shovel of dirt into a box with a wire mesh grill on the bottom and then you slush it up and down in the water to wash off the dirt and then see the stones. Oh my, a huge lump of Amethyst and a huge lump of Citrine. Oh this is such fun. We ended up with a two gallon zip lock bag full of stones, amethyst, citrine, sapphire, emerald, ruby, garnet, gypsum and the list goes on. The owner tells us all what the stones are and stands the Gypsum on a lighted base and it changes colour, just lovely!!!! Of course by the time we get back to the motor home neither of us can remember LOL. We put them on the table on paper towel in the sun to dry and of course take pictures. Oh what a fun time. It was really heavy carrying the stones and one load of laundry back to the camper so we decide to have another cup of coffee and this time we take our bikes back to get the laundry. Wow much easier and it is easy biking as the ground is more or less flat and it is easy biking on the sandy surface.

Some of the dog beds are still a bit damp so we peg them on the fence line in the sun to dry.

We ate dinner which was yummy, liver and onions, and the dogs are all bedded down again we decide to bike ride round and see what else is here. Oh my, the chain is slipping on my bike but as it is flat surface I can still ride without changing gears!! Man this is a new bike and just makes me so cross but there you go!!!!!

We sat and watched another movie and of course drink a bottle of wine. While watching the movie I made a pot of chilli. I cut up the onions and peppers when I cut up the onions for our liver and just put them aside. By the time we got back from bike riding the onion and pepper smell in the motor home was just awful. We lit candles and turned the fan on to get rid of the smell LOL. I am thinking about putting an extractor fan where there is a fan but it just opens and closes so won't take out the smell!! Electric would be better.

I let the chilli simmer for about an hour and we have a little bit before going to bed to taste it.

Good chilli and it will be even better tomorrow.

Hope we don't get indigestion LOL.

Wednesday

We wake up and again the sun is shining but no one is panning for gold yet, guess they wait till a bit later and the water warms up. Well that is my thinking anyway.
We have cereal for breakfast and write our list for the day.

Laundry, our stuff today, all the black clothes we have worn. We want to go panning for Gems again and of course have the dogs to bath, Twister as will show him on Saturday, Sarah, don't know about her yet, McGee, Polly and Diva. That will be a marathon job but it is a nice sunny day so the Chihuahua's can dry in the sun. I will only have to use the dryer on Sarah and Twister. Don't think Diva will have anything to do with the dryer but I will try. She will have to get used to it sometime in her life.

Running behind us is a train track and I counted 110 cars and Pat counted another one with 95 cars. They also run at night but I really only heard two in the night.
We get all the dogs bathed and again ride our bikes up to the office to have another go at Gem Mining. Man this is such fun and again we get a large lump of Amethyst and Citrine. I guess they put that in each bucket so you get something for your money. Again we leave there with large zip lock bags of gems.
Did our laundry and had to hang some of it on the fence. Don't think their dryer is the best it can be but that is fine, we have clean clothes again.

After dinner of sausage and onions and peppers we decide to ride our bikes again. The laundry is all dry now so we put it all away. We put the bikes back on the bike rack so one thing less to do tomorrow again.
We showered again, but have it down to a fine art now but we are running low on propane so I just hope we have enough for the cooking and fridge to run while we are in Hickory. We use a lot of propane when running the water heater and yes we have used it a lot. There doesn't seem to be anywhere here to fill up with propane.

Thursday

Today we pack up and move to Hickory. We are all loaded by 9:30a.m. and stop at the office to pay our bill of course and we have decided to buy t-shirts for the family at home and other trinkets for gifts. Wow I spend $78 and Pat spends $98 but we have t-shirts for the families and a few Christmas gifts which is always handy to have.
Of course our bill included the Gem Mining but we had a good time and have some lovely stones as memories. Hopefully one day we will find someone to make jewelry out of the stones.

We get back on the road and the Hickory Convention Center is only about 45 miles away so we should be there by 11 ish as again we must stop for a couple of things we forgot and of course petrol as we will be running on the generator for the rest of the trip.

Finally arrived and found a nice flat place to park, this car park is a bit on the slope and I don't want to have to put bricks out to drive on. Seems like the fridge is defrosting so we get out the book and read what we are doing wrong. Wow seems like for the fridge to change over to propane you have to press the button. Never done that before but hey it works. I thought if it was on auto it just changed so you learn something new every day!!!

After we are all settled and the dogs done we decide to take the pups over to the building and see what is going on. They walk real well over to the building but when they get inside they have to hug the floor with their bellies. So funny but that is o.k. they will get the idea of it.

Pat got on the computer and we found a Chinese Restaurant that will deliver so we order Shrimp Foo Yong, Sesame Chicken and Sweet and Sour Shrimp. Seems to be taking forever so Pat rings them again and she says the girl is on her way and we see her drive round the building. What a deal, it was only $23.21 and delivered. It was good food but again as always with Chinese, too much food. We decide to save the Sesame Chicken and one of the rice dishes for tomorrow then we only need heat it up after the puppy match as I am sure we won't be back here till about 9:0p.m.

Time to do dishes and the generator won't start, batteries dead. Pat cranks the engine and I start the generator. Well if the battery is the same age as the motor home I guess it is finally shot so will have to replace it when we get home. Just another thing to deal with LOL.

We decide to watch the movie Medicine Man and then go to bed. I get up to close all the vents and windows and realize that I had turned on the vent fan above the pups and of course that is what flattened the battery!!! How stupid of me. That fan has been running since about 11 a.m. this morning and of course that will flatten the battery quicker than anything!!!!!! Glad I found out why the battery was dead but I don't think running the generator will recharge it. I think it will only recharge if the engine is running. Oh well will still have it checked when I get home just to be on the safe side.

Will look under the step and see if I can get to the batteries. Well gee there is only one battery and when you think that has to power everything in here, one battery isn't enough!! Will get it fixed when we get home.

Friday

Pat and I take Diva and Betty over to the building but neither of them are very happy. Plus of course we forget to take some bait for them which would of have helped. We enter them in the puppy match for tonight it is only $5.00 per dog so not a budget killer. Will be fun but guess it will be late getting back to the camper.

About 4p.m. we decide to give all the dogs half rations so they are not starving by the time we get back and we had a little snack. We take it in turns to change clothes while they are outside but nothing fancy. Dress jeans and a nice shirt will work nicely.

We loaded up the trolley and head off to the building for 5:30p.m. I am thinking we will either be first class or the last class!! Guess I am right, we are the last class and there are about 12 breeds in front of us so we get chairs and sit. While they are doing the other breeds we take the kids out one by one to pot even though they did at the camper, putting a lead on them usually makes them want to go. I guess they get nervous the same as us!!! The puppy class will be last so we won't be back to the camper till about 9p.m. if lucky but really do want to see how the two Trixie pups will do.

McGee is in first and then goes back in for Best of Winners against another not so good male. Well gee he gives it to the other male. Oh Pat is disappointed. Remember the rules are different for UKC shows and I am beginning to think this judge has no idea what a Chihuahua should even look like.

Snowball does good and I am pleased with her. She is definitely getting better every time. Just takes a while for that light bulb to go on. Very pleasing. Now Polly's turn and I go in the ring with another long coat as in UKC remember they don't separate the two types. Well we both do our thing and then the judge calls for the computer so he can read the Standard about Chihuahua's. After about ten minutes he points to me as the Champion Winner and also Best of Breed. Another day tomorrow.

Oh wow they are calling for the puppies and we go over to another ring. Well they are doing this different and just putting all the puppies in the ring together. Bet this will spazz out my two pups. Well Diva is doing real well but Betty is just hugging the concrete and no amount of ham is going to make her walk. I go back and put Diva in front and hope that Betty will follow, well just a few steps but that is o.k. The judge gives the win to the two puppy shelties. They always give the wins at puppy matches to the hairy dogs LOL. Oh well another day tomorrow. Now back to the motor home for dinner and of course feed the kids again.

As we walked into the motor home it was 8:59p.m. so I was about right eh.

Pat is so upset about McGee not getting the win that we heat up the Sesame Chicken and rice in the microwave and while that is heating Pat makes slushies. We finish up the Black Cherry rum and start laughing about the happenings of the evening. Have to laugh else you will cry and it is always another judge tomorrow.

Didn't sleep good as I got terrible cramp and had to get out of bed and walk around till it stopped. At least I didn't wake up Pat which was good.

Saturday

Today is Saturday and Mike is supposed to be coming tomorrow to pick up Trixie and the two pups.

We have to be over to the building by 9.0a.m. but I have a feeling we will be the last class to show again!!! For breakfast we decided to wait till we get to the building and buy a biscuit as I am sure we will be the last class.

Today is Twister's turn as he gets dragged along all the time but I don't show him any more. Well time for him to play and he is the fourth class so that breaks it up a bit. Twister is as usual the only Papillon and of course he gets Best Grand Champion and also Best of Breed. He has fun. And loves to show off!!! Pat goes off to get the biscuits for breakfast.

Now we have to wait as again the chi's are the last breed to be shown.

McGee is in first again and just like yesterday he is fine going round the ring. The girl that was here last night isn't here today so McGee wins his class, then I take Snowball in and she again is the only one so then they go in together for Winners Dog and McGee wins, naturally Pat is thrilled. Now Polly's turn and we are in with the same long coat chi and she gets the win. Then I take McGee in for Best of Breed against the long coat and the judge gives it to McGee. Yeah way to go McGee and as you can imagine Pat is thrilled to bits today LOL.

We don't have more than ten minutes to recover and they are calling for Breed Winners which of course is McGee, oh and Twister and I have to go to the trash can as I threw his number away. Luckily it isn't buried phew!! I put the number on Pat and she gets Twister and of course we are last in the ring.

The judge pulls her four out and McGee gets a Third Place Group Win, a lovely green and white rosette. Pat is thrilled and so she should be. The judge comes over to talk to us and we decide to have a picture taken which of course the judge agrees to. McGee stands on the table like a true professional that he has become. Showing him is really going to be fun, providing of course you get a judge knows the standard!!! Well that is always a problem.

We go back to the motor home for lunch and suddenly hear a girl saying the chi's are up next for the second show. Well gee usually they have at least an hour and a half in between shows but not today!!!!! We load up the dogs but not Twister and rush back to the ring. Not good to be late and of course the judge gives me a lecture. Well after that little episode she isn't going to give me a good win, no she gives it to Snowball which really annoys Pat and then gives the Best of Breed to the long coat again. Well that was fast and now we can go back to the motor home and take a nap LOL.

You better believe we won't be coming back to the motor home tomorrow for lunch as usually on a Sunday they run the classes even faster to get the judges back to the airports!!!

We take a nap and don't have to worry about dinner as Pat went over and paid for the Seminar which includes dinner. Not a bad deal for $10.00.
We both lay down for a nap and we have the generator running as also have the air conditioner on. Yes it is very warm here in this tin box LOL.

Have you ever tried to take a nap beside a motorbike race track? Oh this is just awful. we are parked right behind a Harley Davison Motorbike show and also a biker bar. Brmmm Brmm potato, potato all the time so of course neither of us can sleep.
My phone rings and it is a florist and he has a delivery for Pat. Max has sent her a vase of flowers for Easter. Yes tomorrow is Easter Sunday. Good job we didn't sleep eh. It is nice sitting out here in the sun with the dogs but I would rather be sleeping LOL.
Mike rings and needs the address yet again, and says he will be here about 8:0a.m. in the morning!!!! I believe it when I see it. We change our clothes, tidy up a bit so it is clean for when Mike arrives, feed the dogs and go over to the building for the Seminar.

They said the Seminar starts at 6p.m. but they are still running terriers over here. Guess we didn't read the schedule but we don't have terriers anyway.
We run into Doug and Dana and they ask if they can come over to the motor home for a drink and of course we say "come on down". Now I am even happier that we tidied up a bit LOL.
Pat makes slushies and Doug has a beer and we sit and chat!!!! After about 30 minutes talking we all trek over to the building for dinner and the Seminar.

The dinner is really good, chicken, fries, corn, coleslaw, a bread roll and a cup of lemonade and tiramisu for dessert. The seminar is all about genes in terriers as to why they are hairless and really not that interesting to us but it was a good evening. We learnt why the Dalmatian breed has so many dogs with loss of hearing. They really didn't have anything about our breeds but then you never know if we might change one of our breeds LOL I think I have enough dogs at the moment.
We get back to the motor home about 9p.m. and time for a beer and Pat wants to eat chocolate. I rather prefer the chips and dip myself. We finally fell into bed about 11.00p.m. which as you know is late for us!!!!

Tomorrow is another day!!

Sunday

Today is day 19 of our trip. Tomorrow we head for home hoping to have done at least a hundred miles when we leave here this afternoon.

The sun is shining and Mike arrives at 8:30a.m. Course he doesn't bring biscuits for breakfast so guess we will get them over at the building.

Pat and I are already dressed so we load up the trolley and head for the building. Mike says he is tired but that is nothing unusual.

The show in the morning is taking forever as again yes we are the last class. The judge is waiting for the Eskimo dogs to come to the ring as there are juniors with them in another ring. It is protocol for the judge to hold up the class waiting for dogs if they are being shown in another ring in a different event.

Seems to take forever but finally they all come and gee there must be at least 10 of them.

Finally our turn and Snowball gets the win. She now has two wins toward her Championship and McGee has one win. Need him to win this afternoon. Polly goes in and gets her Reserve again. Think I will have Reserve Queen tattooed on my fore head!!

Oh I really hope this doesn't happen this afternoon because we want to pack up and at least do a hundred miles. Best laid plans eh!!!!!!

They finally do the group and then we decide to have some lunch. Not going over to the motor home because of what happened yesterday. After we eat again it is time for taking the dogs out. At least there is a nice grassy area out the front of the building and as long as you pick up after your dog you are allowed to walk on the grass. Of course some people and usually those with big dogs don't pick up after their dogs. That makes me so cross. Pat and Mike go over to the motor home to let the other dogs out!!!!

They put up the boards for the afternoon show and we are at the bottom yet again!!!! Bummer. Oh well nothing we can do so we just sit and watch the other dogs.

Finally our turn and this time McGee gets the win so now he and Snowball have two wins towards their Championship in UKC. Polly gets Reserve again so now we are heading back to the motor home to pack up.

Mike says he wants to take pictures of the dogs so I take each one out for him to do pictures while Pat starts to pack up the camper. At least the sun is shining so I don't mind running the dogs. Just hope he can cut my feet and legs out of the pictures.

Finally all the dogs are done and we are packed up and on the road. Mike is following us and he is going to stay the night with us!! Oh well he will have to sleep in Pat's dirty sheets as I didn't bring clean stuff for him.

We drive for about 50 miles and see a camp site advertised so we turn off. Pat finds the phone number and calls them. When we arrive the road is very very narrow and they give us the choice of two sites. Mike goes and looks as he has a rental car and easier for him to turn round than me!!! We finally find a good grassy spot but there is no dump and we are full. Will have to be real careful as to how many times we use the loo LOL

For dinner we cook up the last of the chilli and then eat chips and dip again with a bottle of wine and beer. It was a good evening watching the movie "Taken" again. Finally all the kids are bedded down and time for us to go to bed. Pat has to share the bed with me but that is fine.

Monday

We all sleep good and time to get up and the sun is shining yet again. Man we have been very lucky with the weather. Only had that one storm and had to pack up with water underfoot so not bad for 20 days eh!!!!!

We get all packed up and on the road by 10a.m. and Mike is going to follow us to the Flying J which is a truck stop so we can get cheap gas and dump our tanks and fill up with Propane as we are almost out. I put the puppies and Trixie in his car and he has all the records etc and I will mail him the ribbons and picture from Trixie's win when I get home. It is sad to see the girls leave but they are five months old, I have had them long enough. It is time for them to grow up and be dogs, hopefully show dogs. Yes I do cry a tear but we have to get on the road and get home.

There isn't even enough propane to keep the fridge going but that is o.k. as we will be home and there really isn't that much food left in there anyway.

As we are driving I look in the wing mirror and see that the awning isn't really up correctly. Pat put it up last night and it isn't tight enough. I pull over and she gets out and gets it up correctly. The wind can pull that awning off in a heartbeat. Mike stops to see what we are doing and

I could have given him the dog food then but didn't think about it. Oh well will give it to him at the truck stop.

Mike rings and says he has to stop for gas now but will catch us up at the Flying J.
The Flying J is further than we thought but there it is and a large camper has just pulled in front of us for the propane. Oh I am going to have to turn and face one way to fill with propane and then turn and face the other way to empty the tanks. Bet this will add about an hour to the trip LOL.
After we have done we went into the store to get some lunch and oh they have a gift store. I buy Eric a couple of t-shirts as they are two for ten dollars which is a bargain. We got coffee, and some fried chicken and fries and doughnuts for dessert. Not a bad lunch at all.
We walk Sarah and Twister as usual and get all settled ready for the trip.
Pat's navigational system, Wonder Woman says we will be home about 3:30p.m. so we will see how she does.

Driving is good and the road surface is good so that it nice.
We talk about all the wins and losses and about how much fun we have had. This is the longest road trip that we have taken and will probably be the last long trip like this.
Now we have to think about puppies expected. Katey, Sayuri and Evie pups are all due within the next two weeks.
Our total mileage done this trip is 1891 over the time of 20 days.
We finally get to Pat's house at 3:40p.m. and I leave and get home by 4.0p.m. Nice to be home but now have to clean out the RV. Well that can wait till tomorrow. All the dogs are happy to be home. Diva has to go in the x-pen in the front yard as I am only going to allow her to run free when the other dogs are up all except Polly of course, they can play together.
Diva is handling it very well being in the x-pen when the other dogs are out. It was fine her running with Sarah and Twister while away but it is a small area, my house is much larger and Sarah can down the pup so easily and don't want her traumatized at all!!!

I take the motor home over to Pat's house so she can get all her stuff out. We stand there and she says that is all and I remind her under the sofa is her dirty laundry and then she has stuff in the bath tub!!! Too funny.

Now we have to wait on puppies.

It is Sunday morning and Katey decided to start with labor. Let's hope this is going to be over during the day and not an all night thing!!!

Katey does well and has the first puppy at 12:10p.m. and the second puppy at 12:30p.m. That is all she has. I give her a shot of oxytocin to clean her out and it also makes the milk drop but she has milk squirting everywhere!!!!

I bed her down in my bathroom with the heating pad and light and she is all set. I am well pleased, two girls as well. These are Grissom pups so now we know that Grissom is fertile and to breed him next time to Sarah. One girl is dark red sable the same as Grissom and the other girl is a red sable marked like a papillon.

Monday we are taking Evie to be x-rayed. I think it is a bit early as I am sure she isn't due till the 19th April and Sayuri on the 20th April. Well the x-ray shows three pups and they really look huge. Meryll tells us to keep her advised incase we need a c-section.

By the time Thursday comes around still no pups and Meryll rings and says that we should take Evie in for a progesterone test done which will tell us when within hours when to expect the pups. I told Pat that I didn't think they were due till the 19th and of course she then checks her diary and agrees so I am thinking Evie will go Friday. The progesterone test says within 12 to 24 hours!! Well gee anyone can say that!!!

Friday morning comes and about 11:30a.m. Pat rings to say that Evie is having contractions. Yes I am in the car. She finally starts pushing and a bubble comes out but no pup so we give her a shot of Oxytocin to hopefully move things along. Max comes back to the house and he brings us Chinese lunch which is good. Still nothing with Evie and at 2.0p.m. I suggest that we ring the vet and get over there as obviously nothing has moved and I really don't like it. We ring the vet and get over there and Dr. Lessinger is of course in Richmond at a meeting so Dr Gibson comes in and takes Evie for x-ray. She comes back and says the head is stuck in the pelvis and yes a c-section is of course necessary. Oh my just what we didn't want. I go outside and stop at the desk and Terry, she has been with Meryll since the year dot, tells me that Meryll is on her way to do the surgery and I am just stunned of course!!!!!!!!!!!!!!

Dr Gibson keeps Evie sedated enough that when Meryll finally arrives and does the surgery, all three pups are born alive!!!!!! Way to go, we are thrilled, two girls and one boy all doing well. They bring Evie back to us and while she is still under the sedation, we put the pups on her to nurse and hopefully when Evie wakes up she will accept them without a problem.

We take them home and get them settled in Pat's bedroom. These are huge pups weighing in at 5 ounces each, the first one weighing 5 ½ ounces, huge for Chihuahua pups!!!

I have rung Pat this morning and they are all doing well. She tells me that they are going to resurface her road so has to move the motor home. She is going to put it in the Colonial Williamsburg secure parking for the three days.

Now we have to wait for Sayuri. No I am not having her x-rayed as it really stresses them out and Sayuri is a great dog for getting stressed.
Katey pups are doing well and they are 9 days old now. Getting to be fat blobs weighing in at 12 ounces!!!!
Monday morning and I think Sayuri is going to have her pups today!!!!!! Doing the usual shuddering and shaking so I ring Pat and she comes over about 10:30a.m.
Well time for coffee and we both sit and chat and hope that we at least have one pup before mid day. Yeah one arrives at ll:55a.m. Good girl Sayuri and it is a boy. We get him all cleaned up and weigh him and he is only 3 ounces. Very small considering Pat's chi pups were 5 ounces each.
Well he is doing fine and on the heating pad and Sayuri has another one again a boy weighing at 3 1/8 ounce. Oh my they are so nicely nicely marked. The have wide white muzzles and wide white blazes. I think they are both black and white but hard to tell just yet.
Eric suggests burgers from McDonald's so off he goes.
We enjoy lunch and sitting watching Sayuri and she is doing well. After we finish we take her out to walk around some. Usually it helps.
Get back inside and she has another pup which is a female this time. Oh my, it is dead. Pat works hard on it but it isn't even taking a breath. I guess it was in the canal too long so I am giving Sayuri a shot of Oxytocin so if there is another one it should come on down quickly.
Yes she has another one and it is a boy again. Well gee three boys!!!! This one is again only 3 ounces. We get them all nursing nicely and I go into the bedroom to get her crate ready as she will have to stay in the bedroom as Katey is in the bathroom.
They are nursing nicely so all should go well. I will take her some food and water in the crate.
She is nicely bedded down and Pat leaves for home.

While we were messing with pups Max went over to the parking garage and he can't get the camper to crank. Dead battery. Like we have been saying if it isn't plugged into power then the battery goes dead!!!

The next day Pat goes over with Max and they jump start the motor home, Pat leaves to go to the hospital for a mammogram and Max stays with the camper till she gets back. He meets her at the gate as she can't get in without a key. Oh dear Max has locked the camper with it running and of course the spare keys are inside!!! Pat walks round and remembered she didn't lock the window over the dining room table so Max gets the window open and the screen out and gives Pat a boost into the window. Now you have to realize we are talking at least 5 feet off the ground and Pat is half in and half out of the window when the security guard comes and asks what they are doing!!!!!!!!!!!!!!! Pat has all her crates on the table so has to push them off the table to get her body through the window. I would have loved to be there to see!!

The moral of this story is "Stand and Think"!!!!!!!!

Pat lost the keys at a dog show a year ago so when at a show, so when got home we both had new keys cut and the spare is in the gas compartment which is never locked!!!! When I reminded her it was there she just about freaked out!!!! Too funny eh!!!!!

Today the Sayuri pups are two days old and they are not doing well. She has inverted tits and will only let them nurse if I have her on the bed. She goes to the back of the crate and gets under the crate pad. This is not good. Pat is on her way over and we will decide what to do.
Pat is taking the one boy home and I am putting the other two on Katey and then putting one of Katey pups on Sayuri. As the Katey pup is 10 days old she should be able to nurse and with any luck pull out the inverted tits!! Well that is what I am hoping.
Today is day three, I kept getting up in the night and putting them both on tits but Katey keeps pushing this one away!!! I sit on the toilet and watch. He had a poo and Katey sniffed it and then pushed him away. She kept picking him up in her mouth and putting him on the other side of the crate!!! I keep putting him on a tit and go back to bed. We will see in the morning. Well morning comes and of course he is dead!!! There must have been something wrong with him else she would not have kept pushing him away!!
Gee now we are down to two!!!!
This one seems to be strong even though he is down to 2 ¾ ounces now. At least he seems able to suck and that is a good sign I hope.
The puppy that I put on Sayuri, I weigh her and she has gained ¾ of an ounce over night so I guess she must be getting milk. It looks like Sayuri's

tits seem to be coming out a bit more with this pup nursing. Sayuri can't get away from this pup as she is strong and determined to suckle!!!

Today is day four, Thursday and the little boy seems to be doing well but he is only up to 2 7/8 ounces. I was hoping by this morning he would be at 3 ounces. I kept getting up through the night and making sure he was nursing but of course I can't see what is happening with the pup as they are in the bathroom. Well I get her bedded down and both of them fed and have to go to work today.
I finally get home and let all the kids out and of course Katey and Sayuri. While they are out I weigh the pups and oh my, the little boy is at 3 ounces. I am thrilled. Sayuri's pup has gone up another ¾ of an ounce so I am sure she is doing fine and Sayuri's tits really seem much larger today. Course she is still at the back of the crate but the pup finds her to nurse LOL.

Today is Friday and I am taking Pat out for lunch for her birthday treat. I ring Pat to tell her that I will pick her up about mid day and we are going to our favorite Chinese restaurant. I have a couple of errands to run first and as I pull out of the driveway Pat calls my cell phone to tell me the puppy she had has finally passed away!!!!! Well Pat gave it all she could with getting up and feeding him every two hours or so. Just think there was something wrong with them as they are just not thriving like they should.

We have a good lunch and chit chat and have a drink called the Flaming Volcano and it is very yummy.
I finally drop Pat off and pick up the pup as he will be buried in the back yard with the others.
I let all the dogs out and go back to check on the pup with Katey and he is still at 3 ounces. Very disappointing but there you go.

By the evening the pup is down to 2 7/8 ounces by 8:0p.m. Well I guess he will be dead by the morning!!!! How upsetting but Katey is doing all she can. By the time we go to bed he is down to 2 ¾ ounces so I am sure he will be dead in the morning.
I just remembered that I gave Pat a bottle of Fading Puppy Syndrome stuff and have emailed her to ask for it. Hey can't hurt to try it.
I have given the pup some plain yoghurt. I tried to get it in him with a syringe but didn't work so had to put it in his mouth with my finger. Will see if that helps but I don't hold out much hope.

When I got up this morning, Saturday, Pat is sitting in the drive and she has bought over the fading puppy stuff. I haven't checked the pup yet but am sure he will be dead. I didn't get up in the night as didn't want to deal with it if he was dead!!!

I go into the bathroom and my, the pup is still alive and up to 3 ounces again!!! Well gee I guess giving him the yoghurt must have helped. We will try the fading puppy stuff and the yoghurt and see what happens. It can't make him any worse than he is and I just have to try something. I still haven't taken off the due claws. If he ever gets to four ounces then I will take them off. No point in stressing him any more than he is stressed now.

Today is Sunday and the pup is up to 3 5/8 ounces. I have been giving him the yoghurt and the fading puppy stuff. Three times the yoghurt today and then the fading puppy in between.

We will just have to see how he is in the morning. Trouble is every time I go in the bathroom I want to see him sucking on a tit and sometimes I know he is full but I still have to put him on a tit!!!

Today is Wednesday and would you believe the pup is up to 5 1/8 ounces! Just amazing.

His name is going to be Pour Quoi Luck of the Draw and Rambo as a call name which I think is well deserved. Going to take the due claws off this evening. Never thought this day would come for him.

Today is also a sad day. I took my first papillon, Zeley to the vet today to be put to sleep. Zeley has been a wonderful dog for me and it is not fair for me to let her suffer any more. She was blind, deaf and could no longer poo without a lot of difficulty. She is now buried in the back yard with the other past dogs that have gone on to Rainbow Bridge. I bought a lovely plant to also put in the hole which is called a Scotch Broom and will flower in April and May which is very fitting. It will flower every year for me to see from the kitchen window and remember Zeley in her younger days. Zena went down the road to return a video and she bought me back a lovely flowering fuscia in a hanging basket. Just lovely.

The end of wonderful friendship with a wonderful dog who did me proud. No she was not a Champion as I couldn't find the majors in those days either and you only needed 5 for a 3 point major, now you need 12!!!.

Rest in peace my beloved Zeley

Tomorrow I am taking my stuff over to Pat to put in her motor home as on Friday about 1:30p.m. as we are leaving for the Chesapeake dog show. Yes we are going in Pat's motor home as she has had it fixed and the generator and everything is running fine!!!!!

Pat and I have the only Chihuahua's on Saturday but there are four females on Sunday which is two points. Now Tibetan Spaniels, there are 10 females entered which is a 3 point major and yes Sarah needs that three point major. I have asked Sue Whaley to show her again but she is not going to Chesapeake this year. What a bummer. Oh well have to do it myself!!!!

May

So this morning I get up and it is Friday and we are leaving today for Chesapeake dog show.

It is only 56 miles away so we don't leave here till about 1:30p.m. because they won't let us park till 3:0p.m. so no point in getting there too early.

I am going to bath Sarah this morning so she is nice and fluffy for the show. Her coat is really growing but as she is now in season and is outside with Chloe, Pat's papillon who has been bred to Mio. Chloe was well pleased to have a playmate.

The Sayuri puppy, Rambo is up to 6 ½ ounces so I am ever hopeful that he will do well while I am away. I know Zena will take care of him.

Eric takes me down to Bloom's car park to meet Pat and off we go.

It was a good trip and luckily the tunnel wasn't backed up. Oh how I hate driving through that stupid tunnel.

We arrive at 2:30p.m. but they let us park and we are next to our friends, Maynard Woods, the Pomeranian guys and they are so nice and always pleasant to Pat and I.

We just get all the x-pens out and Pat tells me to start the generator and as I do Maynard is knocking on the door because our exhaust from the generator will blow right in his door so we decide to turn around. Should have decided that 20 minutes ago eh!! Oh well we undo all the pens and turn the motor home round so now we have our x-pens facing each other so lets hope our dogs don't try to eat their poms LOL.

We finally get all set up and Pat tells me to turn on the generator and the AC while she puts the jacks out under the back and the tip out!!!

The generator will start and run for about 15 minutes but as soon as you turn on the AC it just stops. Pat keeps trying and of course then it floods with petrol so we decide to leave it and just let it cool down for 15 minutes or so!!! Pat is so upset as this was supposed to be all fixed and now we have to ring Max and get him to come and bring the house generator as we can't stay here over the weekend with no AC as it is supposed to be in the 90 degree range on Sunday!!!!

Max and Hunter arrive with the generator and Max and Pat get it all going and we have AC. Patrick will come tomorrow, Saturday and see if he can fix the generator on the motor home.

They finally leave at about 10 o'clock and we sit outside with the dogs and chatting with Maynard of course about the dogs LOL.

We finally get to bed about 11p.m.

Saturday

Morning comes of course all too soon and no I didn't sleep very good at all last night. It is so hot in here even with the AC on and the fan up the front between the two seats. Pat leaves about 8:25a.m. to go over to the ring for stewarding and I groom up Sarah and run wet wipes over the chi's. I have to take them all over to the ring as they show within one class of each other. Oh it is going to be hot for them over there so let's hope I can get the trolley under the tent.

Sarah is the first to show and of course I want this win to finish Sarah to her Championship.

I walk her around and as usual she is barking and lunging at any big dog she can see!!! So nice that she is debarked. It sure is hot standing waiting and no they wouldn't let me put the trolley under the tent.

Finally we go in and I get second out of two. Typical but there you go. No Championship for Sarah today. I won't bother to show her under this judge again.

Finally it is Diva's turn and she has been in the sun way too long and really doesn't want to walk round and yesterday when we bought them over here she was just fine. Oh well she gets a first place ribbon and a Winners ribbon as she is the only dog. The breed dog comes in and we go round again and Diva gets Best of Opposite Sex LOL. Well a hard decision as there were only two dogs in the class. I am pleased with her and hopefully she will do better tomorrow.

McGee is the only male and he performs just perfectly. He is so cute. Hopefully he will get Best of Winners when he goes back in against the winner of the girls.

Pat hands me Snowball. She isn't much better today but at least she walks round the ring. Then I turn to Pat to hand me Polly and there has been an incident.

Pat had Polly and Snowball in her arms and a man trod on Polly's lead and pulled her out of Pat's arms and she flew through the air and hit the floor on her side. Pat thought she was dead.

Of course I didn't find this out till we were on our way back to the motor home. I wondered why Polly was a bit spazzy in the ring. Still she won the points and McGee got Best of Breed and Best of Winners, giving him the point from the females and Polly got Best of Opposite Sex. Snowball gets Reserve.

I am at least happy Polly is o.k. and not too shook up to at least go round the ring!!!

Pat wants me to take McGee to Group as he will be in the toy group and also the Best Bred By Exhibitor Group as well. I hate going to groups but for Pat and his first time we will go. I have put a flannel in the fridge and when I take him back I can have him sitting on a cold towel and that will keep him cooler.

Patrick comes to try and fix the generator but it seems now it is the starter solenoid that has gone and he will fix it on Monday after we get home. He is also going to have to come on Sunday to take the generator home as there is no way I can help Pat lift it on the back of the motor home as I have had back surgery and it isn't happening!!!

Took McGee to the two Groups but no we didn't get placed as usual LOL. Still he was good and it was fun. The judge that did Group today is our judge for tomorrow so that might work in our favor but doubt she will remember me or the dog LOL

Pat finally comes back at 4p.m. and is just exhausted so I make her a cup of coffee and tell her to lay down and rest on the sofa!!!!

We finally get up at 6:30p.m. and let the dogs out and cook dinner. Tonight is liver and onions and gravy and it is well yummy!!!!!

Pat makes slushies while we watch a movie. We also chow down on chips and dip which is good. More slushies as well, to finish the evening. Watched a strange movie called Men who stare at Goats and it was a very strange movie. No not one that we will go out and buy. Finally turned the generator off about 10:30p.m. and went to bed!!!!

Sunday

Of course morning comes all too soon and Pat has to be over to the ring by 8:25a.m.

This morning Sarah shows first but I am going to watch and when they start showing the Pugs

I will take her over as not going to bother with a crate today.

Yes it is going to be another very hot one!!!

I get dressed and groom up Sarah just a bit. Wipe her bummy as she is in season. While drinking my coffee I see that the Pugs are about to go in so off I go with Sarah.

As usual she is barking and jumping and doing a lot of peeing but that is good.

Finally our turn to go in and we get second out of two!!!! Bummer. They all go in for Winners Bitch and the dog in the ring with me wins so I have to go back in for reserve and yeah we get Reserve!!

Well not what I wanted but there you go.

I take Sarah over to the Superintendents office and give them our entries for Manassas and Hampton shows. Yes I have entered Sarah, Polly and Diva expensive but have to finish Sarah and Polly. I am ever hopeful that it will be majors in both at one of the shows. Sarah is going to be bred anyway so after the end of May first week in June, Charlottesville will be her last show.

I take Sarah back to the motor home to be in the cool and change clothes. Think I will go over and have a chat with an old friend called Jackie. She has papillons and they are showing at 11a.m.

Gee it is hot and I really wish I had bought some no sleeve t-shirts but I didn't. I have a yellow one that is very thin and that will do. It was nice to talk to Jackie again and she really has some nice dogs. Of course there is a very small entry so she wins Best of Breed.

We talked about my losing the pups from Sayuri and she says she had the same problem and after doing research it comes from bugs getting in through the umbilical cord and that really makes sense as one of the puppies was bleeding under the umbilical cord, under the skin. It is nice to at least have some foreclosure about why they died. When I get home I will bleach everything like Jackie says and be more diligent about picking up after the dogs. Bleach the concrete etc so the dogs aren't contaminating anything in the house. Nice to hear that it isn't just me losing pups!!!!!

I bought some French Fries which were just yummy and then I watched the Pomeranians and then head back to get the chi's for their class at 12.45p.m.
Another cup of coffee and I have to change my clothes again!!!!
When I got up this morning I put two towels in the freezer so the pups will have a cold towel to lay on in the crates. Will hopefully not be over there long as the long coat, Diva will be the first to show at 12:45p.m.
Pat comes back at 12:20p.m. with a plate of food which doesn't look very appetizing but hey it is free!!!
Pat helps me get the crates out and we load up the trolley and head off over there and the time is 12:35p.m. so we wont have long to wait!!!
I feel so bad for Pat having to work outside in this heat. Even under the tent here it must be in the 90 degree mark!!! It is still stifling hot.

Diva is first and today she is much better than yesterday. Actually walks all round the ring today and stands on the table real good. I am very pleased with her. We then go back in the ring with the Breed dog and of course Diva is raring to go behind the other dog!!!! Well now Diva has two blue ribbons and two purple ribbons and two Best of Opposite ribbons but no points LOL.
That is fine as she did good and it is practice. She will only get better as she gets older.
We have to stand and watch one class and then it is us again.
This time we have the trolley under the tent so now no one can pull Polly out of Pat's arms. Yes I will get Eric to shorten the lead when I get home.
Time to go in with McGee and he is the only male as the other one didn't show up!!!
Then I take Snowball and she isn't too terrible but this will be her last show. Again no other dogs so she wins her class. Now time for Polly and again no show with the other dog so she wins her class and now time for Polly and Snowball and Polly gets the one point. There was no point in my pulling Polly as then it would have been no points so Snowball wouldn't have got any points either!!!!
Time for Polly and McGee to go for Best of Breed. This time I take Polly and let Pat be on the lead with McGee. We have to pick them up so the judge can look at heads!!! Poor Pat hasn't had to do this before so not very good at showing just his head!! I will have to teach her how to do that!!!! McGee gets Best of Breed, Best of Winners which gives him the

female point as well and Polly gets Best of Opposite Sex. A good day, points on both the dogs!!!!

Pat and I go back to the motor home and unload the trolley and get the crates inside in the cool.
Pat has to go back and she will have to stay for helping with Group. It will probably be 4 p.m. before she gets back.
I start cleaning up inside and put stuff away as Patrick is supposed to be coming later to help pack up the generator. He finally arrives about 3p.m. so we have to sit and wait for Pat. I watch the Groups and when it gets to Best in Show we will start taking the x-pens down so all ready to get rolling when she gets back!!!!!
Pat comes across just as we have got all the x-pens folded up and ready to put on the back.
She needs to be in the AC for about ten minuets and of course change her clothes as I am sure she is very hot.
I get her a bottle of water and she tells me that she is just exhausted and next time she isn't staying to do the Groups.
We get all packed up and Patrick disconnects the generator and hooks up the front battery and Pat gets in to start it!!!!!!!!!!!!!

DEAD, yet again. I should have got Patrick to crank the engine before we disconnected the generator but I didn't think about it as he said by disconnecting the front battery it would stay charged!!! Well that didn't happen eh!!!
We have two battery charger packs and neither of them would crank the engine so then Patrick hooked up the jumper cables to Pat's van and eventually it started!!!!!
Way to go now we can go home.

We get on the road and Hunter is driving Pat's van with Patrick as co pilot. Hope he does o.k. We get about 20 miles and the traffic starts to slow up and there is one of those flashing signs which say "6 mile back up"!! Oh just wonderful. We are within half a mile of the bridge and now the traffic is stopped and I tell Pat to take it out of drive and put it in park. Please don't turn the engine off else we might not get it going again!!! As we sit and watch about 6 or 7 cars in front of us there is a load of steam and looks like some one has over heated. Sure hope they can push it to the side of the road else we won't be able to get past!!!!
Suddenly the lights turn green and the traffic starts moving and this poor guy is stuck in the middle of the road. We are right at the beginning of

the bridge and there is just enough room for us to get round him. Poor guy, we know the feeling well.

Pat calls Patrick and they are about a mile behind us and have just started moving as well.
We finally get home and Eric picks me up from the Bloom's car park. Oh nice to be home.
It is now 6:30p.m. and Zena has the other dogs up so I put these up and Sarah outside of course and get them their food.

Zena follows me into the bathroom and of course I have to pick up Rambo to weigh him and he is up to 7 ½ ounces. How thrilling. I am sure he will be fine now.

Well we handed our entries in for Manassas and Hampton and then when we get home I guess we will have to think about Charlottesville the first weekend of June. That means we will be away three weekends in a row!!! That will be hard going.

Now I have to breed Sarah to Grissom.

The puppy, Rambo, is doing fine and up to 9 ounces and is gaining every day. I am thrilled with him and hope that Niki will be as well when she sees him.

May

Wednesday

Today is Wednesday, Pat and I are getting ready for going to Manassas. It is not good numbers for either of the chi's but for Sarah it is a major both days which is thrilling. Yes I have already asked Sue Whaley to show her.
Well about 5p.m. Max rang me to ask if he could borrow my spare tire for our trip which of course I agreed.
Yes now I spend all evening wondering why he wants my spare tire but I am sure Pat will tell me all about it tomorrow when we leave as we are taking her motor home this weekend. Yes we have electric which is why we are leaving a day early.

Thursday morning comes round and I have a 10a.m. appointment to get my nails done and have the two chi's to bath and also have to get groceries. It is 9a.m. and Zena has just left and the phone rings and it is Pat saying not to worry about the spare tire and she will explain when we meet. That is good as now I can bath the chi's without worrying about having to stop. Polly is a breeze to bath but Diva is very opinionated and does not like it one bit but she is going to have to get used to it eh!!!!

Finally get her done and then change clothes to go and get my nails done. I will go to the bank afterwards and then get the groceries. Nice because that will give my nails a good time to set hard. I nearly always bash them up with the seatbelt.

I did Sarah last night and claws on everyone, even the pups.

Everything is done and in the car except the dogs. Wait till Pat rings before I put them in and she rings right at 11:55a.m.

Eric helps me load the dogs and get Sayuri and her pup as they are going as well and off we go to Bloom's car park to meet Pat. I pull in and we can't see Pat and I have just gone about four feet past the entrance so put the car in reverse to back up!!! BANG goes the car as I have hit the car behind me. Crap. I jump out and the man gets out but luckily because I wasn't going fast at all there are no marks on his car nor mine and he offers to point me in the right direction as it is obvious that I am lost!!! Well he shouldn't have been so close to me eh!!! With all that Pat drives into the parking lot and we move on LOL.

Yes I was very very lucky that there was no damage to either car.

We got all loaded up and we left. Both not at our best I might add LOL. Oh to sit and relax and drink my coffee. We head of to I-95 which of course is a road that I hate but the traffic is so far good. We are leaving at exit 104 as there is a Flying J truck stop and we plan to empty the tanks, fill with propane and get petrol and of course something to eat for lunch.

Would you believe it took us an hour messing round turning this way for propane and then turn round again to dump the tanks and then turn around again to get in line for petrol. Still all good and we got fried chicken and fries and of course coffee for lunch.

We get on the road again and Wonder Woman (navigational system) says we will be there at 3:30p.m. which is good.

We get a good parking space, a bit unlevel so have to use our orange building blocks on one side to make the motor home level. Pat and I are getting good at this. Trouble is if the motor home isn't level then the fridge won't work and that is the last thing you need not to be working.

When Pat had her yard sale last weekend she found an old baby play pen in the shed and we had decided to use it instead of the x-pen hoping it won't make as much mess with the litter as the x-pen does. It seems to work well and we put Pat's chi pups in it and my tibion pup in it. Will be interesting to see who is first to use the litter tray. They are all in shock but they will be better tomorrow I am sure.

I can't believe that Sayuri is actually letting the chi pups nurse as well when she wouldn't let her own pups nurse after she had them. Amazing what motherhood does to them.

Pat starts cooking fried chicken and oh my, it is just wonderful. No we didn't set off the smoke alarm nor burn the camper down and had a great dinner.

We saw Vince outside and I quickly wrapped up the left over two pieces of chicken and run them out to Vince. He was thrilled and did us good as he didn't charge us a parking fee for Thursday night.

We do the dishes and open a bottle of wine to drink while we watched a movie. It was an old favorite, Kiss the Girls with Brad Pit and Morgan Freeman. We finally got to bed at just after mid night which was a real late night for us but we aren't showing till Saturday so can have a day of rest tomorrow.

Friday

Morning comes and it is a lovely day. We sit and eat breakfast without hurrying and then decide that we need to trim up the chi's. Really can't do it outside as I really can't see with the sun shining like this so we go inside to do them. We trim a lot of hair of Polly and trim up Diva's whiskers just a bit more as I did miss a couple. They both look good.

Now we are going to put the dogs up and go bike riding round to see what is going on and where the rings are that we show in tomorrow. As usual I can't get up a couple of the hills but that is o.k. too and Pat is very understanding.

We visit one of the trade stands and I end up buying a lovely gold dog lead for Diva and the lady gives me a bottle of shampoo to try. Nice. When we get back I will get the money for the lead and take it back. Our ring for the chi's is in the building and then Sarah is outside under the tent. Going to be hot tomorrow as well so hope we don't have to wait too long as with her being black as well she attracts the sun!!!

We get the money and take it back to the trade stand then come back and have lunch.

I did salad with cold roast pork chopped up on the top and it was very very good.

After we had cleaned up the dishes we decided to take a nap. So far the motor home is running smoothly with the AC on but not much air in the bedroom so I have the fan blowing.

After our nap we have dinner which tonight is liver and onions and peppers. Oh yummy.

Pat made smoothies and we had a beer with our dinner which was good.

We sat outside for about 45 minutes with the dogs and then decided to watch a movie and then of course bed time.

While watching the movie we ate chips and dip which was yummy. We watched Missing with Tommy Lee Jones, not one of his best but still enjoyable.

Saturday

Morning comes oh too early and we have to be over at the building by 8:30a.m. but there are 12 in front of us.

McGee is in first and in the Bred By Exhibitor class and wins his class. We go back in for Winners Dog and yeah McGee wins. Well gee would you believe there are only 3 female smooth coats and they are all in the Bred By Exhibitor class. Well Polly ends up third, this judge went for tiny tiny dogs. Good for McGee but my Polly is a bit on the sturdy side LOL which is why she is only fed green beans.

We hang around as the long coats are next after the Havanese class so no point in taking them back.

Now it is time for Diva and she really isn't doing very well. Not only is she hugging the concrete but she is swimming with her front legs. Oh well she is still a baby but not doing too well at this. I think she needs walking on concrete to build up some muscle. Hopefully she will walk a bit better tomorrow.

Now they are done and I came back to Pat to see her holding a Papillon for Tracy Burdick. Tracy had asked Pat to hold the dog while she was in the ring and of course Pat never says no to anyone. Tracy came back and then asked Pat if she won the next class with the dog she had would Pat take the dog she was holding, back in the ring!! Well I could see the look of panic on Pat's face so asked Tracy if she would rather I take in the dog. That was fine so I got my bait, as you know we use ham. Well this dog has died and gone to heaven with this ham. He is being very attentive and of course is just gorgeous as are all Tracy dogs. We go back in for Winners Dog and we all go round and the judge asks me to put him back on the table and then up and back and then back in line. The dog is good and very attentive to me. We are all in line and the judge points to me for the win. Well all the girls clap and cheer. I find very amusing as it is me they are clapping for, not the dog, because I don't show Papillons any more. Some of the girls even came over to the motor home to ask me when I was going to show Papillons again. Too funny for words. Yes it was exciting and I do like to win.

Well now we have to go back to the motor home, have a sandwich and then go and show Sarah. She is under the tents in ring 7.

We have a sandwich for lunch and then trot off over to Ring 7. It is hot out here. We take the crate because Sarah gets too wound up if she isn't in the crate. Pat goes back for the chairs.

Yes I have asked Sue Whaley to show Sarah as I think she stands more of a chance than me.

The males go in and then the classes before the Open class which Sarah is in. Gee my heart is pacing. Sue comes and gets Sarah and Pat and I are just sitting shaking hoping that Sue gets the win. Oh my Sue is in the ring and going down on the ground, on one knee and I know that will spaz Sarah out as she has never had anyone go down on the ground with her. Yes her tail drops. Oh well she ends up third out of four. Bummer but there you go, Sue has told Pat that we will be going out to dinner this evening. Well Karen was supposed to be coming to see the pups so will she be here before we go to dinner. Who knows?

We trudge back to the motor home, very disappointed but another day tomorrow.

After we have the dogs out we decide to take a nap just in case Karen comes. At least we will feel a bit better by the time we go out to dinner.

Wow I wake up and it is four thirty and no phone call from Karen. We take the dogs out and give them a handful of dry food because Whitney came over as we were putting the dogs up to say they will pick us up at 5:0p.m. Pat and I get dressed and they arrive to take us to dinner. We really didn't want to go but there you go, have to be polite. I just hate it that Sue won't let us pay our share. Oh well we enjoy dinner and finally get back to the camper at 8:30p.m. and Karen is waiting for us.

Sue stays while Karen gets her Chihuahuas out and then she comes into the motor home to see the pups of Pat's. Of course she just adores Calleigh, the tibbion pup.

Karen loves the pups and she finally leaves at 9:30p.m. because it starts to rain. We still have to feed the dogs and get them out before it really pours with rain.

Pat and I sit and chat about the pups and what Karen is going to do and finally go to bed.

Not such an early day tomorrow, which is good. But tomorrow Sarah shows at 10:30a.m. and the smooth coats don't show till 1:15p.m. That means it will be late in the day before we can leave here.

Sunday

What an awful night we have had. The rain never stopped and then thunder and lightening and then my puppy, Calleigh decided she wanted to be in with Sayuri then she wanted to be in the play pen with the pups. I don't think Pat and I have had more than four hours sleep all night long.

At least now it has stopped raining but it also means the ground is going to be so wet to show Sarah as I can't see it being much dryer by 10:15a.m.

Pat and load up Diva and Sarah and head off to the ring which for Diva is indoors. Not going to be really worth it as only two females. Still good practice and let's hope she walks better today.

There are three males and they go in and now it is Diva's turn. Well today she walks much better but is still not good. The judge grunts about her teeth and I tell him that she is booked in on Tuesday to have the baby teeth taken out. Well a surprise that Junko wins, of course and then Diva gets Reserve which is fine too.

Now we go over to the field for Sarah to show. I take her out as soon as we get there because it is starting to rain and really need her to pee so that I can towel her dry before time to show. She pees twice and I towel her dry and brush her and put her back in the crate till her turn.

Sue sends Whitney over to get Sarah and just as I tell Whitney to carry her, Sarah takes a lunge at a big dog she sees. Caught Whitney off guard but all was o.k.

Now it's time for Sarah to go in. Yesterday at dinner I did tell Sue that it was not good to go down on the floor with Sarah and she agreed.

They all go round, Sarah is first in line and the judge tells the contestants to stand under the tent out of the rain and Sue is down on the ground with Sarah about 4 feet from the table which the judge is using. Pat went up to stand by the steward to see Sarah and every time a dog goes on the table the judge looks at the dog and then at Sarah. Oh my heart is pounding. They all go round again and she says that is the way I put them, one two and three with Sarah being first. Oh my how exciting is this. Now they have to go back in for Winners Bitch and they go round again and the judge points to Sarah as Winners Bitch. OH MY SARAH WON A THREE POINT MAJOR, which now makes her a Champion. They go back in for Best of Breed but Sarah didn't get placed.

Yes of course we have a picture done and Sue is actually smiling in this one. Can't wait for it to come LOL.

WE HAVE A NEW CHAMPION!!!!!!!!!!!!!!! WE HAVE A NEW CHAMPION!!!!!!!!!!

Oh I am so thrilled and it was worth every penny of paying Sue to show her.

This was a good weekend. Now we can go home happy with a new Champion and points on McGee.

Our next show is Hampton VA and Pat will be working at that one as a Steward.

I ring home and tell them and we will go out to eat tonight as no I am not cooking.

We have a good drive home even though we are on I-95 and get home at 6p.m. which isn't too bad.

Zena meets me at the car park and we take the dogs home, let them run around and then feed them and go out to eat. We are going to Red Lobster to celebrate finishing Sarah!!!!!

Thursday

I get over to Pat leaving the house just before 10a.m. Our plan is to stop at WaWa for petrol as they are only charging $2.48 per gallon whereas on this side of town it is $2.69 per gallon.

Well I have over full on the petrol tank so we won't be stopping there.

By the time I get to Pat's I have no brakes and they are smoking and smell awful. I ring Danny and he rings Pete who put on the new brakes for me and he says he will be at Pat's in fifteen minutes and there he is. One of the brake lines was leaking and he fixes it but still not right so drains the lines and then it seems to be working good. Great. Well glad I left early.

We head off down the road and will stop at Sam's club to get the wine for Sue Whaley. As we are going to Sam's I decide to ask them to put in a new battery under the step as obviously mine is shot. By the time I had put the dogs in the RV there wasn't enough power to put the step in without my starting the engine. Need to have it replaced.

We finally park but it wasn't easy as this is 38ft long and their car parking area for repairs is not good. As we pull up two men come out saying they can smell burning. Well it is my brakes of course and I try to explain and ask them about the battery. They tell us to go inside and they will put it on for me. We both march inside and then suddenly realize we have left the door open with all the dogs and our stuff in there!! Pat decides to go back while I pay for the battery which was only $77.47 and this is one huge battery.
I go and get the wine etc and then get back to Pat at the RV. Well nothing is simple. The last person that put this battery in here cross threaded the nut on the terminal. A fifteen minute job ends up being 45 minutes!! If he had a hacksaw it would have been cut off in ten minutes but no they don't have hacksaws in Sam's car department!!! Oh well it is finally done and we are on the road again. Not far to the Coliseum and we get there just after 1:00p.m. which is good.
It is a nice day and we get all set up and the generator starts first time with this new battery. Yeah it was worth the money LOL.

We had a good dinner, Chilli and salad and a bottle of wine which Sue had given us. Her brother has a vineyard and makes wine but does not sell to the public and every now and then Sue gives us a bottle and it is to die for!!! It is made from muscadine berries and is just lovely.
We watch a movie and finally go to bed. Oh it has started raining again so let's hope we can sleep through it this time.

Friday

As usual morning comes round all too soon, but at least we did sleep even though rained, but not for long. Dry this morning and Pat has to be over to the ring by 8:20a.m. but I am not showing till 9:30a.m. and only have to take the smooth coats over as Diva and Sarah don't show till this afternoon.

I get the crates out and loaded on the trolley to see Pat coming.

McGee is first and then there is another open male. We go back in for the points and McGee wins which is great. I then take Polly in and she is the only female so then we go back in with McGee for Best of Breed. I put Pat on the end of Polly as really want McGee to win as Polly only needs a major to finish. McGee gets Best of Breed which is great and Polly gets Best of Opposite Sex.

Pat is thrilled and yes now I have to take him to Group but it is inside so that is cool!!!

I can have some lunch and then it will be time to take Sarah and Diva back to show. I get them loaded up on the trolley and off we go to the building. At least it is all on the flat so not a hard pull.

We get in the building and over to the ring and then I take Sarah and Diva outside as Sarah always poos when she gets on the lead. Yeah way to go Sarah, a lot better out here than in the ring!!

Well Diva is not very good at all and slinking round the ring again. I sure hope she grows out of this as it does not look pretty at all.

Time for Sarah and we have to wait a long time as there are five classes before she goes in for Best of Breed as now she is Champion we don't show till the end. She is good but keeps laying down. I think she is tired as now she is pregnant and all the excitement of being in the building etc just tires her out. Oh well I will show her tomorrow but not the rest of the week. Wow we get a ribbon for Select Dog which means she has 3 points towards getting her Grand Champion award which is a new thing that they have started doing. Don't ask me to explain as all I know is you need 25 points and they can only be given to Champions. Well nice for Sarah and now time to go back to the motor home and then get McGee for Group. The toys are second class so shouldn't be too long.

I have a good system for putting the crates back in the motor home without straining my back. I take the crates off the trolley and put the trolley outside and then do up the fence. I let the dogs out of the crates and then put the crates one at a time in the motor home. It makes my life much easier not having to lift the crate with the dog in it LOL. Smart don't you think???

Time for coffee and let the dogs out before taking McGee over there. I won't take a crate, just walk him over there and take a towel to put on my lap. It is 1:30p.m. and time to go over to the ring. Guess Pat is working the Groups today.

I get over there to see that Pat is yes working Groups so she won't be back to the motor home till about 4:30p.m. Gee hard work being a steward for very little money.

My turn to go in the ring and as I am the smallest dog I go on the end with the Pekinese behind me. McGee does really well and I am proud of him but of course we don't get a placement. In fact I have this judge tomorrow for the class so that will be interesting.

I get back to the motor home and let all the dogs out and sit outside with them for about 15 minutes. Oh boy it sure is hot out here so real glad the air conditioning is working inside.

We all go inside and I put the dogs up, put Evie in with the pups for ten minutes to nurse them and then I am going to take a nap and put the heating pad on my back. It really is helping and of course I am still taking the Motrin to reduce the swelling.

Pat finally comes back at 4:30p.m. Don't know why I lay down as I can't sleep if she isn't here but it makes my back feel a lot better LOL.

I make Pat a cup of coffee and then we have to start cooking fried chicken for dinner. We have bought enough for Sue and Vince so when we have cooked enough I will take it over to the building for them.

The chicken looks just yummy and when it has cooled a bit I got out some plastic plates to put it on to take it over the building. I didn't want to give them my china plates as don't know when I will get them back. We put tin foil over it to keep it hot and boy it sure is hot. Sue and Vince are thrilled and I get back to see how Pat is doing with cooking ours.

Boy there sure is a lot of chicken but man it tastes so good. Not quite as good as when we were in Manassas as this seems to be a bit more salty. Pat says that is because it was sitting in the salt water for two days instead of just the one. Oh well it still tastes good. The three pieces that are left Pat takes over to the Shih Tzu lady and of course she is thrilled as well. It was good and even better with a bottle of beer.

We get cleaned up quick as didn't want that oil sitting for too long.

It is time to watch a movie after we take the dogs out of course.

Saturday

I am not going to show Sarah again as with her being pregnant it really isn't good to keep taking her to the ring!! After her win yesterday that is all I needed.

Well the two smooth coat chi' show first this morning but Diva doesn't show till 12:15p.m. so will take her back on her own after lunch. No point in dragging a crate over!!!!

Pat left at about 8:15a.m. this morning but she said she would come back to help me load the guys on the trolley. I get dressed and have one last cup of coffee and now time to load the guys up. Get everything done and the door locked and look up to see Pat coming across the car park again. I call to tell her to wait there as no point in walking all the way over here just to turn around again.

The judge today is the same judge I had in Group yesterday so this should be interesting.

Well it is only going to be one point again for McGee but let's hope that he gets Best of Breed and then goes to Group again.

I take him in and put him on the table and the judge says "this is a lovely boy, I only remember the good dogs and saw you in Group yesterday". Of course I smile and say thank you, I like him too. Then we go back in for Best of Breed and again McGee wins and Polly gets Best of Opposite. The judge says to me "I really like this boy and the reason I didn't place you in Group is because he is still immature, well only 8 months what do you expect but he will get Group placing when he is older. Well nice but we have to start somewhere eh!!

Still Pat was thrilled of course and we will go to Group again this afternoon. Hopefully Pat will be finished by then.

Now time to go back to the motor home and have some lunch and then take Diva back for her class.

At least it is nice and cool in the motor home as it sure is hot out there. Made a sub sandwich for lunch and then change my clothes again ready to show Diva.

She walks over to the building nicely but doesn't show nicely at all. Tomorrow I am going to sit over here with her for at least an hour before she shows so she gets this in her head. Why do I have to have the difficult dogs??????????

Oh well there you go. I take her back to the motor home and have about an hour or more before time to go back with McGee.

It is time for another cup of coffee of course. I will be swimming in the stuff by this evening.

The time is 3:00p.m. and I need to get over to the building for Group. As I walk through the door some girl says that they are having the Toy Group in the ring now so of course I hustle over to the ring and they are just finishing the last Group and then time for the Toys. As usual we go on the end and I see Pat coming over to the ring. Gee she has finished so can get to sit and watch her dog go round the ring. He shows beautifully as usual but no Group placing. Oh well he did well for such a young dog.

Pat and I walk back and now time to take a nap. Of course Pat is exhausted and she has had no lunch so I make her a sandwich and then we talk about the dogs and problems that she had as a Steward.

Time for a nap.

We have a nice evening again watching another movie after we took drinks over to Sue and Whitney. We sat and chatted about the day and of course dogs. It has cooled down a lot but now it is starting to rain so we all pack up and go back to the appropriate Motor homes.

Pat and I sit and watch a movie and have a cup of coffee to take our pills and finally go to bed.

It is another day tomorrow and another judge LOL.

Sunday

Pat leaves early again and the chi's show at 10a.m. today. Again Diva doesn't show till 12:15p.m. so I will just walk over McGee and Polly and then walk Diva over later on. Good for Polly to walk as she needs to poo when she is on the lead LOL. Only had her do it once in the ring but it isn't going to happen again!!!

I see Pat walking towards me and she waits of course. No point in wasting steps LOL.

Well it is the same two males today and the same two females for Polly. McGee ends up winning the point and then he goes back in against the females and ends up winning Best of Breed with Polly getting Best of Opposite Sex. Pat is pleased of course and the Toys are the second Group today so we will be done early LOL. Pat will also be finished just after lunch so she will be able to go over with me and sit and watch.

I take the kids back over to the motor home, have another cup of coffee and then brush up Diva a bit before taking her over.

I know she doesn't show till 12:15p.m. but I am taking her over about 11:30a.m. so she can be a bit more used to the building. Don't think it is going to help any but I am trying eh!!!

So strange, Diva is a spitfire outside the ring but when you take her in the ring she acts so stupid and nervous!!!! I always carry them into the ring because we have had the small dogs jumped so many times just as you are about to walk in the ring so I know it isn't because of the gates!!! She is just pulling my chain a bit like Polly did but this is much worse and I don't like it!!!

Well strange, one of the long coat males leaves the ring, said his dog got scared so no point in showing him. Felt bad as that means that there will be no points for the males. The female class is won by a little cream girl which is quite cute!!!!

Oh well there you go, I will have to rethink this situation a bit. I take Diva back to the motor home and of course outside she is just full of life again. I just get my clothes changed and Pat comes back so we can have lunch and take a much needed nap!!! Well no nap as I forgot we have to go back for Group with McGee. The Toy Group is again third in line so have about an hour before I have to take him over there. At least this time Pat can sit and watch. He does well going round the ring but again doesn't get pulled for a win. Oh well I have to remember he is a baby. Now it is time to go back and have a nap LOL

After our nap we sit outside with the dogs and the girls that have the trailer next to us, come over to chat and of course talk about their losses over the weekend and the problems they had with their trailer. They also give us a very nice vodka ice tea drink. No I do not like ice tea at all but this was a really nice drink. It starts to rain so we go back to the campers and Pat and I watch a movie as usual and then go to bed.

Monday

Today is the last day of showing and sure hope Pat has an early finish today so we can pack up and get home. Ironic isn't it that we can't wait to get away but when the last day comes we can't wait to pack up and get home. Today the smooth coats show again at 8:15a.m. and Diva is again at 12:15p.m. I probably won't go to Group today if we win as I want to come back and get as much packed up so Pat doesn't have much to do when she gets back.

As I am walking over to the building, one of the other competitors comes running out and asks me to go to the Judge with him so he can have our ring time changed till after the last breed!!!
Well crap that means I will have to wait 30-40 minutes before we show. Oh well there you go. Have to be cordial to other competitors but I bet they wouldn't do it for me!!!!!!!!

Finally time for the smooth coats and of course McGee is his usual great self. Love the way he stands on the table. He is getting better, every now and then he will back away from the judge but he is still only 8 months old!!!!!
We go back in for the points and the Judge gives the points to the other dog!!!! Well I guess that is what you get for asking to have the class moved to the end!!! Time for Polly and again she ends up with Best of Opposite Sex. Well now at least I don't have to worry about going to Group LOL. Well always the way, but nice on the last day not to have to worry. Still have to show Diva and can't see her being any better today!!! Still I will bring her over about 30 minutes again before she is to show. Now back to the motor home.

Time for a cup of coffee and a sandwich and then time to take Diva back over to the building. I walk her of course as no point in taking a crate. She is really good outside the building but then fall's apart when time to go in the ring!!!! If this doesn't get any better when we go to Charlottesville the situation will have to be re-evaluated!!! I am not going to spend a fortune showing her if she doesn't want to do it and make up points for other people!!!!

As I expected Diva really isn't much better. At least today she does walk round the ring with her tail up but won't come back to the judge again. She is better on the table today as well. We will see how she does in Charlottesville and then decide.
Boy it is still hot out here but at least Pat is inside with the air conditioning. I will start packing up. Pat comes back about 2:0p.m. and all we have left to do is put the x-pens in the holes and then we are ready to go.

Pat needs a cup of coffee first and change her clothes. We sit and chat for a bit and then get loaded up to go home. It is an easy trip home as really only about 25 miles LOL.
Next trip will be Charlottesville which is next weekend. At least we came home with points on McGee and three Best of Breeds so we had a good four days showing. Oh and a SEL on Sarah, she always gets forgotten.

Pat is coming over on Monday to help me cleanout the motor home so we are ready to leave for Charlottesville on Friday as I have to work Tuesday and Wednesday.

Pat arrives to help clean out the motor home and there is enough dog food on the floor and the bed above the cab to fill a bag. Hair everywhere and we take down the air conditioner cover to clean it and again it is full of hair!!!

Finally get it all clean and spiffy for our next trip.

June

Friday

Today we leave for Charlottesville. I arrived at Pat's just after 10.0a.m. as planned and we load up her stuff and the dogs. It is only a two day show so we really don't have to take that many clothes but of course you can never rely on what the weather will do. I am expecting it to be hot!! Don't need much food either as only a two day show so I went and got what we needed.

We have a tank full of petrol so no need to stop but we will have to fill up when we get there as running on the generator all weekend and if it is very hot then we might need to run it at night.

We have a good trip except that Miss Lolla again brings us off at Pan Tops in Charlottesville which means we have to sit in traffic to get up onto US 29. Well I can't get over to the gas stations. They are all on the other side of the road!!! I am pretty sure there is one further up the road on this side LOL

Well gee I can see the Racetrack and we haven't passed a gas station. We pull in and Vince tells us to go back down the hill and there is one on the left. Gee I hate driving up and down this hilly narrow road and we have to go back down!!! Off we go and about two miles and there is a gas station so we fill up.

We finally get back to the Racetrack and get set up and it is only 2:30p.m. so we can get the dogs out and have some lunch and then a nap LOL!!!!

I was right it sure is hot up here. The dogs only want to be out here for a few minutes and then back into the air conditioning. Smart dogs eh!!!!

We have dinner and then after taking the dogs out we watch a movie. While we have the movie on we let the pups out to run around. They are

so funny but of course Pat gets up to get a drink and treads in shit LOL
LOL. They love to chew on the shoe laces in the sneakers and of course
the mats!!! Was a good movie and now time to take the guys out and go
to bed. At least not too an early start tomorrow. We show at 9:30a.m. and
I can walk the smooth coats over and come back for Diva which is good
for her!!!! I am really hoping she will be better as it is outside.

We have a good night and it really isn't as hot as I thought it would be.
Pat wakes me up at about 7a.m. and we have coffee and cereal before she
has to leave. It is going to be hard on her in this heat but there you go.

It is time for me to get dressed and head over to the ring. At least I can
see who is in the ring so I don't have to wait over there for too long in
this heat which is nice!!!
I take McGee in and he is really good even though a couple of times he
sniffs the ground as he is going round. We go back in for the points and
McGee wins. Now Polly's turn and she is good. She wins and gets Best
of Opposite and McGee gets Best of Breed again so we will have to do
Group this afternoon. At least I can watch and see what Group is in so I
don't have to be over there in this heat with him.

Just as we are leaving, the couple that are coming to see Chloe and
hopefully take her home arrive. Thank goodness Pat is here to chat to
them while I am showing.
I take them back to the motor home and get Diva. Let's hope she is
going to play today.
OOOH a bit of a breeze but I don't think it will last long!!!!
Time for Diva. Well she walks round the ring nice but won't stand on the
table yet again and won't come back to the judge!!!!! So upsetting but
she is in season so will be going home with Pat to stay with Abby in Pat's
bedroom. It is just too hot to put her in the laundry room.

As I am leaving the ring a friend who was showing a long coat and a
smooth coat comes over and offers to have Diva in his van before showing
tomorrow to see how she does being away from me!! Good idea and I
will take him up on it.

We go back to the motor home and the people want to see Chloe so I
bring her out and we sit and chat for about 45 minuets and then they
leave with Chloe. I hope this will be o.k. It is best that I dealt with it as I
don't think Pat would have been able to let her go. Chloe was Heathers

dog and she has really pined since Heather left. They walked away from the motor home with Chloe on a lead and Chloe never looked back.

Pat comes back for lunch and we talk about how her morning is going but she looks exhausted being out in the heat for so long. It is all very well saying she is in the shade but still in the heat!!!! She cries a bit about Chloe but I tell her they are nice people and I am sure they will look after her well.

No I did not show Sarah as she is really feeling it in this heat being pregnant and all. Being black as well she really does not do well in this heat!! Best she stays inside in the AC.

I watch from the window and count the Groups and then it is time to take McGee over.

Timed it just right ready to walk in the ring and Pat is still in another ring Stewarding.

He goes round nicely and stands nicely waiting his turn to go on the table. I am very pleased with him. Of course we don't get placed but it is still good practice for him.

I take him back to the motor home and Pat walks in just as I am letting the dogs out again.

She is exhausted and needs a long cold drink and then a nap!!!! After our nap and dinner we are going to make some English Tea and take it over to Sue and Whitney.

We have dinner and do the dogs and then make the English Tea. I had already soaked the fruit in Vodka so we just had to mix it in the pitcher. I have also bought some plastic cups, even though I don't like drinking out of plastic, you can't go carrying glasses all over the place. If there is any left when we come back, Pat and I can drink it out of a glass LOL.

We sit and chat till it starts to rain and then of course we put all the chairs under her canopy and we head back to the motor home. Well I thought it was going to rain for a long time and cool it down but it just makes the grass a bit wet.

We let the dogs out and then watch another movie and play with the puppies. Debbie rang and says she is coming in the morning and bringing biscuits. I told her we are showing at just after 9:00a.m. so you need to be on time LOL.

The puppies are having a blast running back and fourth. I opened the x-pen so they couldn't get into the bathroom area as really don't want

them peeing or pooping on the mat in the bathroom and not seeing it!!!!! One of us would be bound to step in it!!!
Strange movie but there you go. We put the pups up and then let all the dogs out and go to bed!!!!

Sunday

Morning comes and Pat and I have our coffee and cereal and then of course Pat has to leave to go and Steward.
Debbie is coming this morning and bringing Gary with her, he has one of the Sarah and Twister pups and it will be fun to see him again. He will be six months old now.

I get dressed and just as I am finished Debbie and Gary arrive. We have to time to chat for about 10 minutes and then my turn to take the Smooth Coats over to the ring. I have already taken Diva over to my friends van so don't have to worry about her, I'll eat my biscuit when we get back.
Debbie and Gary go over to the ring to watch the Papillons and I meet them over there. I ask Debbie to hold Polly and McGee while I go and get my numbers. As I come back I see a circle of people as Polly has slipped the lead. As soon as she sees me she drops to the ground and I pick her up. We all have a good laugh and I make a fuss of Polly. She is o.k. but a bit spazzed with all that happening. We stand them on the table till it is our turn.

McGee is first and Pat is holding Polly so nothing else can happen to her LOL. McGee is as usual his perfect self and again wins the point. Then it is Polly's turn and she walks nicely but is still a bit unsettled when it comes to standing on the table. We do our up and back but she is not going to walk back to the Judge so don't guess we will win this one LOL. No the Judge gives it to the other dog. Oh well that is what happens when accidents happen before you go in the ring.

Pat goes over and gets Diva for me from the van and then it is her turn to go in the ring. Pat stands with McGee and Polly so nothing can happen to them while I am in the ring with Diva. She walks really nicely today and is so happy to see me. Stands on the table better than yesterday but again won't come back to the Judge. I will have to rethink this deal.

We all go back to the motor home to chat while Pat has a small break. Hopefully she won't be too late finishing. It is even hotter than yesterday.

After Pat leaves Debbie, Gary and I go and walk round the trade stands and get a bottle of water to drink. Yes I did change my clothes. Not much different at the trade stands so we go back to the motor home and chat and then Debbie and Gary leave.

Debbie says she has another lady for Chloe if these people don't work out as hoped.

It is so hot I am not going to take McGee over for Group as I want to get as much packed up as possible so we can leave when Pat finishes.

I get everything put away except for the x-pens as can't take them down till the dogs have been out one last time.

Pat comes back and we have a cup of coffee and she changes her clothes and we let the dogs out!!!!!

Now time to go home. We should be home about 4:30p.m. if there is no traffic back up!!

There is no traffic as such and we have a good ride home. Again we have had a good trip winning two Best of Breeds and points on McGee. No points on Polly as on Saturday she was the only female again.

Our next show will be Richmond on June 26th so we have two weeks rest in between.

Friday

I get all my dogs loaded up and we set off over to Pat's house to load up her stuff and the dogs of course. We fill up with water and head of to Wall Mart as we didn't get groceries yet. It wasn't worth it just for two days. Wow we only spent $37 so that was good. We get back to the motor home and set off to Richmond.

Not a long trip as it is only 56 miles but still much easier to stay in the motor home than drive back and fourth every day, especially seeing as on Sunday we show at 8:30a.m.

We get a good parking spot even though it is still quite a long walk to the building, we don't have to take the trolley as again we are only showing Polly and McGee.

We get all set up and man it is hot here so we have the generator running and the air conditioner going which is good.

We have dinner and decided to go and see if we could find Sue before watching a movie. We walked all round the building and find her trailer parking spot but no Sue. Finally saw Vince and he told us she had gone shopping two hours ago LOL. Oh well we will see her tomorrow.

Time for a beer and watch our movie. Tomorrow my friend Kim is coming so we won't have time for watching tv.

Saturday

Well we turned off our generator but no one else did and trying to sleep with all the noise of other people's generator's is not easy!!!!!! This won't happen tomorrow night I can assure you.

Morning comes round all too soon and Pat leaves for the Stewarding meeting and I have to get myself dressed ready to go over to the building. Yes the generator is on and the ac belting away. It is going to be another scorcher today.

Pat comes back just as I am walking out the door so we can walk over together. We are only taking McGee and Polly so there is no need for the trolley.

Timed it just right and only have a few minutes to wait. Well gee just the two males again today and two females. Hardly worth the effort but then Pat is stewarding so we had to come.

Way to go McGee gets Best of Winners so now it is Polly's turn. She also gets Best of Winners and now time for Best of Breed which McGee wins and Polly gets Best of Opposite.

Well now I have to take McGee to Group this afternoon.

I got back to the motor home and Kim had rung to say she would be here about mid day.

Kim is coming with Maverick and Lacy and is bringing Chinese for lunch and I expect we will have enough left over for dinner this evening.

I tidy up of course and let all the dogs out and Kim rings to say she is running late so will be about 1p.m. instead of noon!!!! Well I guess I will let the dogs out again and then they will be done when she gets here!!!

It is so hot out here that I just can't stand to be out here more than a few minutes!!!! NO our generator will not be turned off tonight!!!!

Well 1p.m. comes and Kim rings to say she is running late and should be here about 2.0p.m. I am going to be starving by the time she gets here LOL.

Yeah 2:00p.m. and Kim has arrived. We sit and chat and enjoy the Chinese food. The dog's get to play outside but only for a few minutes as it is so hot. Lacy looks lovely and so of course does Maverick. I think he is one of the best dogs I have produced. He is just lovely.

Time gets on and before you know it, it is 3:30p.m. and I have to get ready to go over for Group.

We just leave the motor home to see Pat coming. She has finished for the day but now of course we have to go over for Group. That is o.k. as she can just sit and relax. Well my timing isn't very good as we have three Groups to go through before my turn.

Kim decides to go and do some shopping just as it is my turn to go in the ring!! McGee behaves beautifully but I have to stop him hoovering as he goes round the ring. So many treats have been dropped on the floor he wants to pick them all up!!! We do our up and back and go to the end of the line and then the Judge picks his four and of course doesn't include us!! Oh well we did our best.

Kim is still shopping so I take McGee back to the motor home and let all the dogs out and change my clothes by the time Kim and Pat arrive back. Much too hot to sit outside, Kim had a good time shopping LOL.

It is nearly 5:0p.m. so we decide to feed the dogs and then divide the Chinese that is left between us all and eat and drink.

Wow Kim has bought us a bottle of Champagne which cost $150 and she has also bought glass Champagne glasses to drink it out of. Oh yummy and I am not much of a Champagne drinker but this is just lovely. We sit and chat and laugh and have a good time. It gets round to 8:45p.m. and Kim decides she has to make a move home.

We give Lacy lots of kisses goodbye and of course Maverick. Oh how I love that dog.

Now time to let the dogs out and clean up the kitchen. Wow plates and glasses everywhere but we had a fun time, we don't get to visit that often with Kim so it was nice that she took time to come and visit us at this show.

We got all the kitchen cleaned up and sit and have a cup of coffee and take our pills. I am going to have to drink some water as I think the Chinese was a bit salty!! Just hate that!!!

Oh nice to get to bed tonight!!!! Yes we did not turn the generator off or the air conditioning so it is nice and comfortable in here!!! We can hear other generators running as well so that is good.

Sunday

Morning comes all too fast and Pat again has to leave. Again I am showing early so will have to get my butt in gear. I get dressed and then let all the dogs out as usual. Oh it is hot already and humid so going to be a long hard day again. Man I am ready for winter and we are only in June!!!!!!
I get over to the building and see Pat coming towards me. We are getting good at timing this as I don't think she needs to walk all the way across the car part to just turn round and walk all the way back LOL.
Just as I walk across the arena one of the other competitors comes up to me and says we have to go and speak to the judge about moving the chi's to the last class. Well gee have to do this again but what can I say.
Now I have to sit and wait for about an hour but that is o.k. Payback is a bitch and I will want something from him one day!!
Finally our turn to go in the ring and gee the other guy wins!!!!!!!!!! Well there you go that means he has to go to Group instead of me LOL.
Polly wins her class but doesn't get any points today!!!!

I will take them back to the motor home and the air conditioning LOL. I get back and let all the dogs out. It is even too hot to let the pups out to play so they will just have to play inside later on, oh forgot they will have to wait till even later as we are leaving when Pat has finished working!!!!
I start getting everything put away and then start packing up outside but it is so hot.
Pat comes back at 3:30p.m. So we sit and have a cup of coffee and chat while she relaxes for five minutes before we start sweating getting all packed up. At least it is a short drive home.
The drive home is uneventful which is good and we finally get to Pat's house about 4:30p.m.
Now our next trip is Bell Alton and we leave for that on Wednesday. Only three days and I am working on Tuesday and Wednesday so Pat is coming over on Monday and we will clean up the motor home together. It really is much more fun doing it together and we get it done much faster.

Wednesday

Wow Wednesday came round real fast. I didn't get home from work till mid day but that gave me enough time to get in the shower, pack up the dogs and be out of the house and leaving the 7 Eleven by 1:0p.m. Phew. Get to Pat's and we get all loaded up and on the road. Have a few more clothes for this trip as it is a four day show and you never know what the weather will do.

It really is a good drive to Bell Alton as it is only just over 140 miles. We go on Rte I-17 and then I-301 which mean you have to go over that awful bridge. I just hold onto the steering wheel and keep looking at the car in front. Oh how I hate driving over bridges. Now we are in Maryland and only about 10 miles to go. The dogs are all good, even Twister is being quiet.

We arrive at 4:45p.m. and there are still 6 coaches in front of us to be parked but that is fine.
We get a good spot, under some oak trees and only about 200 yards walk to the building which is good for us.
We get all set up and time for a beer!!!! We decide to walk over and see if Sue is there so Pat can find out what time she has to be there for the morning hound show!!!! They will also have a showing of the fox hounds and Master of Hounds at the front gate and then a blessing of the dogs so we would really like to know what time that is as well. At least it will be cool in the morning.
Well typical no Sue but that is o.k. Pat can go over early in the morning and get the information that she needs.

A nice walk back to the motor home and dinner. Feed the dogs first of course. It is so much cooler under these trees. I have also bought two more windscreen covers to put over the windows in the bedroom and Pat will have to help me with that.
Dinner was good, salad with cold roast pork on the top and a nice bottle of Duplin wine. A nice evening, watching a movie, and nice to be able to take the dogs out without sweating when doing it LOL. Nice being under the trees as usually we are by the barn and very humid there.
There is no wind but I am still putting the awning up as don't trust it one bit!!! Easier to do it before we go to bed than have to get up in the night!!!! Wow sure is dark under these trees!!!!!!

Also the advantage of being under the trees, there are no bugs!!!!

Thursday

As usual morning comes all too soon but Pat has already been over to see Sue and no, she isn't working today!!! Well I thought that was why we had to come on Wednesday because Sue wanted Pat to work the hound show. Oh well there you go.

We hear the announcement on the loudspeaker and the hounds and horses are arriving in about 15 minutes. Pat and I hurry with breakfast and coffee and then take the camera up to the main gate.
Oh what a sight, about 20 fox hounds and three people on horses. Well I know it is hot but it would have been nice if they had worn their red coats etc still it is nice. The Preacher at least has his gold robe on which is very impressive. He blesses the hounds and the hunt and then we head back to the camper. We decide on another cup of coffee and then we are going to take our chairs down to the tent and watch some of the hounds. It isn't too hot and there are tents around we can sit under. I need to take my credit card as I really need to buy a new mat for outside. Mine is just about worn out and it is about 4 years old now!!! Every time we come home I put it on the line and spray it with bleach water and then wash it. Well doesn't take long before the bleach rots the plastic. Still it has been good to me so we will leave it behind when we pack up.

We sit and watch the hounds, the English Foxhounds and the American Foxhounds which are so different to one another. I bought a mat, a blue one this time. It is a bit smaller but that is fine too. Very hard to find the 6 ft by 15 ft which is what I had before.
Pat goes off to the restaurant and brings back a portion of French Fries each. Yummy. Well we have sat here for three hours so I think it is time to go back and let the dogs out etc. Oh yes and have a sandwich and take a nap LOL. Before we take a nap I am going to put Diva and Polly on the building blocks. These are blocks of wood that you make the dog stand on without falling off. Once they learn to balance and relax it usually helps with them standing on the table to be examined. Diva is doing real well and after the third time she is actually standing and relaxing which is good. Polly is used to it so she does well.

We finally got up and took the dogs out and sat outside in the shade from the tree!! It is so nice not to be sitting and sweating all the time. Even the air conditioning goes off every now and then.

Dinner was good and we had slushies to go with it.

After dinner we took the dogs for a walk, well two of them anyway and Twister. He doesn't walk just jumps up and down. Don't know where he gets the energy from. No wonder he has muscles in his back legs to die for!!!!

We sit and watch a movie and then go to bed. Pat has an early start in the morning again.

Friday

Time again to get up and Pat is off as usual.

I am not showing till 10:0a.m. so can lounge about for a bit. I eat breakfast and then get myself ready for the ring. I let the dogs out again and get the bait ready for the bag. We are only showing Diva, McGee and Polly today so it will be a short time showing. Afterwards I can go and watch some of the showing where Pat is stewarding.

Pat comes back just as I am leaving the motor home. She takes Polly and I take Diva and McGee. We are only about 200 yards from the building and it is nice and grassy so they can pee again. Polly always pees when on the lead so that is good.

The first to show today is the smooth coats, McGee and Polly. McGee is first and there are four males which is two points. McGee goes back in and wins Winners Dog for two more points.

Next is Polly and she wins her class and then gets Reserve. I take McGee back in for Best of Breed and he wins. Yeah way to go McGee, now I have to take him to group and it will be hot out there so have to time it right.

Now it is time for Diva. This will be interesting to see how she does.

Oh my, she stands on the table like a rock, must be because of the building blocks LOL. Now to walk round the ring, this will be interesting but hey she does very well. Guess she is trying to show me how good she can be because I said I am going to re home her as a pet. Wow we even get Reserve.

Well that wasn't a bad morning. I am well pleased. The building is just lovely as there is only one ring so plenty of room to have the dogs standing on the ground which is really good for them before going in the ring, especially Polly. Usually the buildings are so crowded and so many people with big dogs not paying attention you can't put the little guys on the ground. This was nice.

I take the kids back to the motor home and let all the others out. Change my clothes and have a cup of coffee of course. I put all the dogs back up and feed Sarah as I forgot her this morning.

It is ll:30a.m and I am going over to the tent to see where Pat is stewarding and watch for a bit.

Pat is in Ring 3 and a new breed, Icelandic Sheepdogs. Well not something that I would want but a nice looking dog. Very much like the Border Collie dog. Wow these people really need some handling lessons. It is obvious these are pets as these people have no idea how to handle them in the show ring. Well it is a new breed recognized by the AKC so in a few months there will be a lot more and of course the handlers will get hold of them.

Pat is now finished so she can go and pick up her lunch and we are going back so we can sit and let her rest in the ac for a while.

Group starts at 1:15p.m. but the Toy Group is the last so will have to time this just right so McGee doesn't have to hang around in the heat.

We sit and chat for a while and of course laugh about the Icelandic Sheepdogs and then Pat has to go back. Hopefully she will be finished by the time I get to go over for Group. At least it isn't as hot as it was in Richmond but it is outside for the Group classes.

Pat comes back to the motor home at 2:30p.m. and we will leave at 3:00p.m. for the Group Classes.

Timed it just right and the last class is just finishing. We all go in and no, McGee didn't get placed but he did good going round the ring.

Back to the motor home and time for a nap LOL. Pat is so tired and she needs to rest. We let all the dogs out first and have a cup of coffee and of course change clothes. Don't know what we are having for dinner but it will be good I am sure.

Now time for a beer before dinner.

We have a nice relaxing evening and then go to bed!!! Tomorrow we don't show till 12:15p.m. and Diva isn't showing any more. I should have entered her after being so good today.

Saturday

Morning comes again and Pat has to be out of here by 7:30a.m. I am not showing till 12:15p.m. so will be a good morning. I get dressed and decide to go over and get a sandwich for breakfast. Oh it is a good bacon and egg sandwich, much better than cereal LOL.

Just after I get back to the motor home Karen arrives with all her dogs. At least she puts them in another pen so I don't have to worry about our dogs. She is doing a demonstration in one of the Buildings called Meet the Breeds and she has a wonderful display. I got out the trolley for her to put all her stuff on instead of making six trips!!!! She left about 10:0a.m. and will be back just before I go to show.

Pat comes back at about 11:30a.m. as it is now her lunch break. She bought back a plate of food and eats while I get dressed. I let the dogs out again as best to be safe than sorry. I wipe McGee over with a wet wipe as he is so dusty from playing in the dirt.

Time to go over to the ring and Pat doesn't have to be back till 1:15p.m. so that is good.

We take the kids over on leads again and it is so nice to have so much room in the building for them to be on the ground.

McGee is first and oh boy he gets second out of two!! That is a blow but there you go. There is a professional handler showing a smooth coat male and oh guess what, he wins the points. We won't bother to show to this judge again. Let's see what he does with Polly. Well no surprise there we get second out of two as well. Well at least we won't have to go to Group again LOL.

Pat is disappointed but there you go. Tomorrow is another day and another judge and tomorrow it is a major so we have to try real hard. We take the kids back and then Pat has to leave to finish her day stewarding. I change my clothes and then go over to buy the tickets for the Crab Fest this evening.

I saw Sue on the way back and she said to tell Pat that she was buying her ticket for dinner this evening. Well blow me down I have just bought the tickets. I get back to the motor home, Pat comes back at about 2:30p.m. so an early day for her. We have a cup of coffee and sit and chat and then take a nap!!! Sounds good to me eh!!! Karen says she is going shopping so that will give us a bit of a nap.

Karen says she will give me the money for the extra ticket so that is good. Pat gives me $15 of it so we ended up only paying $15 each for the dinner.
Get bit of a nap but with Karen here and all her dogs it is hard to sleep.

Dinner is at 5:30p.m. so we need to feed the dogs and get dressed.
Pat and I mixed up the English Tea and it was really rather good with the adding of a bit of orange juice as well. Just hope we can get some ice over there, they usually have plenty.

As we are walking over we see Sue and she gives Pat her wrist band. Karen and I have green ones, Pat's is yellow LOL. Sue goes and gets a couple of cups with ice in and we pour her a drink. I went over to the table and got cups of ice for the three of us. We get in line for dinner and it looks very inviting. Fried chicken, fried fish, shrimp with the skin on in spices, fried shrimp, green beans, red skin potatoes with butter and herbs, hush puppies, bread rolls, pasta salad, and lemonade or ice tea. Very yummy. While we are eating they come and put blue crabs on the table for you to pick at. No not my kind of thing, very messy for very little food. I went back and got more fried chicken which was just yummy. Pat is very good and picking at the crabs and gives me the occasional piece of meat.

We are sitting with our friends Sandy and Norb Novocin, Tibetan spaniel people and very nice folks. We all enjoy the English Tea which we bought, with lots of laughing and chatting. We didn't really care much for the music. Sue came and visited for about ten minutes and was then off to party. Whitney came to get her sip of English Tea and chatted for a few minutes. The food was really good this year, I don't know who the caterers were but they did an excellent job and will have to tell Sue how much we enjoyed it. We finally decided to call it a night and go back to the motor home about 8:30p.m. We still have to pack Karen up with all her dogs and the two puppies that she is taking back. Plus I need a cup of coffee LOL.
When we get back we let all the kids out and Karen's dogs as she has at least a two and a half hour drive and with puppies that is a long time.
Wow she has nine crates to go in that little car!!! We get it all packed and tied down and Karen leaves. Pat is upset to see the pups leave but they now start their new life.

We have another glass of wine and sit and chat for a bit. It nice sitting outside and we can see the fireworks going off in different places around us. It is so nice here. When the fireworks have stopped then we will let the kids out again. Don't need any one scared from the fireworks even though they are a long way away!!!

Now it is time for bed again as another day tomorrow.

Sunday

Now today is a special day as it is the last chance to finish McGee as it is a major for males and if Polly is good, it can cross over and give her the last major she needs to finish.

There is no point in me getting nervous as that doesn't do any good at all. We don't show till 12:45p.m. so I might as well get dressed and go over and see how Pat is doing. Oh it is much hotter today. She is in ring 3 again and the Icelandic Sheepdogs are about to go in. I watch them and then tell Pat I have to go back to the motor home as nearly time to get dressed. I start walking back and she meets me and Sue says for Pat to go in and get lunch for me and Sue also gives me two free tickets for ice cream. Hopefully, I will get that when I finish showing.

Lunch wasn't bad but not as good as last night LOL.

Time for me to get dressed and over to the building. We let the dogs out for one last time before leaving. Pat is finished for the day so we can go together.

We walk the kids over and of course Polly has to pee, bless her. The building is nice and really not many people which is good as the kids can be on the ground. Well it looks like everyone has picked up their numbers so the major seems to be holding.

McGee is first of course and there are three of us in the class. Oh my I get third out of three! Oh what a blow for Pat. Now Polly's turn and she gets second out of two. Well this judge is very political and gives the points in the males to the professional handler and also the professional handler in the females. Bummer Bummer.

Pat is so upset but another day tomorrow but again it isn't a major.

We head back to the motor home to have a cup of coffee and take a nap. Pat is exhausted but also very upset at not finishing McGee. We will just have to come out again after we breed Polly at the end of August. Two friends come back with us for a chat and of course to see the puppies. I am hoping they will want to breed to Henry or perhaps McGee later down the road. They are also interested in visiting with Diva. I told Dawn she is for sale but to a pet home as I don't think she will ever be a show dog. Mind you after the way she showed on Friday, I might well be wrong. We talk and they of course admire the puppies and think that Rambo is a long coat Chihuahua which of course he isn't LOL. Dawn asks if she can show Diva and she will pay the entry fees etc. I told her that isn't fair and perhaps she can show her and then when I breed her give her a puppy back!!! She thinks that is too much but we arrange to meet her on the way home tomorrow. They leave after about an hour and we decide to take a nap. It was a very pleasant chat with them. We have planned to call Dawn after we leave here and meet her in Fredericksburg to give her Diva. Now I have to sit and write out a contract for her. I am thrilled as at least Diva gets the chance to show.

After the nap Pat is a bit happier and again back to making plans LOL. Monday, tomorrow is our last day and hopefully Pat won't be working too late so we can get on the road and get home.
Tonight for dinner we are having steak and of course some wine. We sit and watch a movie while I am trying to write this contract. Oh man it would take me 15 minutes at most on the computer and so far I have taken an hour and that is only one copy LOL LOL.
Time for bed and the contract is written. Just hope she doesn't ring in the morning with a change of plan.

Monday

Morning comes fast and today we show at 9:0a.m. but McGee is the only one showing today so that will be a breeze eh!!!!
Pat of course has left and I have to get dressed and then let the critters out again.
I take McGee over to the building and I am only in there for a few minutes and a real nice man comes over and says he really likes McGee. I am stunned. He has a female long coat that he is showing, can't say that I have ever seen him before so have no idea who he is.
The long coats are first so I watch and he gets Best of Winners which gives him two points as there were four male long coats but he was the only female. Cool win for him.

Now it is McGee's turn so let's hope today is good. We win our class of two which is better than yesterday LOL. We then go in for points and McGee gets Winners Dog. We go back in and McGee gets Best of Breed again. Now I am sure Pat will be pleased with this win but it isn't a major!!!!!

We leave the building and I trot McGee over to where Pat is working and she is thrilled of course. She tells me that she will be doing Group this afternoon but it is going to be inside and asks of course if I will go. Hey inside is good so of course we will go. I can't go home without her LOL.

I bought another bacon and egg sandwich on the way back to the motor home. The dogs will have to wait till I have eaten it LOL. They will survive. It was a good sandwich and coffee and I feel good so time to let the kids out again!!!

After letting the kids out I will go over and visit with Pat and see if she knows what time she will be finished today!!! Oh today it is much hotter than it has been the rest of the week. Phew bet it is in the 90 deg range. Over at the tent Pat is in ring 3 again. She always seems to get the working dogs and when we have toy dogs it just seems strange. Most people that steward are working towards being a judge whereas Pat is doing it just for the money.

She finishes at ll:30a.m and we can go back to the motor home for lunch. Pat picks hers up on the way back and I make a sandwich for me. We have plenty of ham left and bread rolls so that will do. We sit and chat and Pat tells me that she has to Steward the Group rings because one of the girls has left to start her vacation. Well the Groups are going to be indoors so that will be nice. Yes I will take McGee as with Pat Stewarding, there is no reason not to show him. Never know it might be our one time of getting a group placement. Yeah right!!!!!

Pat leaves to go back and I start putting stuff away and cleaning up. I have even cleaned out the fridge which is good. It saves doing it when I get home. Folded up the mat from outside and put it by the trash can. Not taking that home. The only thing we will have to do will be put the x-pens away when Pat gets back. Group starts at 1:15p.m. and Toys are the last Group so I need to go over there about 2:30p.m. Time for another cup of coffee.

I have all the inside cleaned and sorted, Pat's stuff is on the bed in the back so she can just pick it up when we get to her house. The kitchen is clean apart from our coffee cups as we will have one before we leave.

Time to get dressed again and go over to the building for Group. I give McGee a good wipe over with a wet wipe when they all come in from outside. With his lovely white coat he really gets grungy rolling around in the dirt outside. Love wet wipes. Everyone is in their crates and the crates are all ready for travelling. Will let them all out again when I get back as surely Pat won't be far behind!!!!

McGee and I walk over to the building and oh boy it is hot out here. Nice with the air conditioning on inside the building. Wow not very many people at all which is nice. At least there is a chair for me to sit on and have McGee on my lap. My turn and don't hold out much hope as the judge is the judge we had on Sunday and he was very political so I am guessing the wins will go to the professional handlers.

McGee does well and doesn't really look for food on the floor at all. I am very pleased with him but no we don't get placed. Pat has to finish up with Best in Show and then she will be back.

I take McGee back and let all the kids out and put the kettle on for a drink for Pat before we leave. She just needs to sit for a few minutes and cool down before we start packing up.

Pat comes back at 3:00p.m. and we should be out of here by 4p.m. and then ring Dawn and tell her to meet us at the Fresh Market stand in Fredericksburg.

We get all packed up and on the road and Pat rings Dawn to tell her we are finally on the road. The time is 4:05 p.m., not bad eh!!!!

We should be at the Farmers Market by about 4:35p.m.

Oh my I have to drive over that awful bridge again. Well it isn't quite so bad going this way but I just hate going over bridges.

There is no traffic on this side of the road but the other side is backed up for about 5 miles. Glad we are going this way LOL.

We arrive at the Farmers Market and Pat goes off inside to get some fresh vegetables to take home.

Dawn finally arrives. Yes we have the generator on and the air conditioning going as it is about 98 degrees out there!!!!

Dawn comes in and has bought me a crate pad and some dog harnesses. Wow no one has ever bought me gifts before when picking up a dog!!! We sit down and I get the contract out and Dawn says she has changed her mind!!! Well gee I spent two hours writing the contract and now she wants a different one LOL. Well if she wants to buy the dog instead what can I say except that I am not selling her as show dog per say!!!! Yes I write it in the contract. Dawn is just smitten with Diva and says, "You know when you see a dog and your heart tells you, you have to have it?? Well that is how I feel about Diva" I am really thrilled as that is what Niki has always told me about buying a dog.

We get the new contract written and I give her Diva. Not the registration papers but I will send her copies of that and the shot record and rabies certificate etc when I get home. I am just amazed but really very pleased that Diva will have a chance at showing. Dawn has also agreed to breed

Diva the first time either to Pat's Henry or McGee so that will be good. Wow is all I can say!!!!!!

Back on the road and at this rate we should be home by about 6:30p.m. if we are lucky and there are no hold ups!!!!!!
Finally get to Pat's house at 6:45p.m. then home for me. When I get home and start getting the dogs out I look at the back wheels by the side door and again the wheel is leaking oil, and smoking!!!! This just isn't good!!!!! I mean new rotors, new brake pads and a new caliper and it is still leaking and smoking. Will have to call Pete again and see what he says.

Tomorrow I have to take Sarah for her x-ray to see how many pups she is having and that they are all heading in the right direction.
Wow Sarah is expecting four pups, may be five but I am thinking four. Let's hope all goes well. I think she will have them Wednesday, tomorrow.

Wednesday comes and about mid day I decide that Sarah is going to have her puppies today. I call Pat and tell her not to rush but she will have them today. Pat comes over about 1:0p.m. and I do have Sarah in the crate and she seems to have small contractions but nothing really forceful.

We decide to take her out to walk around and pee and of course I didn't have her on a lead and she decided to go under the azalea bushes in the front yard. Crap I can't get down there so go round the other side of the yard and try to make her go over to Pat. We finally get hold of her and there is a pup half hanging out!!!!!! We carry her in and put her back in the whelping crate!!!! Wow it is a female tri colour just like Sarah and weighs 5.1/2 ounces. Well done now three left to go.
The next one takes another hour to come but it is another female and the same, a tri like Sarah and weighing 5.7/8 ounces, huge which is why it took so long. Glad she is doing o.k. though. Pat is so good at getting them going. Wow only 15 minutes and the third one is coming. Pat and I just look in amazement, don't think either of us want to touch it as all we can see is white!!! Oh my, this pup is black and white and Pat and I both stand and look in amazement. Neither of us wanted to touch the pup LOL. Pat looks at me and says "Twister didn't get to her this time did he??" Of course he didn't as she went out in the laundry room. Again it is a female. I know these are all Tibetan spaniels because I put the sperm in there myself. Sarah was put out in the laundry room the second day she came into season so I know Twister did not get to her at all!!!!!

Now you have to remember that Grissom's father is a red and white so it is in his genes to throw coloured dogs. This is a lovely puppy and weighs 5.1/2 ounces. Well still one to go and think we might need to take her out again. Yes not falling into that trap again, she is going out on the lead LOL. She pees and we bring her in and she starts pushing again. Great out comes a dark sable male pup. Oh this is going to be the same colour as Grissom and he weighs 5 ¾ ounces. Way to go Sarah. Yes both Pat and I are thrilled and to have three females is just amazing and a Grissom Jnr. Oh I am so thrilled. Will have to take pictures and send them to Niki. She will be thrilled with the parti-colour.

Now time to bed them down in the bathroom and feed Sarah. I thank Pat and she has rung Max to come and get her. She is such a gem as this is a hard thing to do on your own. Sarah and pups are resting nicely. Now I just need Polly to wait to come into season until the pups are at least six weeks old and have had their first shot. I want to take them to Niki for her to see when we take Polly for breeding. Fingers crossed it will all work out.

Well after talking to Pete we have decided that I have to take the motor home down to Williamsburg Ford for them to have a look at the brakes to decide what is going on. They end up having the motor home for a week and finally decide that it is a hub seal and the ABS sensor and ends up costing another $345. Well have to have brakes right!!! Well on the drive home it didn't leak and I rang Pete and he said he didn't think he would ever have found the problem and was glad I had told him.

At least he is honest and now the brakes are fixed. We won't be going anywhere for a while as we have to wait for Polly to come in season to take her and Rambo to Kansas. We will be going in my car as it is better on petrol and should cost us about $300 in petrol for the round trip.

The Sarah pups are four weeks old today and they are doing well. They are all within ¾ of an ounce of each other which is good. I had to move them into the bedroom in the x-pen because it was getting too hot for them in the bathroom. I can't wait for Niki to see them. Of course I am very partial to the black and white girl although she now has brown eyebrows, which means she is a black and white with tan markings. They all look like they have nice heads, as Tibetan spaniels are called a "head breed" which means the judge is always comparing the heads on all the entries.

The pups are five weeks old today and tomorrow I will move them into the x-pen in the dining room. Sarah really isn't into feeding them much now so time for them to be out in the world so to speak!!!!

Wow are they ever screaming at their new surroundings!! Well they will get used to it!!!

Today is August the 16th and unfortunately Polly has come into season. I was hoping she would hold out till at least the 24th but best laid plans eh!!!

We are now planning to be leaving here on the 21st or 22nd August to go to visit Niki in her new house and dog building to breed Polly to her little long coat boy Leroy Brown.

The tibby pups will be six weeks on Wednesday 18th so I will give them their first shot. Hopefully it will be enough immunity for our trip. We will not of course put them down on any ground while travelling and when we get to Niki's they will be in the house so not in contact with any other dogs. Only the house dogs but of course my puppies will be in the x-pen all the time.

Tuesday

Today is August 24th and I am on my way over to Pat's house to pick her and her dogs up ready to drive to Kansas!

Polly is finally in season and we are on our trip to Niki in Kansas. We are also taking Rambo, my Papillon out of Sayuri and Mio for her. He has grown into a lovely boy with the care from Pat as he has been living with her till now.

We also have the four tibbie pups and of course Sarah. Pat has bought Lolla as she is also in season, Snowball, also in season and of course McGee who will be left in Kansas for Mike to pick up.

The car is well packed, everything is in a bag so we don't have to cart too much into the motel room.

We are trying to drive at least 600 miles today which means stopping round about 7:00p.m. if all goes well. My friend Jeanne had a trip map done from the AAA and it shows all the road works and hold ups so we should do well. Pat can tell how many miles from each place that we go through which is really cool. I can't read a map which is why I do the driving LOL.

So far everyone is being quiet which is good. We have Sarah and the pups in Mikes trolley which I am also leaving in Kansas. I have had it in my shed for the last 6 years so time for it to go!!!

Polly is in the top half and Lolla and Snowball in the other half. When we stop, it is easy to get them out. Of course Sarah has to go on a lead as soon as you open the door else she will run!!!

Rambo and McGee are in crates behind the seats and then our stuff is in the middle. Probably have to repack it after we stop as the stuff never seems to go back the way it was!!!

We also have my small black x-pen to let them out to pot when we stop. We will have to stop at least every 250 miles because I have only a 12 gallon petrol tank in this car.
Driving is good and there is hardly any traffic to speak off.

Well our first stop is in fact at a Flying J gas station that we have been to before!!!! Just goes to show being on the road so much we know where most of the gas stations are. We fill up and get back on the road. No need to let the dogs out just yet. We went inside and bought some stuff for lunch and also some t-shirts to take home as gifts. That is my shopping done LOL.
Well time is ticking on and it is nearly 6:0p.m. so time to find a Motel 6. Pat puts it into Lolla (navigational system) and she pulls up a Motel 6 about 50 miles further on. That is good, we will have done 589 miles. It is a bit short of our estimated 600 miles but good enough.
The dogs need to get out and we need to rest as well.

The first little trauma was as we opened the back door and started getting out our stuff, a bottle of wine fell on the floor and smashed. Oh Pat was so upset. Then as we went to lift out the trolley she noticed that a bottle of Skin So Soft, Avon that she had bought for the flying bugs had leaked out all over the bedding underneath the crates!! Smelled lovely but it was an unopened bottle so have no idea why it leaked. It was also on the t-shirts that I had just bought. Pat took the bedding and put it in the washer at the Motel so at least it was clean even though it smelt lovely!!!!

It isn't a bad motel but I don't think either of us are going to use the bath tub!!! It is not very nice at all. Still the dogs can run and play. We bought in the trolley and the x-pen. The pups are in the x-pen and Lolla and Snowball in one side at the top and Polly in the other. Then on top of the trolley we have McGee and Rambo in their crates.
We had to lug all this through the lobby and I was just dying incase they wanted to charge us a deposit for the dogs but in fact everyone was very helpful holding open the doors etc.
Of course we checked under the beds and they are solid sided so that is good, no pups can get underneath. We also checked under the bedding for bed bugs. I am paranoid about bugs!!!!!!!!

We ordered in Chinese for dinner and it was very good but a lot of food which obviously we didn't eat it all. The man on the desk told us it would be a lot of food but we didn't listen to him LOL. It was good.

We are both exhausted, don't know why as just sitting in the car and driving but it does make me very tired. We decided to go to bed about 10.0p.m. which is early for us. I start collecting pups for the x-pen and we are one short. Grissom Jnr is no where to be seen and now I am wondering if he went out the door when I paid the man for dinner. We look all over and then Pat hears him whimpering. He has crawled over the piece of wood frame and got inside the bed frame. How the hell are we going to get him out!!! I can just get my hand in the hole so he comes to my hand and I grab him by the head and pull him out!! Oh well there is a nice trauma for the pup but what else could I do!!!!! Wow now we can go to bed!!!!

Wednesday

Wow we actually slept till 7:15a.m. My, that is really unusual for Pat but we were both tired.
We drag everything outside. I stay outside with the dogs and pack the car as Pat brings the stuff outside. On her last trip the guy at the desk says he has a trolley if she needs it!! Fine to tell her now after the sixth trip back to the room!!!!!
Oh my, it is 8:30a.m. and has taken us nearly an hour to pack the stupid car but at least now when we stop it should be easier.
We are on the road and need to find a McDonalds for breakfast and coffee. Yeah, one just down the street before we get back on the highway. Two bacon egg and cheese biscuits, and two large coffees with four creams in each. Yummy.

Back on the road and today we need to do at least enough miles to get into Kansas so we will only have two or three hundred miles to drive on Thursday. I really would like to get there before lunch but you know how that goes.
Time to stop for gas again and we find a Flying J station. Their gas is usually a couple of cents cheaper than anywhere else. So far we have paid $2.44 and $2.32 so doing well.
It really is easy driving and Pat drives this time while I try to take a nap. At least having the pillow I can lean it against the window and rest my head on it. It makes it nice and soft to lean on up against the window.

Pat drives till time to stop again and this time we have to let all the kids out. Sarah has been real good staying in the back with the pups but every now and then you can hear her squeak as one of the pups bites her. Pat puts the x-pen up and I get Sarah out on the lead of course and pass the pups to her. Everyone is out and they are all doing well and doing their business. Amazing how people have to come over and ask if they are for sale!!! Sorry no!!!!

We get everyone back in the car and go over the road to McDonalds to get something for lunch. They have these new wrap things so that sounds good. Yes more coffee. We get back on the road and it is again smooth sailing. Wow hardly any traffic to speak of and even when we come up to road works at least the traffic keeps moving.

We plug on and by 7:00p.m. we decide it is time to again find a Motel 6. Pat again plugs it into Lolla and there is one 30 miles up the road. Pat rings them and they are just one block off the highway which is good as the other motel we had to drive nearly 10 miles to get to it. Need one off the highway. We finally arrive and wow a ground floor room and door to the outside which is great. Oh it has laminate flooring which is great. Oh look at the crap under the beds but that is o.k. as Pat and I can clean that up. Oh so much easier when one of the pups pees on the floor to just wipe it up. Oh look at the lovely corner shower. Oh this is nice.

We order Chinese again but this time only one dish and a small soup and two pancake rolls which we can eat. Oh yummy and only $14.00 so a deal. We have a beer and sit and watch a bit of TV but again too tired to do much. Pat works it out and we have about 320 miles to do tomorrow which is cool. We should be there by about mid day if all goes well.

We both have showers and it is lovely except for some reason the water is all on the floor, it has come outside the curtain when I showered so I ended up using all the towels to mop up the water!! What a mess.

Finally get all the kids put up and time for bed. No one hiding today!!!!

Thursday

Morning comes real early but Pat has the kettle on and is dressed by the time I wake up. Can't do much before I have my coffee but the kids are all running around. We get dressed and put all the dogs up and start packing the car. Wow, have this down to a science now, I know where everything goes and we are on the road by 8:15a.m. Wow, better than yesterday because we didn't have to lug all the stuff through the motel. Just open the door and take it out. Everything is in and I take the keys back, well plastic cards and we are on the road again.

Yes breakfast of course is a must so we are looking and can't find a McDonalds. There is a Taco Bell which is closed, Hardy's is closed so we decide to drive down the road a bit and see what there is. Get back on the highway as there is bound to be a sign for something at the next exit.
Yeah McDonalds at the next exit so off we go. Just can't drive without eating and a coffee for the road.

Today is Thursday and we are on the last part of our trip to Niki's house and getting excited to be there.
We will have to stop one more time for gas again and we will let the dogs out so at least they will be able to wait a few minutes while we decide where we are putting them in the house.
We have to drive through Great Bend to get there and we see a Wall Mart so we decide to stop and get the groceries for the meals which we said we would cook. Not bad, we only spent $48.99 and Pat found two pairs of shoes for $3.00 each for Dee Dee. She will be thrilled with them.

O.K. so what is wrong with Lolla. She can't find the stupid farm!!!!!! We ring Niki but of course she can't hear the phone outside in the Kennel so we have to wait for her to ring us back. I think we have done at least 20 miles in the wrong direction!!
Yeah Niki rings and puts Fred on the phone and tells Pat where we should be. Yes 10 miles in the wrong direction. Man there is nothing here but driveways and none of them have a black metal gate and two concrete posts. Oh there it is, just stopped in time and turned in and the gate opens up. Majic!!!
As we drive up the driveway we both are in amazement at the size of the kennel. It sure is big!!!

We say our hello's and hugs and Niki shows us to the bedroom in the back, well the front of the house and that is where we will put the trolley and of course the dogs. She says to put up the x-pen in the dining room for the tibbie puppies. That will be nice for them.

The house is lovely and Fred has done a grand job on laying the laminate flooring. It really is nice. It is an old house and was purchased as a kit from the Sears and Roebuck Catalogue in 1934 so yes it is old but solid as a rock. Niki had all the inside dark wood paneling painted white and it really is nice. There is a very old spiral staircase to the upstairs and of course Pat and I have to climb up and see. Oh so cute, there are five single beds up there. Would be so great for kids.

We get all the dogs set up and then of course have to go and visit the kennel. Oh my it is lovely but all the barking dogs is deafening LOL. Well what do you expect when there are at least 75 dogs out there and we are the strangers in their home. We take our dogs out in the grass area but this isn't going to work as it will disturb her dogs so we will borrow an x-pen and put it up by the front door of the house and then we only have to carry them from the bedroom through two doors to the yard.

Niki introduces us to all the dogs but man we can't remember one dogs name from another. I do know some of them as of course I have four dogs from Niki so know the dogs that are on my pedigrees. Really is strange to put a dog's face to a name which you know so well but have never seen the dog!!!!

Tuesday

Of course you know me, it is definitely time for coffee and Niki puts together a lunch spread fit for a King. Yummy, cold cuts and potato salad and chips and salsa, all of which Pat and I enjoy.

It is so much fun to sit and chat about the trip and of course talk about the puppies which are screaming to get out.

We finally finish eating and clear the table and then Pat and I take our dogs outside. Of course we have Sarah on a lead and she isn't very enthused about that at all but there is no fenced in area so she cannot be loose. One x-pen is a bit small so I go and ask Niki if she has another one that we can borrow and that is much better.
After doing the dogs we take Polly inside to meet with Leroy to see if she is ready to be bred.
Not quite ready so tomorrow we will AI her. Leroy Brown is a red and white long coat Chihuahua and very nice. They should make nice puppies.

The kitchen to the Kennel is very, very nice and there is an industrial front load washer and dryer which works overtime LOL. Niki reckons to do at least 12 loads of laundry a day. To do all that you need an industrial washer and dryer. Attached to the kitchen is a very nice office area where we are sitting and watching the pups play. We have the tibbie pups, Rambo, Dilly, which is going home with me. She is a long coat cream and white Chihuahua, Stella who is a tri coloured Papillon that weighs about 1 pound and is three months old. A tiny, tiny little girl. She is a SuSu pup. Then we have Hannah and Snickers, both papillons. Hannah belongs to Barbara and Snickers is Niki's tiny girl again. They are all having the best time and we sit and chat.

It is time to put the little ones up and then go and let our guys out for a run around. We now have two x-pens put together to make a larger area for them to run. Course all the girls want to do is hump each other but that is o.k. They are having fun and it is outside and not in a crate for a while.

I walk Sarah on a lead, wish I had bought a retractable lead but didn't think of it. She will just have to deal with the short lead. Most of the time all she wants to do is roll in the grass LOL.

After about 30 minutes, even though it is nice out here, no humidity which I love, we decide to take them back in and perhaps sort out our laundry. We have some dirty beds and of course some of our own stuff. We sort out the dog stuff first and then put all ours in a bag as it will have to sit in line for a gap between loads that Niki does.

Pat comes into the bedroom and says that Niki has a tri coloured female chi that has never been on a lead and of course Pat wants to take her out to lead break her and ask if I want to take Dilly which of course is a great idea. I get leads from the car and we take them outside. We decide to go over by the barn as it is away from the kennel and they don't need to hear any of the barking. Of course Dilly is fine on the lead but Nancy will have none of it. Pat lay's down on the floor and I carry Nancy away from her and Pat calls her and I tell her to go to the Mountain. Dilly is having a fun time running and jumping which is fine with me. Nancy is getting better and better and I have a feeling that this will be Pat's pet project while we are here. Niki is just amazed at the progress we made with her.

Pat and I start laying the table for dinner. Niki has a lovely beef pot roast cooking in the oven with potatoes and carrots. Smells lovely.
Pat and I feed our dogs and of course the tibbie pups which are in the dining room. Hopefully they will be quiet during dinner and then we will get them out to play a bit after dinner.

Pat and I make our English Tea while Niki is dishing up dinner. She lays it all out on the center island buffet style which is so much easier.
Everyone gets a plate and we head off to the dining room to eat. So nice sitting round the table and chatting mostly about dogs and of course our trips to dog shows. The English Tea is yummy, of course we finish it up.
Wow it is nine o'clock and we need to get the kids out and think about going to bed. It has been a long day for Pat and me so we also need to get to bed. Pat and I help clear the table and then go to get our dogs out. Great they have eaten all their food which is good. They are good eaters for the most part.
It is so nice out here and the sky is clear and you can see all the stars. Just a slight breeze which is nice and funnily enough there doesn't seem to be any bugs. Well none that are biting me and I am usually the first to get bitten. We get all the dogs up and go and say good night to Niki and Fred. We are just exhausted so time for bed.
By the time we get ourselves organized and in bed it is 10p.m. Sure hope I sleep good tonight!!!!!

Friday

Wow I wake up and look at the clock and it is 7:30a.m. Wow I sure did sleep good. Hope Pat slept as good, of course she is already up. You know me, I turn over and go back to sleep. Just another 30 minutes and I will be ready to go LOL.
Pat comes in with a cup of coffee at 8:30a.m. and says it is a lovely day and she is going to take the dogs out. She tells me that she has already walked Nancy and took her all the way to the lake and back and she did real well. Pat is so thrilled at her progress.

I get my stuff together and go and get a shower. Oh so nice to be in a clean shower rather than the hotel. I have to borrow Barbara's hair dryer as Niki's is in her van. Pat and I have decided that we are going to try and get ourselves to the Wall Mart in Great Bend.
We have a list of groceries and of course a list of stuff for Niki. Will be nice to get out and see what is out there.

I let the pups run around for a while so that I can clean the pen out. Man they sure make a mess even though they use the litter tray they seem to trump the dust and food all over the place. Sure looks like a nice bed when I get all the clean bedding down LOL. I put the kids back and feed them and they are happy to nap.

Pat and I have our list and Niki comes in and say breakfast is on the table. Oh my, she has made the best eggs with cheese and ham and a touch of taco sauce on them, toast and jelly. Oh my, what a spread. Yummy. Of course Pat and I have coffee. Fred is eating sugar coated puff wheat and he throws a handful into the pups and of course we all laugh watching them eat it and get it stuck to their coats. Grissom Jnr gets it all stuck to his belly and is running round trying to get it off!! It is too funny for words. Just love watching puppies play.
Will have to add sugar puffed wheat to the shopping list.
We clear the table and get the list from Niki and off we go with directions from Fred as how to get there. Barbara is leaving at the same time and she will drop us off at Wall Mart.

We set off in the car and plug Wall Mart into Lolla. She is taking us the same way that Fred told us to go and that means she should bring us home the same way LOL. Yeah right, she couldn't find the farm on the way here so what makes me think she will find it when we come home. Pat and I note landmarks like those bales of hay in that field and that barn LOL.
Wow easier than I thought and man they have built a lot in Great Bend since I was here last which was nearly four years ago.
We wave goodbye to Barbara and head off to Wall Mart. We find everything we need and ask where there is a wine store because I would like to take a couple of bottles of wine home from Kansas. We have seen quite a few wineries advertised on those big bill boards while on the road so would be nice to take a bottle home for Jeanne and Jim.

The wine store is only a mile up the road and we need to get petrol and it next to the gas station. We buy two bottles of wine and it says Kansas Winery so that will do. Man it isn't cheap like the stuff Pat and I drink but that is o.k.
We then decide we have to find the Family Dollar store as Niki says they have the best chocolate marshmallow biscuits. Yummy. Well we drive about a mile oh and there it is. Great, they have them so we buy four packets. That should keep us all going, LOL. Well we have been gone nearly two hours so I think it is time to head back.

Yes Lolla is doing well but of course we are watching for our landmarks like those bails of hay LOL. Think they were on the other side of the road coming!!!! Remember we followed Barbara so we still need to pay attention to the things on the side of the road. Oh hay bales, I remember them.

Course Pat laughs and says "they were on the other side of the road coming"
We make another turn and I remember this is a long road and wow, there
are the brick pillars and the black iron fence. The gate opens because Niki
rang and said she would open the gate for us so we didn't have to wait or
call incase they didn't hear the phone as no reception in the kennel.

Wow we made it without having to ring and say we were lost. Well done
Lolla!

Niki is thrilled with all we bought and I start making the Shepherds Pie
for dinner. Doesn't take me long, takes longer peeling the potatoes as
I don't really have a good sharp knife to peel with. Oh well just keep
going. Get it all done and put together and ready to go in the over about
5p.m. so we can eat about 6 ish which is good as the dogs will be done
by then. Now it is time to breed Polly and looks like I will have to AI her
(artificially inseminate) as Leroy doesn't seem to be interested in doing
it naturally. Well that is fine, at least you know it is done.

Pat and I decide to go and take a nap, I think the trip has finally got to
us. We had fun shopping so now time to rest.
We wake up and it is 4:30p.m. so I have to get up and go and turn the
oven on. Hopefully I can find another pan to put the Shepherds Pie in
as don't want it bubbling over the oven. Found another pan and put it in
the oven at 5p.m. and we can eat about 6p.m. which will be good as the
dogs will be done for a few hours anyway!!! Pat and I take our dogs out
and feed them so they will be done as well.
We open a bottle of wine and sit and eat and chat. Glad that Niki likes
the Shepherds Pie, just another easy quick English dish. So nice to sit
and chat without having to rush to do something.
We all laugh and decide to open another bottle of wine, yummy. Well
none of us are driving so it really doesn't matter!!!! We finally clear the
table and time to take the dogs out again and then on to bed. Oh a tiring
day. Pat and I chat about all the things that have happened and finally
fall asleep. It is so quiet here and also dark!!!!

Saturday

Wow the sun is shining again. The weather has been so good to us since
we left it is unreal.

Pat comes in carrying coffee for me as usual. Wow I am so spoiled and will miss this when I get home. I am used to jumping up and getting dogs out and cleaning puppy pens before I even make my first cup of coffee!!!!
We take the dogs out and Pat says that Niki is cooking breakfast so need to hustle. She hates it if we are not ready to sit. I quickly do the pup's pen and put them in and feed them. Course they are waiting for their sugar puffs!!! Fred loves feeding them LOL.

Pat and I quickly lay the table for breakfast which is lovely, toast and jelly, bagels and muffins with lots of coffee as usual. Great! We talk about our things to do today. Firstly we have to breed Polly again and then Pat and I are going fishing in the pond across the way. Oh how exciting. Dishes are done and we get Polly and Leroy for breeding. Tonight we are going to breed Lolla as well. This will be her last chance as she didn't take the last time either.
Afterwards Pat says she is taking Nancy out again so we also take Dilly walking. Fun and Nancy is doing so well.
Before we go fishing I have to get all the chilli stuff in the pot so it can cook real slow!!! Will be even better tomorrow.

That is done and now Niki is packing us a lunch to take out to the dock so we can go fishing.
Fred found the fishing poles and we have two and we are using chicken skin as bait. Probably won't catch anything but it will be fun. We drive round to the pond and spray ourselves for bugs as Niki said there are a lot of mosquitoes but so far we haven't been bitten at all and I really thought we would get bitten in the evenings when we take the dogs out. You remember how they love to bite me!!!!

Well first of all we have to figure out how the stupid things work. I keep getting a bird's nest on the reel which isn't good. Finally get it sorted out and we both cast out. Just don't seem to be able to get it out in the middle but perhaps better fishing in the banks. I want to say Eric always told me when it is hot like this the fish go to the banks for shelter and where it is cooler.
Wow all of a sudden my rod bends and I can't wind up the stupid reel. Pat comes running over and I pull the line to the side of the dock but then the line breaks and gone!!! I have always seen the rod bend like that on the telly but never seen it do that in life!!! Wow what a rush.

So now we only have one rod so Pat has a turn while I eat my lunch. Oh Niki has put beer in here as well so that is cool. Wow sure is hot here and Pat is standing in the shade of the building which is good. She shouldn't stand in the sun too much.

Lunch is yummy but the chocolate cookies are melting LOL.

O.K. time for Pat to eat and me try to fish again. We have had one good bite so now time to try again. Oh wow, another bite, careful now don't break the line again else we will be done. I slowly wind it in and oh I can see it in the water. Pat comes over and grabs the line and pulls the fish onto the deck. Oh my, this is a huge fish, Pat says it is a wide mouth bass and must weigh about 7 pounds. We decide to keep it and take it to the house to cook for dinner!!! I know Niki told us to throw them back but this is a big fish. I take a picture of Pat holding the fish and we go back to fishing again. At least we still have the hook and line LOL. After about another fifteen minutes without a bite we decide that we are both cooked and time to go back and take a nap. I know the sun is not good for Pat so we go back.

Niki is thrilled with the fish as long as I cook it LOL. Pat and I go and lay down, too much sun.

Of course we take the dogs out first as they have been shut in for about two hours. We sit on the front porch and watch the dogs. I don't think I can stand too much to walk Sarah. I have bad problems with moving water and standing on that dock looking at all that moving water is just way too much for me, hence need to sleep it off!!!!

We both hit the bed and go to sleep immediately, yes unusual for me!!!!

We wake up about 4:30p.m. and of course first thing is to let the dogs out again. I take the dogs out and Pat goes to make coffee because I am dying for a cup as usual. The weather is still nice and nice to sit out here on the porch and watch the dogs play. Still having to walk Sarah of course!!!! I take them in and we feed them their dinner. This evening we have to breed Lolla again.

Well I go to cut up the fish and can't find a sharp enough knife to even cut it open!!! Oh well it was a good idea and would have been nice but there you go. In the bin!!!

For dinner Niki is making what she calls "The Poor Mans Steak Sub Sandwich." Smells just wonderful.

Pat and I lay the table, being a glass table it has to be cleaned every time. Glass tables are always so pretty when laid.

We open a bottle of wine and sit and laugh and chat like old friends should. Such a wonderful evening and dinner is just yummy.

We clear the table and Niki does the dishes, oh there is no water!!!!! Oh my, wonder why there is no water. Fred makes a few phone calls and then drives to the main road. We all carry on and breed Lolla.

When he comes back he says there is a water main broken up the road but they are there working on it. Niki is having a melt down because she can't wash the dishes before putting them in the dishwasher so we have another glass of wine LOL. It gets round to 10:30p.m. and Pat and I decide to go to bed. No point in worrying about the water till morning. We take the dogs out one more time before bed and then climb into bed. MMMMM so nice to be in a nice bed. Naturally we lay there talking and giggling as usual about what we have done today. Such a shame about the fish but there you go. We have some nice pictures of it and good to be able to tell the story of the rod bending in half. Now Pat has to get up to pee again LOL.

She comes back and says Fred has just taken a shower and the water is on so Niki is in the kitchen putting the dishes in the dishwasher. Now she can go to sleep happy!!!

We have decided to breed Snowball to McGee tomorrow and again on Monday morning before we leave. Cutting it close but still two breeding's is better than one or none!!

So we have bred Polly three times to LeRoy, Lolla to Leroy twice and McGee to Snowball twice. Not bad, now let's hope they all take.

Yes we have decided to go home on Monday. Pat really needs to get home as we have been gone for 8 days on Monday and it will take us three days to get home. Now time for sleep!!!!

Sunday

I wake up and as usual Pat is gone. She goes into the kitchen to help with the laundry, all the dirty dog beds from the night. I think she really likes it. She comes in the bedroom with coffee in hand which is lovely. She is such a dear. I get dressed while Pat starts taking out the dogs. Sarah is always last as have to take her out on the lead. So boring for her but there you go.

I give the dogs some food and we go into the dining room and I clean out the pups. They are so happy to be running free for a while. Niki says to bring them in the kitchen while I clean up and change the pee pads.

Need to have them all washed today so they are clean for us to use on the road during the journey home tomorrow.

I go and rescue all the pups and put them back in the x-pen and give them their breakfast, while we eat breakfast I am sure that Fred will give them sugar puffs LOL.

I clean off the dining room table and lay the table for breakfast. Today we are having eggs and hash browns, toast and muffins and of course the usual coffee. So nice to sit and eat breakfast and chat without having to rush anywhere. Pat and I are so used to shoveling the food in and getting dressed for a show.

Niki says that Fred is bringing in the books that she has saved for Pat and also the crates from Niki's truck which holds the popcorn tops for us to look through. Wow where are we going to put all these books on the way home. We will sort it out, not a problem LOL.

The popcorn shirts are just lovely but I really don't look good in the plain colours so I decide not to buy any for me but did get two for Zena. Shame but there you go.

Pat and Niki go through the books and Pat only keeps the ones that she hasn't read or that Niki says are really good. I didn't know Niki was such an avid reader but then one must escape into something eh. Wow still a pile of books LOL. Niki says that she has a lot of wire crates at the house in Great Bend and Fred will go and get them for us to decide which ones we want to take home.

Fred will power wash them and set them in the sun to dry. We have been so lucky with the weather while we have been away.

Time for lunch and we have the left over chilli and chips. Oh yummy. I am so glad that Niki likes my chilli. It does get better having been in the fridge for a couple of days.

Time to take the dogs out again, and breed Snowball to McGee. It is a shame that we have to AI him but we really have no time to see if he will do the job. Just easier and at least we know the job is done.

We decide to take the dogs out again and I have a sneaky feeling Pat is going to ask Niki if she can take Nancy home and Niki has already said that she belongs to Tate and not to Niki. I know this will upset her but just the facts.

Pat is doing fried chicken for dinner tonight so we have to start cooking about 5p.m. so it will be ready by about 6p.m. as it does take a long time to do so much chicken. I think we have enough for six people instead of just three as Fred will not eat it.

He is a butcher by trade so will no eat many meats except ground beef.

Fred takes us on a tour of the gardens to see the fruit trees, all of which need pruning real bad. Some of the pear trees have fruit but it is very small. It is just one of those jobs that Fred has to get done. They have only been moved in just about a week now so all these things take time. Such a lovely place and by this time next year I am sure they will have it all looking real nice.

Pat and I come back to do our dogs and feed them and then start cooking the chicken. Niki is doing salad with it and we have the left over potato salad that Pat made the other day. We all accumulate in the kitchen again and open a bottle of wine while we are waiting for the chicken to cook. Smells yummy.
Been a fun day and it is hard to think that we are going home tomorrow. Fred asks us to go to the Kennel and see the crates that he has power washed and that are now dry. Pat decided to bring home 3 of the 36" crates, 3 of the 24" crates and I decide on 3 of the 24" crates as well. Going to have to be creative to get all this stuff in the car!!!!

Well dinner is ready and we take it all to the dining room. Oh so good and a nice bottle of wine as well. We all sit and laugh about all the things we have done while being here. Seems like only yesterday that we arrived and now we are getting ready to go home.
We finally finish eating and drinking and clear the table. Pat and I have to take our dogs out again and go and get our laundry and sort out our stuff for tomorrow. What we need to be able to get to every night while on the road and what we can pack away!!!! Not worth worrying about tonight.
I go and have a shower and then Pat gets one so we don't have to worry about that in the morning. I really want to be out of here by about 10:30a.m. if at all possible. But you know how that goes.
We take the dogs out one last time and get them settled for the night. Of course Pat and I are so excited about going home that it is hard to sleep. Morning will come all too fast and we need to get a good nights rest before we start on the road again.

Monday

Pat wakes me up with coffee, I am so going to miss this LOL. I get dressed and we take the dogs out and we decide that we will leave the pups in the x-pen for as long as possible and they are they barking up a storm. Niki shouts that breakfast is on the table. Oh my, she has made scrambled eggs and hash browns, my favorite. She really is a great cook in between doing loads of laundry. What a gal!!!!

Pat and I take everything that we are taking home out to the front of the kennel. Luckily the weather is just lovely so we can pack the car without worries. The pups are all barking up a storm but that is fine. I needed to get the x-pen from the dining room and the litter tray and pads etc so they will just have to deal with it!!!!

Oh my how are we going to pack all this stuff in this car?

We have three 36" crates and six 24" crates, books and our bags. We are leaving two dogs here but taking another one home, my long coat Chihuahua Dilly.

We have the 36" crates standing up against the side and then five of the 24" crates laying down with Sarah's crate on top of them. Our bags beside her and then the two small crates which we bought the pups in have stuff in them and they are behind Sarah and then the last 24" crate is on top with the tibby pups in all together. Dilly is beside them behind the drivers seat and then Lola and Snowball are in a crate beside Dilly who is on top of Polly. Wow, can't see out of the back window but that is fine, will just have to use the mirrors.

Wow we finally have it all in and I can shut the back door!!! Not much room for breathing but we will be fine driving home. We don't aim to buy anything else because we don't have any room for any more stuff LOL.

We go into the kitchen to say goodbye to Niki and Fred and of course Rambo and McGee who we are leaving behind. I run back to the bedroom just to check that we have left nothing behind, especially my pillow LOL. Can't sleep without my pillow.

We all cry and finally Pat and I leave, Niki has to stay in the kitchen as she hates goodbyes. It was very hard to say goodbye to the dogs especially McGee but had to be done.

Pat and I get in the car and turn Lola on and drive down the long driveway. There is a strange silence in the car except for the tibby puppies who are screaming. I turn on the radio hoping that will quiet them just a bit. There is no talking between us, just that strange silence as we both recount our visit to Niki and Fred in Kansas.

It is 10:30a.m. and we will drive until we are tired and need dinner. At least we have left at a good time, earlier than I thought so that is good.

As we start heading out of town I see a McDonald's and say to Pat that I really would like a cup of coffee while we are driving. Of course she agrees and we get coffee of course. The puppies finally settle down. I think we are both able now to chat about our trip but of course it is hard because Pat feels so bad about leaving McGee. Just hope that Mike comes and gets him pretty fast. It will take McGee a good few days to get used to the kennel situation. I am sure Niki will have him in the house quite a lot before he leaves.

We decide that we will stop about mid day if we feel hungry and get food and let all the dogs out for a while. Really we can drive for 250 miles before we need petrol so that is a good time to stop. Hopefully we can find another Fly J rest stop. Petrol is cheaper there and they have good munchies.

The silence is finally broken and we recount about our trip. Of course the worst part is leaving behind the puppies but then that is what we came for.

The weather has been just wonderful for our trip and let's hope it is still good for our trip home.

You know I hate driving in the rain. We will drive until about 6:30 to 7:0p.m. and then find a Motel 6 as usual.

Finally everyone is quiet and we are doing well. There really is no traffic to talk about as the roads here are just long and flat LOL. We are planning to be home sometime on Wednesday, no point in killing ourselves driving. OOH there is a Flying J. We really are only half empty but better to fill up here and we can get some lunch as well. Might as well let the dogs out as then we can keep going on the tank full.

Oh wow they have a special on flip flops so Pat buys a couple of pairs for Dee Dee and a pair for herself. I can't walk in them so no point in me buying some. We get some fried chicken wings and some fries and a couple of doughnuts for dessert. No coffee, going to try the cappuccino.

They have it in English Toffee flavor which sounds just yummy. Make a change from coffee.

We go back to the car and drive over to where there is some grass to set up the x-pen for the dogs. So nice that there are grassy areas where we can put the dogs out. Course we try and find a bit with some shade as well, plus where there is no glass or anything bad for the dogs. People throw their trash anywhere these days. Just awful. We get all the dogs out and stand and munch on our chicken. Of course the dogs are busy waiting for scraps of chicken rather than do their business but at least they are stretching their legs a bit before we get going again. Well sorry guys but time to pack up and get going again!!! Everyone is loaded and as usual I walk round to make sure we have left nothing behind. No trash and no x-pen left on the grass LOL.

O.K. so now we keep going till we have had enough and can find a Motel 6.

It is nearly 6:30p.m. and we have decided to find a Motel 6 but we want one this time that is not ten miles off the highway, been there and done that. Too tired to do that tonight. We see a bill board and Pat puts Motel 6 in Lola and gets the phone number and rings them. Yeah only 21 miles down the road and just a turn off the highway which is nice.

We finally arrive and I go and check in to be told we have a nice room with a freshly shampooed carpet. Well could do without that as now I will have to put pee pads down for the dogs and hope they don't miss. Most of the time the pups go back to the litter tray so that is good.

We are both so tired, it is order out, Chinese and then shower and bed. Pat does the ordering while I feed the kids. Sarah doesn't seem so good today, off her food which is unusual and she is throwing up. I think it has something to do with her travelling in the back of the car as I seem to remember she did this on the trip going.

Oh door, here comes our dinner. Very yummy. I will take Sarah out to run a bit and Pat lets the kids out and then we are going to bed. Oh so nice to be laying down, still feel as though we are moving!!!

Tuesday

Morning comes and the sun is shining yet again. Wow we really are lucky with the weather.

Kettle is on and the kids are running around having fun. I have to get clothes on so as to take Sarah out for a pee. Don't want her running with the little guys as she gets too excited and flattens them on the ground. She is still a baby herself so nothing I can do about it. She will get over it.

Pat and I sit and have our coffee and play with the pups while we are packing up our stuff. The longer they have to play then the better they will travel.

Well it is 8:30a.m. and we really need to get on the road. We put all the dogs in their crates and then carry the pups out to the car and then I can get the x-pen up. Wow doesn't take us long to get loaded and we are on the road by 9:0a.m. Well done us. I am getting good at packing the car.

It is going to be a long day today as we must do enough miles so that tomorrow we only have a few miles to drive to get home.

O.K. so where are we stopping for breakfast as that is first on the list LOL. We get back on the highway and there is a sign for McDonalds so we will go off at the next exit. We don't have to do the dogs as only been in the car 30 minutes so they will be fine.

Oh yummy the usual bacon egg and cheese biscuit and large coffee's. Isn't it awful when you have to have a biscuit and coffee to make the drive worth while???? Well I do at least.

Traffic is very light and we are doing well. It is fun to talk about our visit and the trip over all.

Hopefully the next time we stop for gas we can get the dogs out for a bit and just sit and rest and stretch the legs. I get so stiff from sitting in the same position.

Well after about an hour I decide to let Pat drive as I am falling asleep at the wheel. Oh nice to sit on the other side of the car for a while and rest my eyes. Looking at the same white lines on the road and so little traffic it gets very mind boggling. Pat is quite happy to drive till we stop for lunch and or petrol.

Finally time to stop for petrol and we find another Flying J Rest Stop. We park so we can let the dogs out and I run in to use the bathroom. We have learnt to buy our food and anything else first because then we get cents of a gallon of gas. They have a nice selection of chicken and fries, well they call them steak fries and of course Cappuccino. I go back to Pat and we talk about the food while the dogs are playing. Course they never really want to pee and again I have to walk Sarah. Wow the weather is really nice and good that we are parked under a tree for some shade for the dogs. That sun beating down is hot. I stay with the dogs and Pat goes back in to get drinks. She comes back with Cappuccino and oh it is lovely. We stand and drink our drinks and we will get more for on the road. Well the dogs have played for about 35 minutes so I guess now time to put them back in the car and get on the road again. We get them loaded up and drive over to get petrol and food. Food first and we ended up getting four cents of a gallon with our Flying J card. Not a bad deal eh. We fill up with more Cappuccino and chicken wings and steak fries. Not good food but we have to have food that is finger food. Too hard to drive and use a knife and fork to eat LOL.

The dogs are doing well and I am back driving. We need to drive at least till about 6:30p.m. so tomorrow we will only have a few hours on the road to get home. Have to let Pat look at the map and try and figure out where we are and how far we have to go.

Good job her reading the map etc as I wouldn't have a clue as to where we are. You start with a mile marker and an exit and she can work it out from there. Smart cookie.

Guess what, we have done 245 miles so time to stop for petrol yet again. Pat puts into Lolla(GPS) for our next Flying J Truck Stop but don't think there is one near here. Wow 12 miles and away we go. Yes we can make that. Will be nice to let the dogs out again and stretch our legs a bit. Letting the dogs out now and of course us peeing as well means we can drive a bit further.

If we can do another 100 miles Pat reckons that tomorrow we will only have to drive 250 miles which will be good, meaning we will be home about mid day or a bit later but before Dee Dee gets home from school which will be good. Bummer meaning that we will probably have to stop for petrol again but at least the dogs will be o.k. for that length of drive without worrying about getting them out!!!

We've been on the road for about an hour so now it's time for Pat to find a Motel 6. Again Lolla comes into use to find Motel 6. Well the nearest is only 6 miles away and really we need to do a few more miles. O.K. where is the next one. That is 45 miles away so that is the one we are going to. Pat rings them up so that they know we are coming and of course to make sure that it is just off the road and not a 12 mile drive off the interstate. Cool that is where we will stop.

We find the Motel 6 and ask if there is a Wall Mart near by. Well the girl sends us on a route march and we never find a Wall Mart but we do find a grocery store. We need water for the dogs and us of course and we need something for dinner. I am just about all done with fast food. Well their food deli is closed so we will have to find something else. We finally get back to the motel and it is a nice room with a laminate floor again. Oh I do like this as so much easier to clean with the dogs. After we get all set up Pat goes over to the office and they tell her of a Chinese that will deliver and give her a menu. Chinese is fine at least it is edible most of the time. Pat orders while I run and take Sarah out and then we can put them all up while waiting for delivery.

Sarah is being very slow but I know she needs to go so we just walk around on the grass for about 15 minutes and she finally goes. I take her back in and we feed all the dogs and pups and put them up so we can open the door and pay when the delivery comes. We open our beer of course which we bought in the store. The food finally arrives. Such polite people.

We really enjoy the food as usual, way too much but that is o.k. You have to spend a minimum of $13 for them to deliver it so of course we always end up with too much. We get all cleaned up and let the pups out again and I take Sarah out for a walk. Such a nice evening, wish we could sit outside with the dogs but can't do that at a motel. For one reason there isn't a flat piece of grass. All seems to be slopes so the x-pen wouldn't sit right LOL. I take Sarah back and now it is time for bed. We both shower fast and then into bed for a good nights sleep. Tomorrow night we will be sleeping in our own bed.

Wow morning already and it's 7:30a.m. I can't believe that Pat has slept so long. We let the kids out to play and I get dressed while Pat makes the coffee. I have to take Sarah out of course. Wish I had bought a flexi lead for her then she could at least run a bit. I get back to the room and Pat has the coffee made and is packing up our stuff. The kids are still running around and we have fed them so at least they have food in their gut. We should be able to make it all the way home without having to stop and let them out. Pat has worked it out and about 200 miles so that should be good. Of course we have to find breakfast first on the list LOL.
We get the car loaded with the dogs and of course last in is the x-pen and all the bedding. Can empty the litter tray today and we put all the smelly bedding in a plastic bag. I sure will have a lot of laundry when we get home but that is o.k.

We get all loaded and Pat goes over and hands in the key and we get on the road. Breakfast!!!
Well there is a place called the Biscuit Shop so I guess we will go there. We saw it on the way in last night so hopefully it will be good. Pat decides to go and get the breakfast and I will walk Sarah as she still hasn't been to the bathroom. Don't want to have to stop in an hour or more.
Well gee there sure are a lot of people going into the store where Pat is. She finally comes out and says, "We won't bother to shop here again, it cost $10.99 for two biscuits and two coffees and they are not the large coffee either, better be good!" The biscuit is yummy but the coffee is just so so. Down the road we will stop for a Cappuccino which we both love.

Just as Pat comes back to the car I look in the back and realize that my pillow has been left at the motel. I tell Pat and she is just devastated as she knows the love with my pillow. She rings the motel and they say they will just ship it to me C.O.D. which is great. Many thanks and great that their phone number was on the receipt.

It is a good drive and very little traffic yet again. Beginning to get into familiar territory now so we know where we are but I still have to keep asking Pat how many more miles LOL. Keeps her on her toes LOL. Well gee a real bummer, we have only about 80 miles to go but have to stop for petrol yet again. Man I sure wish I had a car with a larger tank. Still getting about 24-25 to the gallon is one of the reasons for having this car and it is loaded beyond being loaded at this moment in time. Yeah we can get another Cappuccino!!!! We don't need to let the dogs out as soon we will be home. I will have to let them out when we get to Pat's as have to take them out before we can get anything else out LOL.

It seems so strange to be nearly home when we have been gone for 11 days. Yes it has been fun but also upsetting to be leaving behind Rambo and also McGee. Still we got to visit with friends and had a fun trip none the less.

Well we are on Rte I-64 and only 36 miles to home. Pat rings Max and he says he will meet us at the house, come home from work early to help us unload the car. Well we have loaded and unloaded it so many times I think we can handle it LOL. Still at least it is a body to carry the stuff into the house.

We set up the x-pen and put all the dogs out in it so as to unload the car. Gee it was easy enough getting these crates in the car but now they have all locked themselves together and don't want to come out. Finally get all the crates out which are Pat's and Pat's stuff. When I get home I will of course sort it all out and see what she has left behind LOL. Never do get it all out in one go.

We load all my dogs back in the car and I leave. A sad leaving but I will talk to Pat tomorrow and probably bring over anything she left in the car.

I ring Eric on the way home to tell him that I will be there in about ten minutes.

Finally I am home with all the tibbie pups, Polly and Dilly and Sarah. Seems like we were away for ages but then it always does.

I have to take the x-pen in the house and set it up for the pups. Sarah and Polly are excited to be home but of course Dilly will go in the x-pen with the tibbie pups as she is too small to be running with the other dogs.

Now we have to wait and see if Polly, Lolla and Snowball are pregnant. Exciting.

AKC / UKC DOG SHOW INFORMATION FOR CONFORMATION SHOWS

American Kennel Club

To obtain a Champion ship on a dog you need fifteen points and this must include two three point majors obtained under two different judges.

Each breed of dog that competes has a certain number of entries for a three point major.
In Papillons it is 11 female dogs and 10 males.
In Chihuahuas it is 5 males and 6 females.
In Tibetan Spaniels it is 7 males and 8 females.

The numbers are different for each State as designated by AKC rules and change annually.
I have no idea how they establish the numbers but sometimes it seems very unfair and sometimes it is very hard to find enough dogs for majors.

United Kennel Club

Now the rules for UKC are very different.
Firstly there are no professional handlers. You can only show a dog if you are the owner or co-owner. Yes I do show the odd dog for friends when they don't have enough people to take dogs back in the ring for Winners Dog or for Best of Breed.

To obtain Championship on a dog you need to earn 100 points.

Their point schedule is Regular Class is   10 points
Best Male or Female   15 points
Then Best of Winners   10 points

This gives you a total of 35 points which means if you win Best of Winners with a Male or a Female, as long as there are at least two dogs of different sex, doing three shows you can make a dog into a Champion.

Most UKC shows we do are five or six shows in a weekend so it is usually easy to make one or two dogs a Champion.

Now to become a Grand Champion you have to win five classes with at least three Champions in the ring and it has to be under at least three different judges.

You don't get any extra points for winning Best of Breed but the points from Best of Breed go towards "Top Ten Points".
These are calculated by the number of dogs that you beat for Best of Breed. i.e. If there are five Chihuahuas in the ring and you win Best of Breed then you win 4 points towards "Top Ten".
At the end of the year the points are added up by UKC and then the top ten dogs get invited to Premier, and is held in Kalamazoo, Michigan.
It is a black tie affair and very exciting to see who wins the Top Ten title.
It is run the same way as a dog show but the first four in Group end up going to the Top Ten finals. Then the 20 entries are in the ring and each dog is judged individually by three judges. All the scores are added up and then everyone lines up for the finally.
Taken from UKC Rulebook © 2006

Edwards Brothers, Inc.
Thorofare, NJ USA
December 9, 2011